CADBURY, KNOX, AND TALBERT

SOCIETY OF BIBLICAL LITERATURE
BIBLICAL SCHOLARSHIP IN NORTH AMERICA

Kent Harold Richards, Editor

Mikeal C. Parsons
Joseph B. Tyson, editors

CADBURY, KNOX, AND TALBERT

American Contributions
to the Study of Acts

Scholars Press
Atlanta, Georgia

CADBURY, KNOX, AND TALBERT

American Contributions
to the Study of Acts

© 1992
The Society of Biblical Literature

Library of Congress Cataloging in Publication Data

Cadbury, Knox, and Talbert : American contributions to the study of
    Acts / Mikeal C. Parsons, Joseph B. Tyson, editors.
    p. cm. -- (Biblical scholarship in North America) (Society
    of Biblical Literature centennial publications)
    Includes bibliographical references.
    ISBN 1-55540-653-X (alk. paper). — ISBN 1-55540-654-8 (pbk.: alk.
    paper)
    1. Cadbury, Henry Joel, 1883-1974. —Contributions in study of Acts.
2. Knox, John, 1900-1990. —Contributions in study of Acts.
3. Talbert, Charles H., 1934-   .—Contributions in study of Acts. 4. bible.
N.T. Acts—Criticism, interpretation, etc.—History—20th century.
I. Parsons, Mikeal Carl, 1957-   . II. Tyson, Joseph B., 1928-
III. Series. IV. Series: Centennial publications (Society of
Biblical Literature)
BS2625.2.C33   1991
226.6'06'09730904—dc20
                                              91-36644
                                              CIP

Printed in the United States of America
on acid-free paper

Ad Memoriam
John Knox
(1900-1990)

LIST OF CONTRIBUTORS

J. Bradley Chance is Associate Professor of New Testament at William Jewell College in Liberty, Missouri. He is the author of *Jerusalem, the Temple and the New Age in Luke-Acts* (Mercer University Press, 1988).

Beverly R. Gaventa is Professor of New Testament Studies at Columbia Theological Seminary in Atlanta, Georgia. She is the author of *From Darkness to Light: Aspects of Conversion in the New Testament* (Fortress, 1986).

Donald L. Jones is Professor of Religion at the University of South Carolina in Columbia, South Carolina. He is the author of numerous articles on the christological titles in Luke-Acts and a forthcoming volume on Luke in the University of South Carolina Press Series on biblical personalities.

John Knox, now deceased, was formerly Professor of New Testament Studies at Union Theological Seminary in New York, NY. He is the author of *Marcion and the New Testament* (University of Chicago Press, 1942) and *Chapters in a Life of Paul* (Abingdon, 1950).

David P. Moessner is Associate Professor of New Testament at Columbia Theological Seminary in Atlanta, Georgia. He is the author of *Lord of the Banquet: The Literary and Theological Significance of the Lukan Travel Narrative* (Fortress, 1989).

Mikeal C. Parsons is Assistant Professor of New Testament at Baylor University in Waco, Texas. He is the author of *The Departure of Jesus in Luke-Acts: The Ascension Narratives in Context* (Sheffield Academic Press, 1987).

Richard I. Pervo is Associate Professor of New Testament and Patristics at Seabury-Western Theological Seminary in Evanston, Illinois. He is the author of *Profit with Delight: The Literary Genre of the Acts of the Apostles* (Fortress, 1987) and *Luke's Story of Paul* (Fortress, 1990).

Vernon K. Robbins is Associate Professor of New Testament in the Department of Religion at Emory University in Atlanta, Georgia. He is the author of *Jesus the Teacher* (Fortress, 1984), and (with Burton Mack), *Patterns of Persuasion in the Gospels* (Polebridge, 1989).

Charles H. Talbert is Professor of Religion at Wake Forest University in Winston-Salem, North Carolina. He is the author of *Reading Luke* (Crossroad Press, 1982) and editor of *Luke-Acts: New Perspectives from the Society of Biblical Literature Seminar* (Crossroad, 1984).

David L. Tiede is President of Luther Northwestern Theological Seminary in Saint Paul, Minnesota. He is the author of *The Charismatic Figure as Miracle Worker* (Scholars Press, 1972), *Prophecy and History in Luke-Acts* (Fortress, 1980) and *Luke*, ACNT (Augsburg, 1988).

John T. Townsend is Professor of New Testament at The Episcopal Seminary in Newton, Massachusetts. He is the author of numerous scholarly articles, including "The Date of Luke-Acts," in *Luke-Acts: New Perspectives from the Society of Biblical Literature Seminar* (Crossroad, 1984).

Joseph B. Tyson is Professor of Religious Studies and Chair of the Department of Religious Studies at Southern Methodist University in Dallas, Texas. He is the author of *The Death of Jesus in Luke-Acts* (University of South Carolina Press, 1986) and editor of *Luke-Acts and the Jewish People: Eight Critical Perspectives* (Augsburg, 1988).

TABLE OF CONTENTS

INTRODUCTION

EDITORS' PREFACE

Eldon Epp has recently described the field of NT Studies as a discipline which is "an inch wide but a mile deep."[1] Among other things, this description suggests that students and professors involved in the academic study of the NT familiarize themselves with the history of interpretation of those documents. The study of the Lukan writings has had a lively and colorful history, and Lukan scholarship has been described at various times as a "storm center,"[2] "shifting sands,"[3] and a "fruitful field."[4] A number of studies have been produced which survey the landscape of Lukan scholarship.[5] Much of the significant research on

---

[1]Eldon Jay Epp, "Editors' Preface," in *The New Testament and Its Modern Interpreters*, eds. Eldon Jay Epp and George W. MacRae (Atlanta: Scholars Press, 1989) xxi.

[2]W. C. van Unnik, "Luke-Acts, a Storm Center in Contemporary Scholarship," in *Studies in Luke-Acts*, eds. L. E. Keck and J. L. Martyn (Nashville: Abingdon, 1966) 15-32.

[3]Charles H. Talbert, "Shifting Sands: The Recent Study of the Gospel of Luke," *Int* 30 (1976) 381-95.

[4]W. Ward Gasque, "A Fruitful Field: Recent Study of the Acts of the Apostles," *Int* 42 (1988) 117-31.

[5]In addition to the histories of scholarship found in the introductions to the standard commentaries on Luke (Fitzmyer, Marshall) and Acts (Haenchen, Conzelmann, Bruce, and Schneider), see the book-length surveys of research by W. Ward Gasque, *A History of the Interpretation of the Acts of the Apostles*, rev. ed. (Peabody, MS: Hendrickson, 1989); Jacob Kremer, ed., *Les Actes des Apôtres: Traditions, rédaction, théologie* BETL 48 (Gembloux, Belgium: Duculot, 1979); Francois Bovon, *Luke the Theologian: Thirty-three years of research (1950-83)*, trans. Ken McKinney (Allison Park, PN: Pickwick Publications, 1987). Other references may be gleaned from the bibliographic surveys by, among others, Paul F. Stuehrenberg, "The Study of Acts before the Reformation: A Bibliographic Introduction," *NovT* 29 (1987) 100-86; Erich Grässer, "Acta Forschung seit 1960," *TRu* 41 (1976) 141-94, 259-90, 42 (1977) 1-68; A. J. Mattill, Jr. and Mary B. Mattill, *A Classified Bibliography of Literature on the Acts of the Apostles*, NTTS 7 (Grand Rapids: Eerdmans, 1965); Günther Wagner, *An Exegetical Bibliography of the*

the Lukan writings during the modern period of critical study has taken place in Germany (Haenchen, Conzelmann), Britain (Bruce, Marshall), and France (Dupont, Bovon), a fact not lost on surveyors of Lukan research. And at times in these surveys, the contributions of American interpreters are eclipsed by the notice taken of the findings of their European, especially German, counterparts.

This volume takes its place alongside these previous studies. Its distinctive contribution, as the title suggests, is in its focus on American contributions to the study of Acts in the twentieth century. Three scholars were chosen as representatives of the rich diversity of American Lukan scholarship: Henry J. Cadbury, John Knox, and Charles H. Talbert. The choice of these three scholars is not intended to diminish the significant contributions of other American scholars in this century, but the work of each does stand in a kind of complementary relationship to the other two. These scholars produced the majority of their work during various points in the twentieth century, Cadbury working during the first third of the century, Knox in the middle third, and Talbert in the context of the latter part of the twentieth century.[6] Equally important are the diverse contributions these three made in the study of Acts: Cadbury in the area of philological and literary analysis of Luke and Acts in their literary environment, Knox in the area of chronology, and Talbert in the area of method. Each one in his own way has deepened and broadened our understanding of the Lukan writings.

This collection of essays grew out of the 1987 meeting of the SBL Acts Group (chaired by Joseph B. Tyson) which focused on American contributions to the study of Acts. Earlier versions of the major papers in this volume by Beverly Gaventa on Cadbury, Joseph Tyson on John Knox, and Mikeal Parsons on Charles Talbert, were presented at that meeting along with earlier versions of the responses by Donald Jones, John Townsend, and Bradley Chance. In preparation for publication, the original papers and responses were revised, and other respondents (Richard Pervo, Vernon Robbins, David Moessner) were added to the original group. Bibliographies of the works by Cadbury, Knox, and Talbert have been added at the end of each respective section. Beverly

---

New Testament: Volume 2: Luke and Acts (Macon, GA: Mercer University Press, 1985); Watson E. Mills, *A Bibliography of the Periodical Literature on the Acts of the Apostles 1962-1984*, NovTSup 58 (Leiden: Brill, 1986).

[6]But while these three do roughly represent these different chronological periods, it should be noted that the three were all contemporaries for nearly a decade during the 1960's.

Gaventa compiled the Cadbury bibliography; Mikeal Parsons compiled the Knox bibliography (building on the bibliography compiled by John Hurd in the 1967 Knox *Festschrift*) and the Talbert bibliography.

In addition, David Tiede has contributed an insightful essay on the future of Lukan research in North America. John Knox and Charles Talbert have also written responses to the evaluations of their own work. The response by John Knox was completed only months before his death in June, 1990. The editors and contributors dedicate this volume to the memory of John Knox, whose distinguished literary career extended across eight decades.

If creative scholarship is defined as seeing what everyone else has seen and thinking what no one else has thought, then the essays collected in this volume bear eloquent testimony to the creative genius of Cadbury, Knox, and Talbert. But all the contributors, each an established Lukan scholar in his or her own right, bring unique perspectives to bear on the current state of research on Acts, as well as different assessments of the contributions of these three scholars to that current state of affairs. The result is a volume which is both a survey of past Lukan research in the American context *and* a showcase of the variety of methods employed in and conclusions drawn from the contemporary study of Acts. The volume is also unusual in its internal coherence. A web of responses to papers, and responses to responses, have contributed to producing a volume with layers of intertextual references between and among the essays, producing an integrity unusual for the typical "collection" of essays. This volume intends to assist students and scholars of Luke and Acts to stand on the shoulders of these giants, and from that vantage point to see more clearly what others have seen of the Lukan landscape in the hopes that future generations of readers, too, may think what others have not thought.

Appreciation is expressed to Kent Richards, General Editor of the American Contributions to Biblical Scholarship Series, and to Scholars Press, for their help in bringing this volume to press. We are especially grateful to the following graduate students at Baylor University who served, at various times, as research assistants for this project: Howie Batson, Duane Brooks, Beverly Burrow, Dennis Horton, David Matson, Sharon Moore, and Leo Percer. Finally, thanks are due to the Baylor University Research and Sabbatical Committees for providing resources necessary to complete this project.

Mikeal C. Parsons   Joseph B. Tyson
Baylor University   Southern Methodist University
Waco, Texas   Dallas, Texas

THE PIONEERING WORK
OF
HENRY J. CADBURY

THE PERIL OF MODERNIZING HENRY JOEL CADBURY

Beverly Roberts Gaventa

Introduction

Recent studies of Luke-Acts testify to a growing interest in the literary character of this early Christian text.[1] While these studies take their impetus from literary criticism of other biblical texts as well as from current literary theory, they frequently connect themselves also to the work of Henry Joel Cadbury. At the outset of his study of literary patterns in Luke-Acts, Charles Talbert has lamented the lack of scholarly interest in the formal patterns within Luke-Acts since the time of Cadbury, who interpreted the Lukan parallels stylistically.[2] In his dissertation on the narrator of Acts, Allen Walworth identified Cadbury as one whose work foreshadowed the current generation of literary interpreters of Luke-Acts, for Cadbury "devoted a lifetime to the elucidation of Luke's literary style."[3] Joseph B. Tyson identified Cadbury, along with Dibelius, as one who paid serious attention to the literary qualities of Luke-Acts.[4]

None of these scholars has claimed to find in Cadbury a misplaced literary critic of the late twentieth-century variety. Nevertheless, the fact that each of them introduces Cadbury at the outset of his work may

---

[1]All references to the work of Henry J. Cadbury in this essay and the responses to it by Jones and Pervo are keyed to the bibliography of Cadbury's writings found on pp. 45-51.

[2]Charles H. Talbert, *Literary Patterns, Theological Themes, and The Genre of Luke-Acts,* SBLMS 20 (Missoula, MT: Scholars Press, 1974) 1-5.

[3] Allen Walworth, *The Narrator of Acts* (Ann Arbor: University Microfilms, 1985) 3-4.

[4] Joseph B. Tyson, *The Death of Jesus in Luke-Acts* (Columbia, SC: University of South Carolina Press, 1986) 25.

not be the result of mere coincidence and suggests that the literary interests of Cadbury are seen as a path not yet taken. According to this view of Lukan scholarship, Cadbury's perspective was lost in the midst of various options in research on Luke-Acts, and needs now to be recovered. Admittedly, his contributions to the study of Luke-Acts were great in their own day (e.g., his study of the so-called "medical" language in Luke), but his importance is only now fully understood.

In the survey that follows, I assess the accuracy of this view of Cadbury's place in Lukan studies. As the title itself indicates, I see a certain "peril" in this interpretation of Cadbury's work.[5] It is appropriate to laud his work and draw upon it, but we need to be careful lest we impute to him a view he actually did not have.

Ranking Cadbury among the leading twentieth-century American contributors to the study of Acts amounts to an understatement. Colleagues, attempting to convey the importance of his contribution to our understanding of Acts, have variously referred to him as "the doyen of Anglo-Saxon research on Acts,"[6] "one of the best specialists on the Acts of the Apostles,"[7] "the most important name in the history of Lucan research in America,"[8] "one of the great pioneers of modern Lucan studies,"[9] and "the high-water mark in Lucan studies."[10]

What makes Cadbury's productivity the more remarkable is that it was carried out in the midst of a life marked by contributions in a variety of other areas as well. Born in 1883 to Anna Kaighn Lowry Cadbury and Joel Cadbury, Jr., a family with a long history of strong Quaker ties, Cadbury graduated from the Penn Charter School in 1899; he earned the B.A. from Haverford College in 1903, and both the M.A. (1904) and the Ph.D. (1914) from Harvard University. In 1916 he married Lydia Caroline Brown, and the two became the parents of four children.

---

[5] "Peril" is admittedly an overstatement when applied to the issue of evaluating and assessing the work of Cadbury. It is worth noting that he also regarded it as an overstatement in his own title, *The Peril of Modernizing Jesus* (1937b). The title was selected by his publisher (1949b).

[6] Ernst Haenchen, *The Acts of the Apostles: A Commentary*, trans. Bernard Noble and Gerald Shinn (Philadelphia: Westminster, 1971) 43.

[7] Jacques Dupont, *The Sources of Acts: The Present Position*, trans. Kathleen Pond (London: Darton, Longman and Todd, 1964) 13.

[8] W. Ward Gasque, *A History of the Criticism of the Acts of the Apostles* (Grand Rapids: Wm. B. Eerdmans, 1975) 168.

[9] Robert Maddox, *The Purpose of Luke-Acts*, ed. by John Riches (Edinburgh: T. and T. Clark, 1982) 1.

[10] Paul W. Walaskay, *'And So We Came to Rome': The Political Perspective of St. Luke*, SNTSMS 49 (London: Cambridge University Press, 1983) 7.

Cadbury taught at the University Latin School in Chicago (1904-1905), at the Westtown School in Pennsylvania (1905-1908), and at Haverford (1910-1919). When what Cadbury termed an "orgy of hate" broke out in the United States against Germans, Cadbury published a letter of protest in the *Philadelphia Public Ledger* (October 12, 1918), an act that led to harsh criticism and his eventual resignation from Haverford. He then joined the faculty of Andover Theological School (1919-26). Following the dissolution of the merger between Harvard Divinity School and the Andover Theological Seminary in 1926, Cadbury taught at Bryn Mawr College until 1934, when he was invited to return to Harvard to succeed James Hardy Ropes as Hollis Professor of Divinity.

Alongside his own teaching and writing, Cadbury served the Society of Biblical Literature as its secretary (1916-33), its president in 1936, and its delegate to the American Council of Learned Societies for some twenty years. On the occasions of the Society's fiftieth anniversary in 1930, its seventy-fifth anniversary in 1955, and its one-hundredth meeting in 1964, Cadbury was among the invited speakers. His presidential address was notable for its plea that biblical scholars not remain indifferent to the social consequences of their work, a plea made specific by reference to developments in Nazi Germany, where, as Cadbury put it, "the figure of Athena was to be replaced by the swastika" (1937a:13). In addition to these contributions to the SBL, he was secretary of the American Schools of Oriental Research (1934-54) and editor of that Society's *Annual* (1927-32). An initiator of the Studiorum Novi Testamenti Societas, he was its president in 1957-58. For over forty years, he served on the Revised Standard Version Bible Committee.

In addition to his NT scholarship, Cadbury wrote extensively on Quaker history, most notably as publisher of the papers of George Fox. A participant in the formation of the American Friends Service Committee, Cadbury visited Germany after World War I to view AFSC centers for feeding young children. From 1928 to 1934, and again from 1944 to 1960, he chaired the AFSC, commuting from Cambridge to Philadelphia for meetings each month during the second period of his chairmanship. If to others this activity seemed incongruous with his life as a biblical scholar, Cadbury's response was, "I am still trying to translate the New Testament" (1947b:171).[11] A history of Harvard

---

[11]For biographical treatments which attend especially to Cadbury's involvement with the Quakers, see the following: Mary Hoxie Jones, "Henry Joel Cadbury: A Biographical Sketch," in *Then and Now: Quaker Essays: Historical*

Divinity School, dedicated to Cadbury upon his retirement in 1954, used
different language to make the same point: "During a half century of
instruction he has known how to balance the scholarly claims of the past
and the urgent necessities of the hour."[12] Following a long and
productive retirement, Cadbury died in 1974. Over the years his many
accomplishments were acknowledged with honorary degrees from
Haverford College, the University of Glasgow, Whittier College,
Swarthmore College, Howard University, and Earlham College.

Any biographical sketch of Cadbury that omitted reference to the
multitudinous Cadbury anecdotes would be the poorer for it. Perhaps
the most revealing of these stories concerns Cadbury's trip to Oslo in
1947 to accept the Nobel Peace Prize on behalf of the AFSC. Lacking the
requisite formal attire for the occasion, Cadbury borrowed a set of
evening clothes from the warehouse where the AFSC was collecting
clothing to be sent to Europe (such clothing was sent for use by European
orchestras). He wore the borrowed clothing for the festivities in Oslo
and then sent it on to its intended destination.[13]

As with other aspects of Cadbury's life, the sheer volume and scope
of his work on Acts are impressive. Even prior to his doctoral
dissertation on Luke's literary style and method (1920c), Cadbury wrote
an article on the Lukan style of the notorious *pericope adulterae* (1917).
Over the next five decades, Cadbury published a number of studies on
Luke-Acts that continue to influence our interpretation. To my
knowledge, his last publications on Luke-Acts appeared in 1972 and
addressed litotes in Luke-Acts and Luke's references to animals (1972a;
1972b).

---

and Contemporary, ed. Anna Brinton (Philadelphia: University of Pennsylvania
Press, 1960) 11-70; Margaret Hope Bacon, "Let This Life Speak: The Legacy of
Henry J. Cadbury," *Friends Journal* 29 (December, 1983) 9-13; idem, *Let This Life
Speak: The Legacy of Henry Joel Cadbury* (Philadelphia: University of
Pennsylvania Press, 1987). For essays written by Cadbury's colleagues at Harvard,
see the following: Amos N. Wilder, "In Memoriam: Henry Joel Cadbury, 1883-
1974," *NTS* 21 (1975) 313-17; idem, "A Grammarian with a Difference," *Harvard
Magazine* (May, 1975) 52; George H. Williams et al., "Henry Joel Cadbury: A New
Testament Scholar and Nobel Laureate," *Harvard Gazette* (February 6, 1976) 7;
George W. MacRae, "Henry Joel Cadbury (1883-1974)," in *Profiles from the
Beloved Community,* eds. G. H. Williams, George W. MacRae, and Paul D.
Hanson (Cambridge: Harvard University, 1976) 13-21. Professor Eldon Epp kindly
drew my attention to the article by George MacRae.
  [12] *The Harvard Divinity School,* ed. George Hunston Williams (Boston:
Beacon, 1954) v.
  [13] Jones, *Let This Life Speak,* 147.

Cadbury left few topics untouched in his work on Luke-Acts. His well-known *The Making of Luke-Acts* (1927b) and *The Book of Acts in History* (1955a) treated the large issues of Luke's literary method and historical context. His many contributions to periodicals and to *The Beginnings of Christianity* addressed issues in Acts as diverse as the use of relative pronouns, the "odor" of the spirit at Pentecost, the titles given to Jesus, and the problematic "we" passages. While his interests are often characterized as literary and historical rather than theological, he wrote on the eschatology of Acts as well as on the religious "interests" evidenced in Luke-Acts. His apparently voracious reading and exacting mastery of detail lend to all of these contributions an encyclopedic quality that enhances their on-going usefulness. To those who read extensively in Cadbury's work it comes as no surprise to find that he frequently greeted colleagues with the salutation, "What have you learned that I ought to know?"[14]

In order to assess Cadbury's contributions to the study of Acts, especially in the context of the current interest in literary criticism, I shall survey his major treatments of Acts. The aim is to understand both the shape and underlying assumptions of Cadbury's work in order to place (in their proper perspective) his contributions to our understanding of the literary character of Luke-Acts.

The Style and Literary Method of Luke

While the second part of Cadbury's dissertation deals exclusively with Luke's use of sources in his Gospel and thus falls outside the scope of this paper, the briefer, first part takes up several problems regarding the vocabulary of both Luke and Acts. The stated aim of both parts of the dissertation is "to examine the work of the *auctor ad Theophilum* as an individual writer of the Hellenistic age" (1920c:v). First, it must be recognized that the NT is a collection of diverse works. Since it does not have a homogeneous style or vocabulary, individual writers must be treated distinctly. Second, Cadbury rejected the category "New Testament Greek," observing that early Christian writers employed the common language of the Roman empire rather than some special "language of the Holy Ghost" (1920c:v).

Following his insistence on the distinctiveness of individual NT writers, Cadbury's first study of Luke's vocabulary attempted to estimate its size relative to the vocabularies of other NT writers. Here

---

[14] Ibid, 110.

he employed various earlier vocabulary studies to show both that Luke's vocabulary is larger than that of any other NT writer, and that the number of words peculiar to Luke is greater than that of any other NT writer. Luke's vocabulary is roughly the same size as that of some writers outside the NT whose works are of about the same length as one or both of Luke's volumes (1920c:1-4).

Cadbury's second study focused on Luke's literary standing by investigating Lukan vocabulary in comparison with Attic Greek. Here again was a departure from earlier studies which compared the vocabulary of the NT as a whole with the vocabulary of classical Greek writings and which judged Luke's vocabulary to be sophisticated, though these previous works in fact only compared Luke with that of other NT writers (1920c:4-6).[15] Cadbury showed that Luke's vocabulary contains many more post-classical words than are found in the Atticists. He also pointed out, however, that many of the post-classical words found in Luke appear solely in those passages that Luke takes from the LXX, Mark or Q. In addition, some of the post-classical words are found prior to 200 CE only in Jewish or Christian texts, and they may be part of a technical vocabulary rather than reflecting Luke's "normal" Greek style. Cadbury's own careful conclusion was that Luke's vocabulary "has its natural affiliation with the Greek of the Bible" but "is not so far removed from the literary style of the Atticists as to be beyond comparison with them" (1920c:37-38).

In the third and best known of these studies of Luke's vocabulary, Cadbury conducted the first thorough and critical investigation of W. K. Hobart's thesis that Luke's vocabulary reflects the training of a physician.[16] Here he demonstrated that the words and phrases Hobart regarded as "medical" are not employed principally or exclusively by medical writers. Indeed, most of them appear frequently in writers who are not medically trained (e.g., in the LXX, Josephus, Plutarch, Lucian). This "medical language" cannot be regarded as demonstrating that the author of Luke and Acts was a physician, although the opposite case,

---

[15] Cadbury also notes here and elsewhere that the uniqueness of a word within the New Testament is better regarded as the result of a statistical accident than as a revealing piece of the author's vocabulary. He makes this point as early as 1917 in "A Possible Case of Lukan Authorship" (1917:242).

[16] W. K. Hobart, "The Medical Language of St. Luke," *The Medical Language of St. Luke* (Dublin: Hodges, Figgis, 1882).

that Luke was *not* a physician, likewise cannot be made from the available evidence (1920c:39-63).[17]

The Making of Luke-Acts

While a number of articles and notes followed Cadbury's dissertation, his next major work was the well-known *The Making of Luke-Acts* (1927b). In the opening pages Cadbury distinguished his work from that of his predecessors, who primarily studied Acts in order to reconstruct the history of early Christianity:

> The present study does not aim to deal as such with the events narrated by this writer [Luke], but with an event of greater significance than many which he records—the making of this work itself (1927b:7).
> [Previous studies of Luke and Acts]...all contribute to our understanding of the making of Luke-Acts. But their scope is not identical with the present inquiry. Their ultimate interest is not the author and his times, but the subject matter of his history. His own interests are considered merely as they color or adulterate his story. He is someone to be allowed for, eliminated and discounted, not someone to be studied and appreciated for his own sake. His literary methods are examined in order that we may discover the earlier sources behind them, or the facts and personalities lying behind the sources. All this is significant and valuable, but when these studies are completed and even while they are going on there is still place for concurrent studies of the historian himself (1927b:7).

Cadbury thus clearly intended to investigate the work of the author of Luke-Acts. He was not interested in the reconstruction of early Christianity or in merely identifying the sources used by Luke; rather, he intended to focus on the author himself.

Cadbury further distinguished his work from that of his predecessors by criticizing the practice of treating the Third Gospel and the Acts of the Apostles in isolation from one another. Since their common authorship is recognized and their interdependence likewise understood, what was needed was a single name. Cadbury offered the apparently novel suggestion that Luke's two-volume work be designated "Luke-Acts" (1927b:7-11).

In the second chapter, he identified four major factors that contribute to any composition: (1) the materials that are available; (2) the conventional means of thought and expression; (3) the individuality of the author; and (4) the author's conscious purpose (1927b:12-17).

---

[17]It is this study, of course, that prompted the familiar quip of Cadbury's students to the effect that he gained his doctor's degree by depriving Luke of his (Wilder, "Henry Joel Cadbury, 1883-1974," 314).

These factors in turn form the major parts of this investigation into the writing of Luke-Acts.

Discussion of the materials available to Luke begins with the several stages of their development. Cadbury compared the process with Luke's own comments in his preface. That is, first come the impressions of those who witness events ("eyewitnesses and ministers of the word"), followed by the transmission of these traditions ("they were delivered to us"), and then the arranging and recording of events ("many have undertaken to compile a narrative") (1927b:23). Even at the stages of eyewitness impressions and early transmission, the motives of early Christians shaped the material they selected and handed on. Cadbury emphasized the complex character of these motives, which ranged from the inherent interest of the events themselves, to an interest in the activities of particular individuals, to a defense of the Christian movement (1927b:34-40). As these motives varied, so did the forms acquired by the stories themselves. In Acts no less than in the Gospel, we can see the "rounding" of stories and the collection of stories into groups "by mortising the joints or by utilizing summaries as both conjunctive and disjunctive interludes" (1927b:59). Many of these stories came to Luke from written sources. It is reasonable to think that Luke had written sources for Acts just as he did, in Mark and Q, for the Gospel. We need not expect to find internal evidence of written sources for Acts, since the passages used from Mark and Q contain no sign that they had been copied (1927b:66).

Whatever materials Luke received, like all authors he employed those materials according to the conventions of his era. These strategies included the common language (vernacular Greek), popular literary forms, a conventional means of using available sources, the composition of appropriate speeches, and other literary formalia (1927b:113-209). The element of convention must be underscored, Cadbury claimed, because the writing process is "hemmed in with the compulsions of convention" (1927b:113).

In addition to the sources available to Luke and the writing conventions of his day, the third factor contributing to Luke's composition was his own "personality":

> The third factor to be considered in the work of Luke is the author's individuality. His sources represent the deeds and records of predecessors. His general language, method and viewpoint he shares with others of his group. There remains, however, something distinctive in his writing, as

there is something distinctive in everyone's writing—his own personality (1927b:213).

The burgeoning interest in psychological analysis during the same period in which Cadbury wrote *Making* makes it important to point out that the term "personality" here refers to the individuality of an author. Nowhere did he engage in speculation about the psychological make-up of Luke.

Luke's personality may be glimpsed through his writing style. While the conventions of the day influenced him, Luke also had an individual way of expressing himself. In this context, Cadbury identified several characteristics of Luke's writing that he later developed more fully in notes and articles. Luke varied his style and vocabulary to make his writing appropriate to the literary setting (1927b:223-4). Even the notorious "we" sections in Acts may be "somehow connected with...mental habits of the editor" (1927b:230; also 1956c). Luke displayed an interest in parallel individuals and parallel scenes, but he also enjoyed contrasting persons within a story (e.g., the rich man and Lazarus) as well as contrasting events (e.g., the "journeys" of Jesus and Paul) (1927b:231-5). In general, Luke's writing has a compelling dramatic quality, but it is difficult to know to what degree this drama derives from Luke and to what extent from his sources. Cadbury several times noted that "the more general traits of his work...were doubtless due to his sources in very large measure. For good or for ill he had to depend on earlier material" (1927b:231).

The following chapters in *Making* explore the secular, social, and theological concerns displayed in Luke-Acts, including such issues as Luke's cosmopolitan outlook, his preoccupation with cities in general and with Jerusalem in particular, his universalism, his concern for outcasts, and his emphasis on the roles of women. Here again Cadbury was careful not to attach too much significance to the interests he identifies, since in some instances Luke's "sources are responsible for his matter, and even when he appears to change his sources the changes are slight..." (1927b:271). He also noted the difficulty of moving beyond these isolated "interests" to an inferred identification of the author (1927b:273).

The final section of *Making* addresses the purpose of Luke-Acts. The form of Luke's work—narrative—"carries with it the intention of supplying information" (1927b:299). In addition, Luke was indebted to his sources even for the purposes that are part of Luke-Acts. Luke's own purposes were "minor and secondary" and "detected rarely, if at all, and only in slight hints and details...." (1927b:300-301). Among Luke's several purposes was the desire to correct Theophilus's misunderstanding about the Christian movement, especially as that misunderstanding focuses on charges that Christians have broken Roman law (1927b:315).

Attempts to identify the "plan" or structure of Luke-Acts are modern devices. Once again, Cadbury insisted that the shape of Luke's work comes from the material he inherited. The omissions which modern interpreters find difficult to understand in Luke's account probably stem from all of the four factors which enter into authorship (materials, convention, personality, and purpose). Luke was also limited in what he could write by the length of the rolls of papyrus that were in use at the time (1927b:320-25).

Making is a rich volume which has now influenced scholarship on Luke for over sixty years. Despite Cadbury's description of his work as having a narrow focus on the author of Luke-Acts, *Making* in fact deals with the author largely by asking what materials he received. It touches on a multitude of issues that subsequent scholars have retrieved and explored, and not always with more insight or depth. The program for the next several decades of Cadbury's own work on Acts emerged from this volume.

The Beginnings of Christianity

Probably Cadbury's best-known contributions to the study of Acts are in *The Beginnings of Christianity*, known by virtually all students of early Christianity. Although the final volume was published in 1933, the fact that *Beginnings* was reprinted again in 1979 indicates its lasting contribution to the field.[18] It is difficult to assess properly Cadbury's contributions to this five-volume work, both because they were numerous and diverse and because the commentary itself (Volume 4) was written by Kirsopp Lake together with Cadbury.

In order to offer some characterization of Cadbury's contributions to these volumes, I have selected three of his notes for comment: "Names for Christians and Christianity in Acts" (1933i), "The Summaries in Acts" (1933j), and "The Speeches in Acts" (1933k). While these studies are adjacent to one another in Volume 5, they differ in method and approach. The study of "Names for Christians and Christianity in Acts"

---

[18]In his survey of the history of the interpretation of Acts, Haenchen comments that the detail of *Beginnings* renders it "now as then, indispensable to the scholar, and ensures its value even on the Continent" (*Acts*, 37).

examines some nineteen different words in Acts, primarily with a view to their linguistic and historical origins. If a term is used in only a few places (e.g., *sozomenoi* in Acts 2:47), it is possibile that its appearance is merely *ad hoc* and that it is not a conventional expression for Christians or Christianity. Some terms may have come to Luke from the sources he employs. Cadbury compares their usage in Acts with that in other early Christian sources, considering the historical origin of each expression (1933i).

"The Summaries in Acts" begins with a point made earlier in *The Making of Luke-Acts*, that the summaries do not provide the structure of Acts. Instead, using K. L. Schmidt's work on Mark, Cadbury compared the summaries with the Markan framework. Luke, especially in the first part of Acts, brought together separate scenes from separate sources. The summaries constitute the "connective tissue by which memorabilia are turned into the beginnings of a continuous narrative" (1933j:395). The summaries were created by a process of "generalization" from adjacent material and are susceptible to very free treatment by the final editor of Acts. When they appear similar to one another, it may be because of Luke's tendency to repetition,[19] but it also may be that he has repeated them from an underlying source. While the summaries are editorial in nature, they may already have been written prior to Luke's final editorial stage (1933j:395-401).

In analyzing the speeches in Acts, Cadbury dealt primarily with the issue of their historicity. Speeches were a literary convention in antiquity, and their presence did not imply that they contained definite information about a particular historical address. Within Acts itself, the occasions on which speeches are given do not lend themselves to the presumption of an immediate written record. While it might be assumed that the speakers reported in their own words, such a report after the fact would diverge to some degree from the actual speech as delivered. Also undermining the assumption of the historicity of the speeches in Acts is the fact that their style is Lukan and that the subject matter of many of the speeches is shared (1933k:405-409).

Cadbury acknowledged and criticized the several arguments made in favor of the historicity of the speeches. He dealt at some length with the argument that the speeches of individual leaders in Acts contain idioms similar to those found in their letters (i.e., Paul's speeches recollect his letters, Peter's recollect 1 Peter, James's recollect the Epistle

---

[19]This is developed further in "Four Features of Lukan Style" (1966a).

of James). A careful examination of the expressions adduced by others showed that the similarities were no more than can be explained by a generally common Christian faith and a common use of contemporary language (1933k:410-15).

Cadbury's contributions to *Beginnings* were consistent with and often built upon the earlier work of his dissertation and of *Making*. In these articles, as in much of *Beginnings*, the focus is almost entirely historical and lexicographical. They do not attempt an analysis either of the theological argument of Acts or of its literary structure.

The Book of Acts in History

While nearly twenty years separate *Beginnings* from *The Book of Acts in History*, this volume flows naturally from Cadbury's earlier work. The basic perspective on Luke-Acts remains unchanged, although the focus shifts. As the title indicates, this volume takes up the place of Acts within history, that is, the "concentric cultural environments" of Acts: "general," Greek, Roman, Jewish, and Christian. In his discussion of the "general" cultural environment Cadbury refers to those many features of Luke-Acts that are not easily identified as either Greek, Roman, Jewish or Christian. "In the ancient as in the modern world cultures and ideas have no frontiers" (1955a:27). While some features may be broadly described as "oriental," others can be classed only as "ancient." For example, the story of the conversion of the Ethiopian eunuch in Acts 8 is a kind of "cultural amalgam" which depends upon the ancient view of Ethiopia as a "peculiar and exotic country" (1955a:15-16).

Discussion of the Hellenic character of Luke-Acts centers primarily on Luke's language. Both Acts 28:2 ("And the natives [*barbaroi*] showed us unusual kindness....") and 21:37-39 suggest that Luke identified with a Greek viewpoint and sympathized with a certain Greek "sense of superiority" (1955a:32). Luke's variation in style derived from the varying cultural contexts in which his narratives occur. In the early chapters of Acts, therefore, the language used has a more Semitic character, perhaps in imitation of the Septuagint. The second half of Acts, by contrast, contains most of those terms and expressions that are associated with Luke's "superior" Greek (1955a:34). While Luke did include quotations from classical Greek literature, these appeared to be quotations such as would have been widely known and referred to in contemporary thought. Luke's discussion of events in various Greek cities shows a familiarity with them and their customs. Luke was "a man of some cultivation, at home in the speech of the current Greek and not to be reckoned a mere barbarian or one ill at ease in the speech and civilization of the far flung area in which the Greek influence had come to dominate" (1955a:53).

The Roman background of Acts is more generalized. While Luke's language and intellectual background are Greek, the broad outline and condition of the contemporary world are Roman. This Roman environment appears in Acts in the rulers who are mentioned, the security of travel, and the Roman roads. Cadbury addressed at some length the issue of Paul's Roman citizenship, assessing various theories concerning the means by which Paul obtained his citizenship. Paul may have had an ancestor among those individuals granted citizenship by virtue of some particular service offered to the state (1955a:75). Luke's positive attitude toward the Roman government derived from the growing and broad appreciation for Rome's "genius...to assimilate into a single citizenship the whole world" (1955a:81-82). If Luke seems to us naive in this optimistic assessment of Rome, it is because he could not anticipate the conflict that would later characterize the relationship between Rome and the church.

In his consideration of the Jewish environment of Acts, Cadbury argued that Luke was knowledgeable about contemporary Judaism. Acts is particularly valuable for its picture of the synagogue in Diaspora Judaism, although the Pentecost account demonstrates that Luke knew of the presence of Diaspora Jews in Jerusalem itself (1955a:86-88). The speeches drew not only upon the LXX, but also upon traditions of contemporary Judaism which are evidenced in Josephus and Philo (1955a:98-106). Luke's story offered a negative response to Judaism, which Luke viewed as the center of opposition to Christianity (1955a:91-92, 106).

Not surprisingly, the discussion of the Christian environment of Acts pertains more to the importance of Acts as a source for Christian history than to the light shed on Acts by other information about early Christianity. A brief review of non-Christian sources and both canonical and non-canonical Christian sources underscored the scantiness of information about Christianity in the first century. This review led to the conclusion that Acts is "our principal narrative source" for knowledge of the period in which gospel materials were being developed and collected. Acts is even more important for interpreting the letters of Paul. "A narrative of Paul's life would be almost impossible without"

Acts. In short, Cadbury argued, "Acts is to Paul's letters what Mark is to Q,—in fact, what biography usually is to letters, what history is to literature" (1955a:122-3). Cadbury did not regard Luke as having had access to Paul's letters; rather, the coincidences between them arise from the genuine agreement of two independent sources. Their differences are sometimes serious but often complementary (1955a:124).

The final chapter of *Acts in History* addressed the subsequent history of Acts. Acts may have played a role in the process of canonizing both the Gospels and the letters of Paul. When separated from the Gospel of Luke, Acts became figuratively the "arch, lintel or keystone" between these two parts of the canon (1955a:143). Cadbury concluded with a discussion of the canonization of Acts and the limited and selective interest in Acts evidenced in the first centuries of Christian history (1955a:158-60).

In some ways this book reveals Cadbury's view of Acts more openly and directly than did *Making*. He identified Luke himself as a Hellene. While Luke knew about contemporary Judaism, he viewed it from the perspective of an outsider and stressed the distance between Christianity and Judaism. *Acts in History* also evinces an optimistic stance toward the history *within* Acts. When Cadbury discussed the importance of Acts for understanding early Christianity, he gave little indication that the accounts in Acts might be unreliable. Instead, he seems to have assumed that Acts can be used to reconstruct the history of early Christianity. This tendency appears also in the treatment of Paul's Roman citizenship, where we see no question about the notion that Tarsus is Paul's home nor problem with Luke's claim that Paul was a Roman citizen.

Acts and Eschatology

Because it deals with an important issue in Luke's theology, I devote separate attention to the single article, "Acts and Eschatology" (1956a). Cadbury's work in the 1920s and 1930s contained little explicit discussion of Luke's theology, although *Making* did devote some chapters to theological and religious characteristics of Luke. Hence, it will be instructive to see how Cadbury addressed the issue of Lukan eschatology just prior to the debate provoked by Conzelmann's *Die Mitte der Zeit*.[20]

---

[20]While Cadbury knew that Conzelmann's work would deal with Lukan eschatology, he had not seen it when he wrote this article. By the time he

His study began by identifying, based on the Gospels, Acts, and the letters of Paul, three convictions shared by early Christians: (1) Jesus had risen from the dead; (2) he would return from heaven; and (3) his followers had received the Holy Spirit. Consistent with Luke's "orderly mind" and "strong belief in objective reality," Luke did not transfer these convictions to the realm of the imagination. Instead, Luke treated these convictions through the use of objective narratives. For example, the gift of the Holy Spirit was not a figurative gift but an objective gift of speaking in particular human languages. Similarly, the risen Jesus was not an apparition, but a real human being who had a physical body (Luke 24:39, 41-43; Acts 10:41) (1956a:303-309).

While Cadbury conceded that Acts itself has little eschatology, he attributed this to the fact that Acts is narrative. The eschatology of Acts, like any of its theological elements, is to be located in the "missionary addresses, though we may legitimately add the conversations and other briefer spoken parts." The narrative does not so much omit eschatological hopes as it assumes them and does not need to restate them (1956a:310). A survey of Acts shows that many of the familiar themes of early Christian eschatology do appear here (e.g., the kingdom of God, the last times, final judgment), which means that Luke was not ignorant of these themes. He may have drawn some of them from his sources, but the eschatology throughout is reasonably consistent and thus indicates the author's acceptance of these teachings (1956a:311-12).

Disagreeing with Dodd's view that Acts contains a realized eschatology, especially in the early speeches, Cadbury insisted that Acts "does not spiritualize away the concrete eschatological hopes of Christianity nor on the other hand does it emphasize their imminence and urgency." Instead, Acts retains "the old and literal expectation but is satisfied to leave the time to God's ordering." The Gospel of Luke discourages a "too early expectation," and Acts does not contradict that view. Nevertheless, Luke did not find the future hope embarrassing, and he did not "blur" its concreteness (1956a:315-16).

Luke accepted the fact of the delay of the parousia, but this acceptance only strengthened "the assurance of the final events." Both the life of Jesus and the story of the early church are part of the assurance about the future that Luke offered. These events of the past "do not reduce the importance of the future, or much alter the nature of

corrected the proofs for the *Festschrift* he was able to supply only the name and bibliographic information for this new work (1956a:320).

its expected fulfilment. The *eschaton* remains intact in the future" (1956a:321).

The contribution of this article, which does not seem to have played a significant role in the on-going debate about Lukan eschatology, is its attention to the varying features of the eschatological elements in Acts. Typically, Cadbury gave careful attention to the details of the text. If those details conflicted with one another, he tried to hold them in tension rather than to over-interpret one element at the expense of another.

Methodologically, this article is consistent with the approach taken in *Making*. It describes features of the text and then draws conclusions about the theological convictions they reflect. While Cadbury said little here about the sources of Acts, he did introduce them as factors to be considered. Unlike the tentative suggestions offered at the conclusion of *Making*, however, this article does not even speculate on the author's setting. It makes no move from the description of eschatology in Acts to a reconstruction of the author's *Sitz im Leben*.

Cadbury here revealed his assumption about where the theology of Acts is located. As noted above, he explained the relative lack of eschatology in Acts as a result of the narrative character of Acts. Apparently this means that narrative does not bear theology. Instead, Cadbury suggested we look to the missionary speeches or other elements of public address and conversation in order to find Luke's theology. While these assumptions are by no means unique to Cadbury, they do indicate his view of the relationship between theology and narrative.

Conclusions

This survey takes into account Cadbury's major contributions to the study of Acts, but it leaves aside numerous articles (see the bibliography below). Most notably omitted from discussion is Cadbury's study of the "we" sections of Acts and his article on Lukan style. Each of these articles builds on observations already present in *Making* and therefore does not require separate discussion. Also omitted is the series of lexical notes published periodically between 1925 and 1972.

Despite the fact that Cadbury's publications on Luke-Acts extend over more than five decades, a striking continuity characterizes those publications. There is little change in Cadbury's work over the years, although he did take up some new issues, particularly in *Acts in History*.

He also expanded his earlier work, as seen especially in "Four Features of Lukan Style," which extends upon some arguments made in *Making*. I do not, however, recall any instance in which Cadbury repudiated a position taken at an earlier period. His work exhibits no fundamental change of perspective or judgment, so that moving from *Making* to *Acts in History* scarcely seems to be crossing several decades.

Another feature of Cadbury's work, and one which may contribute to this continuity, is that he seldom presented his argument as conversation or debate with other scholars. This feature stands out most clearly in the case of the work of Dibelius and Conzelmann. Cadbury certainly knew of Dibelius's work on form criticism (see, for example, 1923a), and "Style Criticism of the Book of Acts" was first published 1923, well before *Making*. The common interests of the two scholars would seem to have made them natural conversation partners, but neither drew on the work of the other. Similarly, Conzelmann and Cadbury made virtually no use of each other's work. As was observed earlier, Cadbury did not have access to Conzelmann's *Die Mitte der Zeit* while writing his essay on the eschatology of Acts, but it is noteworthy that Cadbury's later article on Acts in the *Interpreter's Dictionary of the Bible* (1962a) did not refer to Conzelmann, not even in the bibliography.

This silence with regard to Dibelius and Conzelmann needs to be placed in its proper context. Cadbury did not discuss their work, but he also did not often discuss the work of other scholars. References in the text of Cadbury's writings to the positions of other scholars are extremely rare. Even the footnotes refer largely to items of information found in other scholars' work and seldom to their theses or conclusions. The prime exception to this comes in Cadbury's dissertation, with its extensive refutation of W. K. Hobart's argument for the medical language of Luke. Put concisely, Cadbury engages in conversation with the text and only on rare occasions with fellow scholars.

A third feature of Cadbury's work concerns his view of the text itself. Particularly in *Making* we find a perspective that is best described as form-critical. Since the announced goal of *Making* was to study the author of Luke-Acts, it may seem unusual to link the work with form criticism. Recall, however, that Cadbury began his discussion of authorship by identifying those things used in authorship, namely, the sources. In that discussion, Cadbury spoke of the rounding of episodes and the handing down of traditions. Even when he addressed the "personality" of the author, he again and again spoke of the constraints placed upon the author by his sources. He insisted that our reconstruction of the "interests" of the author may only reflect the interests present in those sources. If there is a polemical edge to Cadbury's view of Acts as presented in *Making*, it came from his desire to show that the material in Acts does not spring full-blown from the author or from some pure and early tradition.

Cadbury did not identify *Making* explicitly with form criticism, and so the names of the emerging form critics did not appear when he introduced his work or intentions for it. This silence should not be understood to dissociate *Making* from form criticism, however, and my earlier comments about Cadbury's usual method of working pertain here. The antecedents for this book are in Dibelius and Bultmann. While Cadbury did not analyze the history of individual units of the text as Bultmann might have, he nevertheless did work with an archaeological view of the text.[21] In Cadbury's case, this archaeological viewpoint appeared in his discussion of the factors involved in authorship. Discussion of the author was at every point shaped by references to the sources which constrained the author and dictated the shape and content of the author's work.

It is difficult to state concisely Cadbury's general theory of Acts, since, as one of his earlier reviewers noted, "the chief criticism which most readers will make of the book is that it so often avoids definite pronouncements."[22] It is clear that he regarded Luke-Acts as having the general purpose of apology. Further, Cadbury understood Luke to be a Hellene who identified with claims of Greek superiority. Luke saw the importance of Jewish tradition and drew upon it in the speeches in particular, but he also understood the Jews to be the opponents of Christianity and clearly viewed them as outsiders.

Perhaps more important than these slender and tentative conclusions about the person of Luke is what this review reveals about Cadbury's methodological stance toward Acts. As we have seen, he associated narrative with the goal or implicit purpose of conveying information about something or someone. It is not surprising, therefore, that Cadbury saw in Luke-Acts the purpose of defending Christianity.

---

[21] In "Between Jesus and the Gospels," Cadbury refers to form criticism as "literary excavation" (1923a:92).

[22] E. F. Scott, "The Genesis of Luke-Acts," *JR* 8 (1928) 286. It is also Scott who comments that *Making* has "more genuine scholarship in it than in nine-tenths of the ostentatiously learned books that are being written today about the New Testament" (285).

The narrative informs Theophilus and other readers so that they may make an accurate judgment about Christianity.

Further, Cadbury characterized Luke's narrative as an "objective" narrative. By "objective" he did not mean that Luke is somehow detached from the story he tells or uninvolved with it, but that Luke describes in an objective way events that others might describe more spiritually or subjectively (e.g., the fulfillment of the promise of the Holy Spirit).

The content, extent, and structure of Acts are determined by the sources to which Luke had access. Cadbury's discussion of the plan and scope of Luke-Acts attempted to see the work as organized around the summary statements or around other patterns. While Cadbury acknowledged the movement in Acts from Jerusalem into the Gentile world, he contended that these stages came to the author from his material.

As noted in the discussion of *Acts in History*, Cadbury, at points, operated with what seems a sometimes naive view of the history *within* Acts. This is most clear in *Acts in History*, where he speculated on the citizenship of Paul without reference to the historical problem created by the fact that only Luke speaks of Paul's citizenship. Again in Cadbury's discussion of the importance of Acts for the study of early Christianity, he seems to have insisted upon the usefulness of Acts because of the scarcity of historical evidence outside the NT. Here, also, Cadbury's investment in the presuppositions of form criticism becomes apparent, since he continued to argue that Luke made use of sources and that these sources have value as historical evidence.

The historical element in Acts, however, is to be distinguished from the speeches, which reveal the theology of Acts. Two important and related points emerge here. One is that the speeches themselves are not to be regarded as historically accurate. The other is that the speeches in Acts are the primary place in which its theology may be located. Cadbury would have found very peculiar the notion that the shape of Luke's story itself reveals something about his theology. For him, the speeches reveal Lukan theology. Even in the speeches we cannot be certain of locating the author's own theological viewpoint, however, since the speeches are also shaped by pre-Lukan tradition.

In many parts of Cadbury's work, especially in *Making*, we find observations about Luke's literary style. As I indicated at the beginning of this paper, these observations have been very important in the development of the literary criticism of Luke-Acts. One thinks especially of Cadbury's work on parallels, repetition, and the "we" sections.

The number and significance of these contributions tempt us to think of him as a literary critic in the contemporary sense. However, this review of his work demonstrates that viewing Cadbury as a literary critic would be modernizing as surely as would Cadbury's own example of a portrait of Mary Magdalene wearing Florentine headdress (1937b:1). What is important about Henry Joel Cadbury is not that he was a literary critic, but that, even in the context of work that is dominated by the concerns of form criticism, history, and lexicography, he offered a multitude of insights that continue to stimulate and instruct our interest in the literary character of Luke-Acts.

THE LEGACY OF HENRY JOEL CADBURY: OR WHAT HE LEARNED THAT WE OUGHT TO KNOW

Donald L. Jones

Introduction

With the thoroughness and attention-to-detail which we have come to expect from her, Beverly Roberts Gaventa performs an important service for all students of Luke-Acts by her careful survey of Henry Joel Cadbury's contributions to the study of Acts. In doing so she has enabled all of us to assess our debt to Cadbury for his more than a half-century of Lukan scholarship. Gaventa discusses Cadbury's contributions under five headings, each bearing the title of one of his major publications. I will follow her outline in my response, occasionally expanding upon her treatment, introducing areas of Cadbury's research which she omits, and referring to other works by him which deal with the topic at hand.

Lukan Vocabulary

Gaventa begins her discussion with Cadbury's dissertation published in 1920, *The Style and Literary Method of Luke*, and focuses on his analysis of Luke's vocabulary—i.e., its size compared with that of other NT authors, its comparison with Attic Greek writers, and the well-known "medical language" investigation (Gaventa, 11-13). While Gaventa fairly summarizes Cadbury's efforts here, a further word should be said about his careful classification of Lukan vocabulary (from *alpha* to *epsilon*) with that of Dio Chrysostom, Lucian, Aristides, Aelian, and Philostratus (1920c:4-39). Cadbury discovered that Luke's vocabulary was more elegant than most of the others, and that ninety percent of his words could be found in the LXX. Luke's Pilate, for example, used several expressions which occur in other Attic writers (1920c:10-17). Luke, as described by Cadbury in *The Making of Luke-Acts*, was "a gentleman of ability and breadth of interest," whose vocabulary "no purist could wholly commend, but no ignorant man could entirely equal it, though he could always understand it" (1927b:220).

Lukan Prefaces

The second part of Gaventa's survey (Gaventa, 13-16) deals with Cadbury's classic book published in 1927, *The Making of Luke-Acts*. This book was developed around four principal factors involved in literary composition: (1) the accessible materials; (2) the conventional media of thought and expression; (3) the individuality of the author; and (4) the author's conscious purpose. In her treatment of the first factor (Gaventa, 13-14), Gaventa notes that Cadbury compared the process of discerning stages in the development of available materials with Luke's own comments in his preface (1:1-4). Since the preface is not discussed elsewhere in her paper, and since it is of major importance in Cadbury's overall interpretation of Luke-Acts, to allow Gaventa's brief analysis to suffice more needs to be said, especially since it is to the preface that one must ultimately turn in order to determine Luke's purpose. Again, Gaventa's discussion of Cadbury's fourth factor, dealing with purpose (Gaventa, 15-16), only alludes tangentially to the preface.

As Cadbury observed, it was the custom in antiquity to prefix to the first volume of a work a preface to the whole, which mentions one's predecessors in the field, as well as the sources upon which the work is based (1927b:358-9; 1922d:491). Luke 1:1-4, then, Cadbury noted, is "the real preface to Acts as well as to the Gospel, written by the author when he contemplated not merely one but both volumes" (1922d:492).

In v. 3 of his preface, Luke explained his credentials: he had "followed all things accurately for some time past." Because he was unable to find a single Hellenistic example of *parēkoloutrēkoti* as meaning "to follow," Cadbury argued that the verb *parēkoloutrēkoti* can only mean "to observe" in the sense of claiming eye-witness status (1922d:501-2). "The writer's information," Cadbury concluded, "had (notice the perfect tense) come to him as the events took place; it was not the result of special reading and study" (1922d:502). I maintain, however, that Cadbury has interpreted the verb too narrowly, especially since in v. 2 Luke distinguished himself from the "eyewitnesses" to Jesus' ministry. Cadbury held out for the possibility that, since the preface refers to both parts of the two-volume work, Luke might well have been referring to his own participation in some of the events described in the latter parts of Acts (1927b:346).

The long word *parēkoloutrēkoti*, Cadbury argued, was due to Luke's desire for sonorous rhetoric in the preface (1922d:496). The rhythm of the sentence requires that the adverb "accurately" *(akribōs)* be taken with "to follow," rather than, as Cadbury suggested, with "to write" *(grapsai)* (1922d:504), indicating that Luke was careful in the investigation of his sources. *Kathexēs*, meaning "orderly, " and not "successively" or "continuously," as Cadbury claimed, should be taken with "to write" to describe the character of the narrative (1922d:505).

Luke's avowed purpose as expressed in his preface, Cadbury said, was "to correct misinformation about Christianity" and to direct an apology to the Roman state (1927b:315). Cadbury cited instances from the papyri where *asphalein* (v. 4) means "the truth," and he claimed that the position of the word at the end of the sentence made it emphatic (1922d:509). So, while Theophilus cannot be identified, there is no reason to doubt that he was a real person. Cadbury's position was that Theophilus was a Roman official who had received unfavorable reports about the activities of the Christians (1921b:439-40).

Lukan Summaries and Speeches

Gaventa's third section (Gaventa, 16-18) is concerned with Cadbury's contributions to the five-volume work, *The Beginnings of Christianity*, published between 1920 and 1933. She selects for comment three of his notes which appear adjacent to one another in Volume 5: "Names for Christians and Christianity in Acts," an examination of the linguistic and historical origins of nineteen different words; "The Summaries in Acts," an analysis of Luke's use of "connective tissue" by which particular incidents received from tradition are incorporated into his narrative; and "The Speeches in Acts," a discussion primarily of the issue of their historicity. Gaventa's treatment of both the summaries and the speeches deserves elaboration—brief in the case of the former and detailed with regard to the latter.

For Cadbury, the summaries in Acts 2:41-47; 4:32-35; and 5:12-16, all exhibited considerable repetition and parallelism by reflecting the unity of the church (e.g., in the sharing of all property). Believing the summaries to have come from the author's hand, Cadbury concluded:

"To Luke himself rather than to his sources must be assigned the origin of these summaries" (1933j:399[n.2]).

Gaventa's summary of Cadbury's note on the speeches touches on some of the key points raised there, but her treatment covers only half of the essay. In order to clarify further what Cadbury understood as the function of the speeches, I will call attention to several issues discussed in the first half of his note in an attempt to complement Gaventa's analysis. Also, since Cadbury's examination of the Acts speeches was, by no means, limited to this note, I will bring together his views on the subject from three additional sources: his essay "The Greek and Jewish Traditions of Writing History" (1922a:7-29), and his books *The Making of Luke-Acts* (1927b) and *The Book of Acts in History* (1955a).

Cadbury described the custom of antiquity as, for the most part, that of inventing speeches without "any real knowledge of what was said" (1933k:405). By composing speeches and placing them on the lips of chief actors when great issues were at stake or great decisions had to be made, historians of antiquity varied their styles and displayed their rhetorical skill. Such discourses became for the historian, as Cadbury put it, "objects of special care and pride" (1927b:184). Cadbury spoke of recasting the substance of an original passage and offered as examples the speech of Caesar to his soldiers in the history of Dio Cassius,[1] which is quite different from the brief address reported by Caesar himself[2] on the same occasion (1922a:13-14), and Josephus' verbose elaboration of Samuel's rebuke of Saul in 1 Sam 15:22 (1927b:153-4).[3]

The prayers offered by David and Solomon in 2 Sam and 1 Kgs are obviously free compositions of the Deuteronomist. And in the work of the Chronicler is to be found "an elaborate example of the employment of sources and the introduction of literary devices." The author, however, according to Cadbury, is "no mere collector; he has a marked style of his own and gives to all the material he uses the impress of his personality" (1922a:16-17). In 1 Macc 3:50-53, the prayer offered by Judas and his company before attacking Gorgias is, Cadbury posited, not unlike the prayer of Peter and John in Acts 4:24-30 (1922a:23).

With regard to the Acts discourses, it was Cadbury's contention that "the elaborate, homogeneous and schematic speeches suggest, if not the rhetoric, at least the free composition of the speeches in Greek and Roman histories" (1922a:15). "More probable than the hypothesis of

---

[1]Dio Cassius, *History*, xxxviii.36-46.

[2]*B.G.* I. 40.

[3]Josephus, *Ant.* 6.7.4 par. 147ff.

much direct recollection of words actually spoken," Cadbury said, "is the surmise that the author has like other historians more or less successfully composed speeches suited to the speakers and occasions out of his own imagination" (1927b:190). Further, "there is no reason to suppose that notes were taken either in short-hand or in long-hand when the speeches were being delivered" (1933k:406). "The voice," he proclaimed, "is the voice of Luke" (1933k:407). Cadbury provided a thorough analysis of the points of comparison between the speeches in Acts and epistles attributed to the same person (1933k:410-13). In the case of Paul, Luke apparently knew the apostle's style and language well enough to have consciously imitated them in his attempt to illuminate the various sides of his ministry and doctrine. Subtle "Paulinisms" in the speech in chap. 13 attest that Luke was attempting to give it a Pauline "ring" (1933k:411).

In the second half of Cadbury's note on the speeches, which is not discussed by Gaventa, are found several important contributions. Cadbury believed that Luke's variation of style to suit the occasion is obvious in his use of proper names. The most famous illustration is Acts 13:9, where Luke employed the ancient counterpart to our term "alias": "Saul, who is also called Paul." Now that Paul's mission among the Gentiles had begun, Luke made the transition from the Hebrew to the Roman name out of his desire to use appropriate nomenclature (1933k:417-18). Luke repeated the account of Paul's conversion three times, Cadbury believed, because it was of crucial importance to him. Regarding the first account (Acts 9:1-19) as the original, Cadbury showed how elements such as reports of Paul's youth and his part in persecuting Christians, lacking in chap. 9, are prefaced to the later accounts (22:3-5 and 26:9-11). He also listed other instances of parallel reports in which the second account supplies items not mentioned in the first (1933k:422-24).

Notwithstanding the various attempts to ascribe the canticles of Luke 1 and 2 to a Semitic source or sources,[4] Cadbury, confident of Luke's ability to write in a Semitic style when it would serve his purpose, made a strong case for their being, in the main, Luke's own compositions

---

[4]See notably the work of Paul Winter: "Some Observations on the Language in the Birth and Infancy Stories of the Third Gospel," *NTS* 1 (1954) 111-21; "Magnificat and Benedictus—Maccabaen Psalms?" *BJRL* 37 (1954/55) 328-47; "The Main Literary Problem of the Lucan Infancy Story," *ATR* 40 (1958) 257-64; "The Proto-Source of Luke I," *NovT* 1 (1956) 184-99; and "On Luke and Lucan Sources," *ZNW* 47 (1956) 217-42.

(1933k:420). In discussing the synagogue sermon at Nazareth (Luke 4:16-30), Cadbury noted that, save for the traditional logion about a prophet being without honor in his own country (v. 24) taken from Mark 6:4, the address is primarily Luke's own elaboration. Cadbury observed that "There is much about the thought of the speech as well as the style that points to the author's free composition" (1927b:189).

Cadbury called attention to several literary devices employed by Luke in the Acts speeches. Among the most striking is the intentional interruption of the speakers following close upon some special word in the speech, e.g., the charge about Jesus in Acts 2:36 "whom you crucified" (1933k:425-26). Another device is Luke's indication to his readers of the close of formal quotations in the speeches by introducing a new vocative, e.g., the long quotation from Joel in Acts 2:17-21 is followed immediately by the address, "Men of Israel" (1933k:426). A third device is the author's use of litotes. Luke, alone of the NT writers, used this feature, which attests to his thorough knowledge of the Greek idiom of his time. The best-known example is Acts 21:39, where Paul boasts of citizenship in Tarsus, "no mean city" (1927b:120-21) .

Mention should also be made of Cadbury's contributions to the study of the Acts speeches in his 1955 volume, *The Book of Acts in History*, which is the focus of the fourth section of Gaventa's paper (Gaventa, 18-20). *History* deals with the general, Greek, Roman, Jewish, and Christian "concentric cultural environments" in Acts. Cadbury claimed, for example, that in fashioning the Stephen speech, Luke was indebted to Hellenistic Jewish sources, including Philo and Josephus, and that among the discrepancies between the OT and Stephen's historical summary is the special prominence given to Shechem (1955a:102-6). With regard to the Areopagus speech, Cadbury provided an enlightening discussion of the philosophical currents at work in Athens, parallels to the address in Greek literature, as well as Luke's use of quotations from the poets (1955a:45-50).

Lukan Eschatology

The last section of Gaventa's paper (Gaventa, 20-22) is devoted to Cadbury's article, "Acts and Eschatology," published in the 1956 C. H. Dodd *Festschrift* (1956a:300-321). While her treatment is fair and helpful, especially at the three points mentioned below, more needs to be said concerning Cadbury's contributions to the study of Lukan eschatology.

Gaventa correctly observes that Cadbury did not view the eschatology of Acts as "realized" (Gaventa, 21). With regard to "when the kingdom of God was coming" (Luke 17:20), Cadbury emphasized that there is no "emphatic change of time from future to present" (1956a:315) and that there is even linguistic support for rendering *entosh humōn* in the following verse "within your power" (1950a:172). The question in Acts 1:6—"Lord, will you at this time restore the kingdom to Israel?"—does not anticipate an imminent fulfillment. Cadbury was right when he remarked that this question "is not corrected by any hint of present partial realization" (1956a:315). But Luke apparently did have in mind some kind of salvation for Israel (see Acts 3:19-21), and he interpreted "the last days" (Acts 2:17) as, in some sense, having already begun. The eschatological drama will continue, and there will be a final intervention of God, but it is not imminent.

Gaventa is also right when she says that, according to Cadbury, the Gospel of Luke discouraged a "too early expectation" (Gaventa, 22). While Luke 9:27 suggests that some of Jesus' hearers will still be alive on that fateful day ("there are some standing here who will not taste of death before they see the kingdom of God"), Cadbury understood the parable of the pounds (Luke 19:22)—told near the end of Jesus' journey to Jerusalem when "they supposed that the kingdom of God was to appear immediately"—as an attempt to explain the delay of the Parousia (1927b:293).

Finally, Gaventa correctly emphasizes Cadbury's forceful warning against "spiritualizing away" Luke's concrete eschatological hopes (Gaventa, 21). As Cadbury put it: "It would be quite contrary to the practice of giving precision of time and place and manner to the divine intervention in history as Luke conceived it. If other Christians ancient or modern have found the primitive emphasis on such a literal future event embarrassing, Luke gives no real countenance to any of their ways of avoiding it" (1956a:315-16).

Lukan Christology

Among the topics not dealt with in Gaventa's paper is Lukan Christology. Such an omission needs correcting because Cadbury's contributions in this area are numerous and significant. His primary discussions of the subject are found in his note, "The Titles of Jesus in Acts" (1933h:354-75) and, to a lesser degree, in *Making*. I will summarize

Cadbury's position on the four major christological titles used in Acts: "Servant," "Lord," "Christ," and "Son of God."

Cadbury insisted that Jesus did not pattern his ministry on the Servant figure, and that other OT texts influenced him as much, if not more, than the Servant Songs of Isa 40-55. Further, there was no separate Servant Christology with which to identify, and all interpretations of Jesus as the Suffering Servant, including that of vicarious suffering and atonement, were introduced later in the early church to explain his death (1933h:364-70). In the OT, according to Cadbury, the term "Servant of the Lord" was a common expression frequently applied to the righteous in general, who are loyal to the service of Yahweh and endure suffering and humiliation for his sake. A partial list of Israelites who are so called includes Moses, David, Isaiah, and Job (1933h:365-67).

In Luke 22:37: "For...this scripture must be fulfilled in me, 'And he was reckoned with transgressors'," we have for the first and only time in the Synoptic Gospels a clear reference to Isa 53:12. Cadbury noted, however, that there is no allusion to the essential function of the Servant: the vicarious bearing of sin (1933h:366). In Acts 8:32-36, the text of Isa 53:7-8, quoted by the Ethiopian eunuch, is applied by Philip to Jesus. Reference to suffering for the sins of others, though, so eloquently expressed both immediately preceding and following the quoted verses, is conspicuous by its absence. Luke, amazingly, has passed over all the passages about vicarious sufferings which abound in Isa 53 (1927b:280[n. 2]). Luke may have had the Septuagint of Isa 52:13 in mind at Acts 3:13, but no use is made here, according to Cadbury, of the most distinctive feature of the Suffering Servant: the atoning value of the Servant's vicarious suffering (1933h:366; 368[n.1]). The idea that Christ died for our sins is striking by its complete absence from the Acts speeches (1927b: 229).

Twice in the missionary speeches of Acts (2:36 and 10:36), "Lord" is applied to Jesus as a title. According to Cadbury, at 2:36 "Lord" was joined with "Christ" with the combination having been derived from the Septuagint of Psalm 2:2 ("against the Lord and his anointed") (1933h:360). Cadbury regarded the abrupt expression "he is Lord of all" in 10:36 as "parenthetical and ejaculatory." Since there is no article, it is uncertain whether "Lord of all" is an actual title. Cadbury gave examples from the Apocrypha and Pseudepigrapha of similar expressions applied to God. He concluded that the occurrences of

"Lord" as a title for Jesus in Acts seem to reveal Luke's own free and unconscious use of the term (1933h:361-62).

Cadbury pointed out three features concerning the use of the title "Christ" in Acts: (1) it is rarely used as a name; (2) it is certainly never used by itself as a name; and (3) it usually bears a fully "messianic" connotation (1933h:357-59). In Luke 4:18, quoted from Isa 61:1, Jesus pronounced in the Nazareth synagogue: "The Spirit of the Lord is upon me, because he has anointed (*echrisen*) me." Cadbury observed that the Holy Spirit and Jesus as the Anointed One are meaningfully linked here by Luke. Jesus is the anointed bearer of the Spirit (1927b:277).

The trial of Jesus before the Council (Luke 22:66b-71) reveals Luke's interest in the title "Son of God." The chief priests and scribes said to him: "If you are the Christ, tell us" (v. 67). He answered them: "If I tell you, you will not believe." Later in the account (v. 70) they asked: "Are you the Son of God, then?" and he responded with: "You say that I am." Cadbury claimed that "Christ" and "Son of God" are used in parallelism here. In Acts 9:20, following his conversion, Paul proclaimed Jesus in the Damascus synagogues saying: "he is the Son of God." Two verses further on Paul is still "proving that Jesus was the Christ," again indicating that for Luke, as Cadbury has noted, "Christ" and "Son of God" are synonymous terms (1933h:363).

Conclusion

In conclusion, permit me a personal word. In her biographical sketch of Cadbury, Gaventa mentions that one of his honorary degrees was conferred by Earlham College, a Quaker institution in Richmond, Indiana. Following the completion of my graduate work at Duke University in the summer of 1966, I accepted a one-year appointment at Earlham's Religion Department. Early in the spring of 1967, I learned that the commencement speaker that year would be none other than Henry Joel Cadbury. This did not particularly surprise me since I knew (as does Gaventa) of his prominence in Quaker circles. But I was eager to meet the man by and about whom I had read so much. My eagerness was heightened the night before commencement when I was invited to a dinner party in his honor. When I was introduced to him as someone who had recently completed a Ph.D. on Luke-Acts, Cadbury greeted me, as Gaventa reminds us he frequently greeted his colleagues, with the words: "What have you learned that I ought to know?" Flattered, and yet at the same time feeling terribly inadequate, I responded: "I have been asking that question of you, sir, for the last three years." Beverly Roberts Gaventa's essay and the two responses in this volume are attempts to recognize the unparalleled contributions of Henry Joel Cadbury to the study of Luke-Acts in the twentieth century, or, to put it another way, "what he learned that we ought to know."

"On Perilous Things":
A Response to
Beverly R. Gaventa[1]

Richard I. Pervo

Gaventa cleverly invokes her thesis by evoking the title of one of her subject's books, albeit his least enduring volume. For Cadbury, "modernizing" was first and foremost the failure to situate texts and movements within their historical parameters. He was at home within the literary remains of the Greco-Roman world and devoted his career to the delineation of its particularities for the purpose of illuminating Christian origins.[2] Cadbury thoroughly discouraged any facile attempts to portray Jesus as an enlightened humanitarian or Luke as a democratic socialist—or as an historian in the tradition of von Ranke. Just as Hobart had failed to establish a comprehensive linguistic field for his investigation of "medical vocabulary," so had Harnack (whose historical methods strongly influenced Cadbury) neglected the apocalyptic background and content of the teaching of Jesus when formulating his lectures on the essence of Christianity.[3] To treat the author of Luke and

---

[1]Shortly after Cadbury's death, Amos Wilder shared his reminiscences with the NT Graduate Seminar at Harvard (where I was then engaged in writing a thesis on Acts). These included many of the anecdotes included in this collection, to which I shall add another: at a banquet in Geneva concluding a post-War conference treating the problem of refugees, Cadbury found himself appointed M.C. Those present included a galaxy of ecclesiastical, military, political, and titular dignitaries. Having no grasp of the requisite protocol, Cadbury, to the delight of some and presumably the horror of others, cut the knot by introducing each of these worthies as "Mister": a splendidly Quaker and democratic resolution.

His status is further confirmed by the attachment to him of a "floating apophthegm." A Harvard Professor of Classics used to enjoy telling an old joke ("Do you believe in infant baptism?" "Believe it? Sir, I have seen it!") as a Cadburian *ipsissimum verbum*.

[2]Gaventa thus correctly sees German Form Criticism as one impetus to his work (Gaventa, 24).

[3]*What is Christianity?*, 1901. A summary of Harnack's views of Jesus' message may be found in his *History of Dogma*, tr. N. Buchanan (New York: Dover, 1900, rp.1961) 1:58-76.

Acts like a modern rationalist was for Cadbury nearly as reprehensible as "modernizing Jesus." This perspective creates the great gulf between him and another historical scholar, W. M. Ramsay.

A Firm Foundation

Cadbury's road to and through the past traveled upon the back of (often unpleasant) facts. He never lost his youthful passion for Philologia.[4] The windows he opened upon the social world of early Christianity admitted the sunshine of lexicography. Even late in his career he could revel in discovering an illustration for "waving garments" (Acts 22:3) in the *Acta Alexandrinorum*.[5]

For Cadbury, as for his long-time colleague A. D. Nock, facts were sacred things and generalizations likely to be goblins.[6] He believed that facts were eternal verities and strove to present them in a timeless manner. This patient and attractive elucidation of small details, skillfully assembled by an apparent master of all that he surveyed, gives Cadbury's writings enduring value and abiding testimony to the importance of data, especially the most implacable and recalcitrant facts.

A Universal Patron

As transparent as his works are, they are also elusive. Cadbury was so discrete in expressing his views that scholars as diverse as Ward Gasque and Ernst Haenchen can read him sympathetically.[7] His writings are apparently ageless windows to the past. They are also mirrors. Small wonder that the

The object of Cadbury's criticism was the old Liberal theology which lived on in this country as if Weiss, Wrede, Bultmann and Barth had not shattered the exegetical bases of its position and as if World War I had not raised fundamental challenges.

[4]Thus, while spurning the fallacy of "modernizing Jesus," Cadbury justified his commitment to causes (a commitment that once cost him his position) by saying, "I'm still trying to translate the New Testament" (Gaventa 10), a statement made the year following the appearance of the RSV NT). This was a metaphor that spoke to him as philosophy or systematic theology did not.

[5]Without, it should be noted, offering any comment upon possible implications of this source for the understanding of Acts (see 1955a:38).

[6]This instinctive distrust of theory may offer a partial explanation for Cadbury's reluctance to recognize the inspiration he received from Bultmann and (especially) Dibelius and for his indifference to Conzelmann. For his view of theories as ephemeral structures, see 1955a:127-28. His sustained hesitation about efforts to classify Ephesians as Deutero-Pauline reveal one weakness of this stance (cf. 1959). The other is, as we should say today, that it is impossible to do scholarship devoid of theory and that it is incumbent upon practitioners to make their theories explicit.

[7]W. Ward Gasque says, "It is difficult to do justice to the immense contribution of H. J. Cadbury to the study of the Lucan writings," *A History of the Criticism of the Acts of the Apostles* (Grand Rapids: Eerdmans, 1975) 185. Note the dedication in the English translation of Haenchen's *Acts*, and the quote from p. 37 cited by Gaventa (Gaventa, 16).

scholars cited by Gaventa (Gaventa, 7-8) hail him as the patron of the literary approach to Luke. In the sixty's one could see in *Making*, Conzelmann *in nuce*.[8] *Profit with Delight*[9] resulted from a vigorous (or reckless, if you will) pursuit of some of Cadbury's suggestions. Because of his comprehensive scope and openness of mind, Cadbury may be claimed as patron by every scholar grinding a particular Lukan axe, including both those who would say "Luke-Acts" and those who prefer "Luke and Acts."[10] Axes of his own Cadbury had, but he ground them so fine that they could remove a head without disturbing the victim.

Cadbury is the forerunner of the contemporary literary approach in regard to the question of historicity. He regarded Luke and Acts as created (which is not to say concocted) products of their author and proceeded from the methodological principle that the works could not be properly understood if merely quarried for factual data or scrutinized for underlying traditions. To state his approach positively, he did not wish to make historicity a bone of contention. It is often possible to read Cadbury as historicizing,[11] and equally

---

[8]See the lengthy discussion of the "Delay of the Parousia" (1927b:286-296), and Gaventa's comments (Gaventa, 20-22). When Cadbury wrote these pages he was dealing with the question of "modernizing" by emphasizing the eschatological dimension of the text rather than working within a context which presumed this character.

[9]Richard I. Pervo, *Profit with Delight: The Literary Genre of the Acts of the Apostles* (Phildelphia: Fortress Press,1987). In particular, this applies to statements like, "Sometimes the fictitious romances offer the best parallel. I do not know where one can get so many illustrations of the idiom and ideas of the author of Acts in 150 pages as in the love story of his near contemporary, Chariton of Aphrodisias" (1955a:8); and in general, to Cadbury's appeal to a variety of genres (1927b:60) and his recognition of the popular character of Luke and Acts (1927b:140-154). *Profit* contains abundant references to Cadbury's works. The dissertations of Douglas R. Edwards (Boston 1987) and Susan M. Praeder (G.T.U. 1980) are further evidence of ripples flowing from that brief allusion to Chariton.

[10]Cadbury is acknowledged as the creator of "Luke-Acts," yet he distinguished them in a number of ways, such as genre (1927b:10, 134), style (1955a:8), and theology (1927b:274-296). In any case, he remains best remembered for his contributions on Acts.

[11]Perhaps least so in *Beginnings* (1922a:4). In her review of the notes in *Beginnings* (1922a:5), Gaventa points to the historical focus (Gaventa, 18). This valid judgment should take into account the purpose of the project, whose originators were Foakes-Jackson and Lake. The object was to write a history of Christian origins, a task then seen to require a historical critique of Acts as a preliminary stage. Thus the now otiose "Part I" of the actual title. Cadbury's contributions to *Beginnings* do not necessarily derive from his own scholarly agenda and ought not be invoked as evidence of his lack of literary interest.

possible to read him as a judicious and sensitive skeptic.[12] In modern terms the question for Cadbury is that of the implied author.[13]

This protean quality has the merits of being all things to all people—an inexhaustible treasure chest providing great rewards on dive after dive into the depths. However, the drawbacks are there also. The problem is not that others may dredge up oyster shells and believe that they have found pearls left by Cadbury; scholars must take responsibility for their views. It is rather that, for example, we did not appreciate how much Cadbury had anticipated Conzelmann until Conzelmann came along and pointed out the issues.[14] By stating his views with such reserve and by diffidently sprinkling his pages with "perhaps," "probably," and "evidently," Cadbury protected himself from possibly exaggerated assertions, but also obscured for his readers some implications worthy of continued investigation.[15]

Luke the Historian

The above remarks do not intend to suggest that Cadbury was an artful dodger. He is the prototype of the leading contemporary approach to Luke and Acts in that he gave primacy to non-historical questions, however without excluding them from his purview. Comments about accuracy appear at the end of *Making*, judiciously stated and judiciously placed to avoid contamination (1927b:364-368—all governed by "*In medio tutissime ibis*"). To some extent this approach, however cloaked in caution, is preferable to those more recent works which leave the reader wondering just what the author thinks "actually happened."

---

[12]Even in his mature years, Cadbury could assert that the "general fitness to its time" of Acts was "really more important than any exact correspondence of its narrative with historical fact" (1955a:4, v). Gaventa (Gaventa, 13) makes the same point, with an apt citation from *Making* (1927b:7). For one example of writing seemingly designed to evoke skepticism, see 1927b:342-343. At the heart of the matter lies Cadbury's insistence that his readers take responsibility for their opinions. As one who was reluctant to cite secondary sources as "proof," he did not make it easy for others to trade on the basis of his authority.

[13]Gaventa's observation that *The Book of Acts in History* (1955a) reflects a nearly credulous approach toward the reliability of Acts (Gaventa, 20) illustrates the dilemma. Her reading is certainly defensible, but it does not take his opening qualifications fully into account. Is this the real Cadbury, firmly convinced of the reliability of Acts but cautious as always, or does he merely illustrate verisimilitude (as the citation in the previous note seems to imply) and leave such judgments in the reader's hands? How reliable is this narrator? The question is only enhanced by the recognition that the older Cadbury appears to have been more conservative than the younger.

[14]Issues that he resolved by erecting a theory of salvation history, a procedure by nature uncongenial to Cadbury, not least when sustained in the face of some inconvenient data.

[15]In literary-critical terms one may speak of the influence of Conzelmann upon Cadbury. For the past twenty five years theological students have nearly always first encountered Conzelmann, even if at second hand and do not come to Cadbury with either blank minds or with the issues of the 1920's.

Forerunner of Redaction Criticism

Perhaps a more precise designation for Cadbury would be the *prodromos* of late Redaction Criticism.[16] One need but glance through the pages of Bultmann's *History of the Synoptic Tradition* and Streeter's *The Four Gospels* to be reminded of the extent to which even the cutting edge of post-World War I scholarship regarded the evangelists as primarily mechanical collectors of traditions and/or arrangers of sources. Gaventa's statement that *Making* deals with the author largely through asking what materials he received (Gaventa, 14) could be misleading, for Cadbury rigorously opposed the use of sources as the principal means for explanations of Luke's writing. This is one aspect of his long opposition to the views of Torrey. If the point of departure was linguistic, the result was a portrait of a conscious author[17] in control of the sources available and selected. This scholarly tradition, represented by Dibelius, Cadbury, Easton, and Haenchen, not only anticipated later Redaction Criticism, but also prepared the ground for its natural heir: literary criticism that is increasingly indifferent to source questions and to the problem of genre(s).[18] This is one instance in which methods developed for the study of Acts have subsequently been applied to the analysis of the Gospels.[19] A relevant example of Cadbury's approach is his observation that the journeys of Paul influenced Luke's portrayal of the journey of Jesus (1927b:231-232).

Had Charles Talbert followed Cadbury to the letter, we should be considerably poorer, for one major difference between the late Harvard Professor and contemporary Acts scholars concerns the plan or plans of Luke and Acts. The patron of Luke-Acts scholarship did not believe that the author followed a plan and dismissed the possibility of a literary structure overarching the entire work (1927b:325).[20] This view dramatically expresses Cadbury's focus upon the minute and the particular. The unity of Luke and Acts discovered by Cadbury is the unity imposed by an author's control of disparate

---

[16]A view shared, with qualifications, by Gasque, *History*, 186.

[17]See Gaventa's remarks on Cadbury's view of Luke as a personality (Gaventa, 14-15). By this term Cadbury did not refer to psychology. The depth of his sophistication emerges in the quote from E. M. Forster (1927b:348-349), a citation that could still inform discussions about the role of the omniscient, anonymous narrators in the biblical tradition.

[18]Haenchen routinely began his analysis of each pericope by dynamiting the structures erected by Source Criticism so that the field of the text itself might come to light, explicitly moving beyond the question of what Luke did with his sources to the question of what Luke wished to accomplish. He did not directly address the question of genre.

[19]The contrary is more customary. See *Profit with Delight,* 2, and the references given there.

[20]Cf. also Gaventa's observation (Gaventa, 15-16). The reference is to C. H. Talbert, *Literary Patterns, Theological Themes and the Genre of Luke-Acts,* SBLMS 20 (Missoula: Scholars, 1974).

materials held together by individual style, personal interests and views, and the force of a single authorial will. His valuable portrait of Luke the author comes from the assembly of a number of details. A fair amount of that assembly must be made by the reader, whence the above-mentioned number of Cadburys to be found in scholarly assessments. All, or at least most of them are authentic, for they are indebted to his basic insight that Luke and Acts must be studied in relation to one another.

Two more of the seeds scattered by this fruitful mind deserve recognition. His discussion of the differences between Luke and Acts foreshadows Canon Criticism, for he has a clear understanding of the canonical function of each work, in particular of the role of Acts as a bridge between Jesus and Paul, Gospels and Epistles, with an implicit recognition of the traditional function of Acts as a hermeneutical key to Paul (1927b:10, 134; Gaventa, 20). He further anticipates modern criticism through the realization that the meaning of a work cannot be determined from biographical information about the author or identification of the author's intentions alone (1955a:136-7). In the last analysis, questions about author, date, and provenience are more important for understanding early church history than for determining the meaning of the work within Christian history.

Polemics and Dependence

Gaventa does well to point out that Cadbury was not only not engaged in written[21] dialogue with other scholars, but was also silent about some of those whose work was most influential upon him. Cadbury was irenic by nature and faith, but he was not unwilling to engage in polemic. His gentle reprimands are often difficult to detect, for many of them emerge in his silences, but this very style often sharpens his polemic. If he was not given his due by Conzelmann (as he was not), it is equally true that Cadbury did not acknowledge his proper debt to Dibelius. In this matter his style was rather British than American—older at any rate, and no longer to be emulated.[22]

Conclusion

Beverly Gaventa has presented a critical sketch of Cadbury's life and work, raising important issues for discussion. My response has attempted to

---

[21]With regard to oral dialogue the question identified by Don Jones reveals an approach that could be interpreted as self-interested. The tales told about the RSV committee adumbrate a tough negotiator rather than a team player.

[22]Gaventa observes that Cadbury did not repudiate his earlier positions (Gaventa, 23). One example occurs in *The Book of Acts in History* (1955a:22f.), where he employs the passive, "A few years ago the view was expressed," to cite his previous view.

offer refining comments to her assessment. If Cadbury sought scholarly immortality through the composition of timeless, academic prose nourished with erudition, seasoned with wit, graced with style, and colored throughout with a sweet reasonableness, he met his life's goal, yet without forsaking his vocation as Christian and citizen. No small part of the nearly universal admiration he receives is due to the recognition that today's academic life makes it all but impossible for any of us to be Cadburys. We cannot master the texts as he did, for secondary literature abounds, challenging new methods demand attention, and the administrative burdens of professorial life have increased vastly.

What have we learned that he did not know? We have learned the values of collaboration and interdisciplinary studies. We have learned that the notion of a single, objective method in which pure logic that confronts naked data is illusory. We have learned that genuine pluralism brings revelation which both distresses and exhilarates. Would H. J. Cadbury despise such learning? Scarcely. The heritage of his writing and his life will continue to remind us that trying to translate the New Testament is still a perilous thing.[23]

---

[23]Members of the scholarly community could both honor Cadbury and enrich ourselves by finding some means for a (presumably photographic) reprint collection of Cadbury's articles and reviews, together with suitable indices.

BIBLIOGRAPHY OF HENRY JOEL CADBURY*

Beverly Roberts Gaventa

1917   "A Possible Case of Lukan Authorship (John 7:53-8:11)." *HTR* 10:237-44.
1918   "Basis of Early Christian Antimilitarism." *JBL* 37:66-94.
1920a   "Luke--Translator or Author?" *AJT* 24: 436-55.
1920b   *National Ideals in the Old Testament.* New York: Scribner's.
1920c   *The Style and Literary Method of Luke.* Part I: *The Diction of Luke and Acts.* HTS 6. Cambridge: Harvard University Press.
1921a   "The Medical Language of Hippocrates." *HTR* 14:106.
1921b   "The Purpose Expressed in Luke's Preface." *The Expositor* (Series 8) 21:431-41.
1922a   "The Composition and Purpose of Acts: The Greek and Jewish Traditions of Writing History." 2:7-29 in *The Beginnings of Christianity.* Part I: *The Acts of the Apostles.* Edited by F. J. Foakes Jackson and Kirsopp Lake. 5 vols. London: Macmillan. (Hereafter cited as *BC.*)
1922b   "The Identity of the Editor of Luke and Acts: The Tradition." *BC* 2:209-264.
1922c   "The Identity of the Editor of Luke and Acts: Subsidiary Points." *BC* 2:349-62 (Co-authored with F. J. Foakes Jackson and Kirsopp Lake).
1922d   "Appendix C: Commentary on the Preface of Luke." *BC* 2:489-510.
1922e   "The Knowledge Claimed in Luke's Preface." *The Expositor* (Series 8) 24:401-20.
1922f   "The Social Translation of the Gospel." *HTR* 15:1-13.
1923a   "Between Jesus and the Gospels." *HTR* 16:81-92.
1923b   "The Relative Pronouns in Acts and Elsewhere." *JBL* 42:150-57.

1924a   "The Ancient Physiological Notions Underlying John I:13 and Hebrews XI:11." *The Expositor* 12:1-10.

1924b   "David's Defense Test." *Christian Century* 41:1302-1304.

1925a   "The Apocalypse, An Appreciation." *Crozer Quarterly* 2:259-64.

1925b   "Jesus and the Prophets." *JR* 5:607-622.

1925c   "Lexical Notes on Luke-Acts. 1." *JBL* 44:214-27.

1926a   "Collation of the Peshitto Texts of Acts." *BC* 3:291-316.

1926b   "Collation of the Vulgate Text of Acts." *BC* 3:276-90.

1926c   "Divine Inspiration in the New Testament." Pp. 369-75 in *An Outline of Christianity: The Story of Our Civilization*. Vol. 4. Ed. Francis J. McConnell. New York: Bethlehem Publishers.

1926d   "Lexical Notes on Luke-Acts. 2. Recent Arguments for Medical Language." *JBL* 45:190-209.

1926e   "Lexical Notes on Luke-Acts. 3. Luke's Interest in Lodging." *JBL* 45:305-322.

1926f   "Questions of Authorship in the New Testament." Pp. 376-84 in *An Outline of Christianity: The Story of Our Civilization*. Vol. 4. Ed. Francis J. McConnell. New York: Bethlehem Publishers.

1926g   "Results of New Testament Research." Pp. 385-94 in *An Outline of Christianity: The Story of Our Civilization*. Vol. 4. Ed. Francis J. McConnell. New York: Bethlehem Publishers.

1927a   "The Bible, Its Nature and Use." Pp. 123-31 in *Religion and Modern Life*. New York: Scribners.

1927b   *The Making of Luke-Acts*. New York: Macmillan.

1927c   "Mark 16:8." *JBL* 46:344-45.

1928a   "Concurrent Phases of Paul's Religion." Pp. 369-89 in *Studies in Early Christianity*, ed. by S.J. Case. New York: The Century Company.

1928b   "The Historic Jesus." [Review of S.J. Case, *Jesus: A New Biography*.] *JR* 8:130-36.

1928c   "The Odor of the Spirit at Pentecost." *JBL* 47:237-56.

1929a   "Egyptian Influence in the Book of Proverbs." *JR* 9:99-108.

1929b   "The Language of the New Testament." Pp. 880-84 in *The Abingdon Bible Commentary*. Edited by Frederick Carl Eiselen, Edwin Lewis, and David G. Downey. Nashville: Abingdon-Cokesbury.

1929c   "Lexical Notes on Luke-Acts. 4. On Direct Quotation, with Some Uses of *hoti* and *ei*." *JBL* 48:412-25.

1929d   "Luke, Gospel of." *Encyclopedia Britannica*. 14th ed. 14:475-78.

1930a   "The Ethics of Paul." *Crozer Quarterly* 7:423-48.

1930b   "*Theatrizo* no longer a New Testament hapaxlegomenon," *ZNW* 29:60-63.

1931   "Erastus of Corinth (Acts 19:22)." *JBL* 50:42-58.

1933a   *English Translation and Commentary. BC* 4 (Co-authored with Kirsopp Lake).

1933b   "Lexical Notes on Luke-Acts. 5. Luke and the Horse-Doctors." *JBL* 52:55-65.

1933c   "Note 7. The Hellenists." *BC* 5:59-74.

1933d   "Note 24. Dust and Garments." *BC* 5:269-77.

1933e   "Note 26. Roman Law and the Trial of Paul." *BC* 5:297-338.

1933f   "Note 27. The Winds." *BC* 5:338-44 (Co-authored with Kirsopp Lake).

1933g   "Note 28. *hupozōmata*." *BC* 5:345-54.

1933h   "Note 29. The Titles of Jesus in Acts." *BC* 5:354-75.

1933i   "Note 30. Names for Christians and Christianity in Acts." *BC* 5:375-92.

1933j   "Note 31. The Summaries in Acts." *BC* 5:392-402.

1933k   "Note 32. The Speeches in Acts." *BC* 5:402-427.

1933l   "Note 36. The Family of the Herods." *BC* 5:487-89.

1933m   "Note 37. Lucius of Cyrene." *BC* 5:489-95.

1933n   "Some Semitic Personal Names in Luke-Acts." Pp. 45-56 in *Amicitiae Corolla. A Volume of Essays Presented to James Rendel Harris on the Occasion of His Eightieth Birthday*. Edited by H. G. Wood. London: University of London Press.

1934   "The Macellum of Corinth." *JBL* 53:134-41.

1935   "Introduction to the New Testament (Special Reading List)." *Bulletin of the General Theological Seminary Library* 28.1:9-14.

1936a   "My Professor's Closet." *Harvard Alumni Bulletin* 39:297-301.

1936b   "The New Testament *Versus* Christianity." Pp. 25-36 in *Harvard Divinity School Annual, 1935-36*.

1937a   "Motives of Biblical Scholarship." *JBL* 56:1-16.

1937b   *The Peril of Modernizing Jesus*. New York: Macmillan.

48   *Beverly Roberts Gaventa*

1937c   "Rebuttal, A Submerged Motif in the Gospels." Pp. 99-109 in *Quantulacumque*. Ed. R.P. Casey. London: Christophers, 1937.
1938   "The Present State of New Testament Studies." Pp. 79-110 in *Haverford Symposium on Archaeology and the Bible*. New Haven: American Society of Oriental Research.
1939   "The Meaning of John 20:23, Matthew 16:19 and Matthew 18:18." *JBL* 58:251-54.
1941   "New Testament Study in the Next Generation." *JR* 21:412-20.
1943   "Review of John Knox, *Marcion and the New Testament*." *JBL* 62:123-27.
1944a   "From Gospel to Gospel." *The New Christianity* 10:1-12.
1944b   "The Informality of Early Christianity." *Crozer Quarterly* 21:246-50.
1946a   "The Bible in English (Special Reading List)." *Bulletin of the General Theological Seminary Library* 38.4:6-8.
1946b   "From One Culture to Another." *The New Christianity* 12:93-99.
1946c   "Revision After Revision." *The American Scholar* 15:298-305.
1946d   "Superfluous *kai* in the Lord's Prayer and Elsewhere." Pp. 41-47 in *Munera Studiosa*. Ed. M. H. Shepherd, Jr., and S. E. Johnson. Cambridge: Episcopal Theological Seminary.
1947a   *Jesus. What Manner of Man*. New York: Macmillan.
1947b   "The New Translation's First Year." *Christian Century* 64:170-71.
1947c   "A Reply to the Review of the New Testament: Revised Standard Version." *The Classical Weekly* 41:92-94.
1948a   "A Possible Perfect in Acts 9:34." *JTS* 49:57-58.
1948b   "Review of H. Sahlin, *Der Messias und das Gottesvolk: Studien zur Proto-lukanischen Theologie*." *JBL* 67:73-74.
1949a   *Gospel Parallels*. Ed. with F. C. Grant and C. T. Craig. New York: Nelson.
1949b   "The Peril of Archaizing Ourselves." *Int* 3:331-38.
1950a   "The Kingdom of God and Ourselves." *Christian Century* 67:172-73.
1950b   "Review of H. Sahlin, *Studien zum dritten Kapitel des Lukasevangeliums*." *JBL* 69:81-82.
1951a   "From Evangelists to Popes." *Harvard Divinity School Bulletin* 48:33-43.

1951b "Mixed Motives in the Gospels." *Proceedings of the American Philosophical Society* 95:117-24.

1951c "The New Testament and Early Christian Literature." *IB* 3:32-42.

1951d "Overconversion in Paul's Churches." Pp. 43-50 in *The Joy of Study: Papers in Honour of F.C. Grant*. Ed. S. E. Johnson. New York: Macmillan.

1951e "The Vocabulary and Grammar of New Testament Greek." *BT* 2:153-59.

1953a "The Danger of Overtranslation." *ExpTim* 64:381.

1953b "Life and Character of Jesus (Special Reading List)." *Bulletin of the General Theological Library* 45.3:4-6.

1953c *A Quaker Approach to the Bible*. Ward Lecture, Guilford, N.C.: Guilford College, 1953.

1953d "Review of L. Girard, *L'Évangile des voyages de Jésus*." *JBL* 72:69.

1953e "Translation Principles of the R.S.V." *Christian Century* 70:1388-90.

1954a "Current Issues in New Testament Studies." *Harvard Divinity School Bulletin* 51:49-64.

1954b "The Single Eye." *HTR* 47:69-74.

1955a *The Book of Acts in History*. New York: Harper.

1955b "The Grandson of Ben Sira." *HTR* 8:219-25.

1955c "New Light on Old Scrolls." *Unitarian Christian* 11:9-12.

1955d "Review of J. C. Dancy, *A Commentary on 1 Maccabees*." *JBL* 74:44.

1956a "Acts and Eschatology." Pp. 300-321 in *The Background of the New Testament and Its Eschatology: Studies in Honour of Charles Harold Dodd*. Eds. W. D. Davies and D. Daube. Cambridge: Cambridge University Press.

1956b "Review of Ernst Haenchen, *Die Apostelgeschichte*." *JBL* 76:65-66.

1956c "'We' and 'I' Passages in Luke-Acts." *NTS* 3:128-32.

1957a "A Liberal Approach to the Bible." *JRT* 14:119-28.

1957b *Quakerism and Early Christianity*. Swarthmore Lecture. London: Allen and Unwin.

1958a "The Exegetical Conscience." *Nexus* 11:3-6.

1958b "A Qumran Parallel to Paul." *HTR* 51:1-2.

1958c "Review of G. Ricciotti, *The Acts of the Apostles: Text and Commentary*; C. H. Rieu, *The Acts of the Apostles, by*

Saint Luke; and C. S. C. Williams, *The Acts of the Apostles.*" *JBL* 77:171-74.

1958d "Some Foibles of New Testament Scholarship." *JBR* 26:213-16.

1959   "The Dilemma of Ephesians." *NTS* 5:91-102.

1960a "Intimations of Immortality in the Thought of Jesus" (The Ingersoll Lecture for 1959). *HTR* 53:1-26.

1960b "New Testament Scholarship: Fifty Years in Retrospect." *JBR* 28:194-98.

1960c "Review of S. V. McCasland, *The Religion of the Bible.*" *JBL* 79:382.

1960d "Soluble Difficulties in the Parables." Pp. 118-23 in *New Testament Sidelights.* Ed. H. K. McArthur. Hartford: Hartford Press.

1961a *Jesus and Judaism.* Shrewsbury Lecture. Indianapolis: Woolman Press, 1961.

1961b "Review of Dom Jacques Dupont, *Les Sources du Livre des Actes: État de la Question.*" *JBL* 80:78-79.

1961c "Review of Hans Conzelmann, *The Theology of St. Luke.*" *JBL* 80:78-79.

1961d "Review of J. C. O'Neill, *The Theology of Acts in Its Historical Setting.*" *JBL* 81:197-98.

1961e "Review of R. C. Dentan, *The Design of the Scriptures: A First Reader in Biblical Theology.*" *JBL* 80:289-90.

1962a "Acts of the Apostles." *IDB* 1:28-42.

1962b "Lexical Notes on Luke-Acts. 6. A Proper Name for Dives." *JBL* 81:399-402.

1962c "The Unappreciated Paul." *Friends Journal* 8:408-11.

1962d "Varieties of Religion in the New Testament." *Friends Journal* 8:120-22.

1963a "Lexical Notes on Luke-Acts. 7. Some Lukan Expressions of Time." *JBL* 82:272-78.

1963b "Looking at the Gospel Backward." *SE* II:47-56.

1964a *The Eclipse of the Historical Jesus.* Haverford Library Lectures. Pendle Hill pamphlet 133. Wallingford, PA: Pendle Hill Publications.

1964b "Gospel Study and Our Image of Early Christianity." *JBL* 83:139-45.

1964c "Review of M. Goguel, *The Primitive Church.*" *JBL* 83:422-23.

1965a "The Name for Dives." *JBL* 84:73.

1965b   "Review of A. Q. Morton and G. H. C. Macgregor, *The Structure of Luke and Acts.*" *JBL* 84:337-38.

1966a   "Four Features of Lucan Style." Pp. 87-102 in *Studies in Luke-Acts: Essays Presented in Honor of Paul Schubert.* Edited by Leander E. Keck and J. Louis Martyn. Nashville: Abingdon Press.

1966b   "Review of J. C. Fenton, *The Gospel of St. Matthew,* D. E. Nineham, *The Gospel of St. Mark,* G. B. Caird, *The Gospel of St. Luke.*" *JTS* 17:138-40.

1966c   "Review of J. P. Hyatt, ed., *The Bible in Modern Scholarship.*" *JBL* 85:236-37.

1967   "Review of Eldon J. Epp, *The Theological Tendency of Codex Bezae Cantabrigiensis in Acts.*" *JBL* 86:112-14.

1968a   *Behind the Gospels.* Pendle Hill pamphlet 160. Wallingford, PA: Pendle Hill Publications.

1969   "Review of J. Neusner (ed.), *Religions in Antiquity: Essays in Memory of Erwin Ramsdell Goodenough.*" *JBL* 88:83-84.

1972a   "Animals and Symbolism in Luke (Lexical Notes on Luke-Acts, 9)." Pp. 3-15 in *Studies in New Testament and Early Christian Literature: Essays in Honor of A. P. Wikgren.* Edited by D. E. Aune. Leiden: E. J. Brill.

1972b   "Litotes in Acts (Lexical Notes on Luke-Acts, 8)." Pp. 58-69 in *Festschrift to Honor F. W. Gingrich.* Eds. E. H. Barth and R. E. Cocroft. Leiden: E. J. Brill.

*This bibliography contains Cadbury's writings on the Bible and related topics. It does not include his extensive writings on the Quakers and their history, except for those few articles in which the two interests intersect. For a bibliography of his writings on the Quakers, see: Margaret Hope Bacon, *Let This Life Speak: The Legacy of Henry Joel Cadbury* (Philadelphia: University of Pennsylvania Press, 1987) 237-43; and "Expanded Bibliography of Henry J. Cadbury, to 1974 and including Quaker History," Quaker Collection, Haverford College Library, 1986. An earlier bibliography that does not cover Quaker writings is "Toward a Bibliography of Henry Joel Cadbury," *Harvard Divinity School Bulletin, 1953-54,* 65-70. I am grateful to my former student assistant, A. Pieter Kiwiet-Pantaleoni, for his work during the initial stages of developing this bibliography.

THE QUESTIONING MIND
OF JOHN KNOX

John Knox and the Acts of the Apostles

Joseph B. Tyson

Introduction

To assess the contribution of John Knox to the study of the book of Acts is to highlight only one of the many contributions this scholar has made to the study of the NT, the history of Christianity, and Christian theology. His interests have ranged from the historical study of Pauline chronology to practical interests in the church's ministry and the integrity of its preaching. He has been equally at home in theoretical studies of Christology and in the appraisal of the bearing of biblical criticism on faith.

Knox has provided us with a penetrating and thoughtful autobiography entitled *Never Far From Home* (1975). Anyone interested in perceiving how he has reflected on his life and values will be deeply affected by this book. I will draw from it to present here only the barest outline of some aspects of a career marked by both genuine integrity and wide interests.

John Knox was born in Frankfort, Kentucky, in 1900. His father was a YMCA secretary who became a minister in the Southern Methodist Church when Knox was five or six years old. He graduated from Randolph-Macon College in 1919 and took his first ministerial appointment, consisting of six rural Methodist churches in eastern West Virginia, the same year. In 1921 he entered Emory Divinity School, where he received his Bachelor of Divinity degree in 1925.

While in his last year at Emory and for two years afterward, he taught in the Department of Religion. The department at that time consisted of E. C. Colwell and John Knox. But Knox was dismissed from the university after writing a letter to an Atlanta newspaper supporting the workers in a local cotton mill. In 1927 he enrolled at the Chicago Divinity School as a Ph.D. candidate, but left after a few months to serve a Methodist church in Bethesda, Maryland. In 1929 he became Chaplain at Fisk University in Nashville, Tennessee—a university founded by Congregationalists for the purpose of educating black students. Knox held this position until 1936, but was given a leave of absence in 1934 to resume his studies at Chicago, where he received his Ph.D. in 1935. E. J. Goodspeed, S. J. Case, H. Willoughby, D. W. Riddle, and E. C. Colwell made up this remarkably creative and productive faculty in NT and early Christian studies. Knox became particularly attracted to the work of Goodspeed, which inspired his own studies, *Philemon Among the Letters of Paul* (1935a) and *Marcion and the New Testament* (1942a).[1]

From 1936 to 1938, Knox served as an editor of *Christian Century* and *Christendom*. After spending a year as Associate Professor of NT at Hartford Theological Foundation, he returned to Chicago in 1939 to assume an appointment as Associate Professor of Homiletics. In 1942 he became Professor of Homiletics and NT.

In 1943 Knox was appointed Baldwin Professor of Sacred Literature at Union Theological Seminary in New York, a position he held until 1966. At Union he joined an illustrious faculty, with the likes of H. S. Coffin, F. C. Grant, R. Niebuhr, P. Tillich, H. P. Van Dusen, and J. Bennett. During these years he served as Associate Editor of *The Interpreter's Bible* and later *The Interpreter's Dictionary of the Bible*. He was also an associate editor and a translator of *The New American Bible*. In 1962 he was ordained to the ministry of the Protestant Episcopal Church, and in 1963 served as president of the SBL. After his retirement from Union in 1966, Knox became Professor of NT at the Episcopal Theological Seminary of the Southwest in Austin, Texas. Since 1972 he lived in Medford, New Jersey, until his death on June 25, 1990. It is to his memory that this volume of essays is dedicated.

Knox's contribution to the study of Acts should be seen within the context of his larger religious and theological concerns. But there is no sense in which these concerns have determined the outcome of his studies. Thus, whether Knox is doing exegetical work, tackling methodological problems, or working out a detailed table of chronological relationships, he adheres strictly to the principles of

---

[1]See also the second edition (1980a). Quotations here are from the first edition.

critical scholarship. In this sense, he links us with that influential group of Chicago scholars with whom he studied over half a century ago.

The purpose of this essay is to call attention to the character of Knox's work on Acts and to attempt a critical assessment of it. This can best be done by concentrating on two specific foci of Knox's work that represent distinctive approaches and contentions. One focus deals with a hypothesis that has met with moderate success among NT scholars, while the other seems to have been largely neglected.[2]

Acts as a Source for Pauline Biography

The first focus to be considered raises a methodological concern having to do with the way in which the book of Acts might be used in the study of Paul. Knox had begun to work out his views on this subject as early as 1936, when he published an article entitled, "'Fourteen Years Later': A Note on the Pauline Chronology" (1936c:341-49). He began the article with a clear methodological statement about the priority of Paul's letters to the book of Acts:

> It does not need to be said that our principal sources for the life of Paul are the letters generally esteemed authentic and the several sections of Luke-Acts that deal with his career. It is equally unnecessary to add that of these the letters are by all odds the more important and in cases of conflict with Acts, whether explicit or implied, are always to be followed (1936c:342).

The force of the article, if persuasive, would be to revolutionize Pauline chronology by identifying the period of fourteen years (Gal 2:1) as the time of Paul's active missionary work. This fourteen-year period had generally been assumed to be a silent period prior to Paul's work among the Gentiles. For Knox, it was precisely the period of the Gentile mission and the time of his greatest literary production.

This article was followed in 1939 by "The Pauline Chronology" (1939a:15-29), where Knox expressed caution about the use of Acts in Pauline studies, but nevertheless hesitated to relegate to it an irrelevant

---

[2]I am greatly indebted to J. C. Hurd, Jr., who has compiled a very helpful and detailed bibliography of Knox's work and reviews of it in *Christian History and Interpretation: Studies Presented to John Knox*, ed. by W. R. Farmer, C. F. D. Moule, and R. R. Niebuhr (Cambridge: Cambridge University, 1967) xxiii-xxxii. A more detailed and unpublished version of the bibliography was kindly made available to me by the library staff at the Episcopal Theological Seminary of the Southwest, Austin, TX. A revised bibliography of Knox's publications appears elsewhere in this volume.

role. He found no reason to doubt the accuracy of the account in Acts about Paul's trial before Gallio in Corinth (18:12-17), although he wanted to locate it at a different time in Paul's career. He was able to work out a Pauline chronology that differed from the traditional one, especially in filling in the fourteen-year period of Gal 2:1 with meaningful activity. At the same time, he also wanted to contend that his chronology, based entirely on a study of Paul's letters, did not significantly conflict with Acts. He wrote:

> Although it is my conviction that students of the life of Paul must rigidly hold themselves to using Acts as a secondary source and must be ready to disregard it whenever the letters give the slightest ground for doing so, nevertheless a chronological arrangement which involved constant or even frequent conflict with the Acts narrative would be open to serious question (1939a:23).

Later he claimed that his new chronology "does not involve wholesale disregard of the statements of Acts" (1939a:26).

At this point it is important to say something about the sometimes misunderstood relationship between this early work of Knox and the work of D. Riddle. In the preface to his *Paul, A Man of Conflict*, published in 1940, Riddle paid more than courteous respect to Knox:

> This book owes a particular debt to my friend and colleague, Professor John Knox. It was Dr. Knox's article, "Fourteen Years Later, A Note on the Pauline Chronology," which stimulated the investigations and largely shaped the basic perceptions upon which the present work is projected. Frequent discussions have been of great assistance. While I assume responsibility for all generalizations, most cordially I share with Dr. Knox any credit which may accrue for what is presented herewith.[3]

There is no reason to doubt the sincerity of Riddle's remarks, especially since the chronology of the relevant publications supports their accuracy. Indeed, it seems likely that Riddle moved the argument about the use of Acts farther along than Knox did, for he maintained that Luke did not intend to write a biography of Paul any more than he intended to write a biography of Jesus in his gospel. Riddle contended that Acts is not useful for understanding Paul himself; rather, it is useful only to the reader who understands its purpose and the relationship of its portrayal of Paul to the overall scheme of the book. Riddle thus adopted the

---

[3]D. W. Riddle, *Paul, Man of Conflict: A Modern Biographical Sketch* (Nashville: Cokesbury, 1940) 9.

methodological stance of confining himself to Paul's letters in writing about Paul.

Knox's fundamental statement about the position of Acts came in his book, *Chapters in a Life of Paul*, an outgrowth of his Quillian Lectures, delivered at Emory University in 1949 (1950a).[4] The book begins with a methodological section on the sources for understanding Paul. Knox first acknowledged that the student of Paul has an apparent advantage over the student of the historical Jesus. The advantage is that, whereas we have no writing directly from Jesus, we have not only letters from Paul himself but also an extensive biography about him. But this advantage is deceptive, since there is no ground for any greater confidence in Acts than in the gospels. Even the epistles in their present form cannot be regarded as exact replicas of Paul's original letters since they have been collected, arranged, and in some cases conflated. The collector (or collectors) of Paul's letters also engaged in pseudepigraphy by including Ephesians as a genuine letter of Paul. These problems with the letters notwithstanding, Knox agreed that the student of Paul is in far better position than the student of Jesus because we have at our disposal letters—Romans, 1-2 Corinthians, Galatians, Philippians, Colossians, 1-2 Thessalonians, and Philemon—that, for the most part, have come to us "substantially as they left their author's hand" (1950a:20f.). He concluded that "they constitute our only primary sources for the life of Paul" (1950a:21).

If pseudepigraphy is to be seen as one way of reinterpreting Paul for the post-Pauline church, biography ought to be seen as another way. Although the author of Acts was not solely interested in writing a biography of Paul, this work is the earliest and worthiest of those biographies that attempt to bring Paul into later times. In approaching the question of its historical reliability, one ought to assume that it is neither more nor less reliable than the Gospel of Luke, and Knox intended this to be an affirmative recognition of substantial reliability. He did, however, call attention to some differences between the writing of the gospel and the writing of Acts. For example, in writing the gospel, Luke drew on earlier materials for his recording of the teaching of Jesus, whereas in Acts he substantially wrote speeches for his heroes, including Paul. In addition, Luke had a well-organized document as a source for the gospel, i.e., the Gospel of Mark, but for Acts, he "probably had available only brief accounts of particular episodes; or, perhaps

---

[4]See also the revised edition (1987a). Quotations here are from the first edition.

occasionally, of short sequences of episodes, as, for example, of some journey of Paul; or, possibly, longer overlapping accounts written from divergent points of view" (1950a:24). Thus, in writing Acts, "it is probable that he was more the author and less the compiler than when he wrote Luke; we may confidently believe that he had fuller control of the arrangement of his materials and was in large part responsible for it" (1950a:24).

If Luke was in substantial control of the arrangement of his materials, what conceptions led him to arrange the materials in the way that he did? Knox found three such conceptions important for the study of Paul. The first was the tendency to emphasize the significance and place of Jerusalem in the history of the early Christian movement. This emphasis, probably born of the need to legitimate Christianity to the Roman officials and thus to connect it with Judaism, is found in the gospel as well as in Acts. In Acts, however, the activities of the Christians in the first seven chapters are confined to Jerusalem, where Paul periodically returns. Knox thus wrote: "Not only is Jerusalem the point from which the world-wide expansion of Christianity takes its start; Jerusalem remains the center of the whole development, the source of direction and control in the expanding church" (1950a:27).

Knox noted a second, related tendency: "It is the view that the Twelve at Jerusalem exercised a careful and authoritative oversight of the entire Christian church" (1950a:27). The authority of Paul is derived from the apostles, and the process of his selection was of a different order from theirs. By emphasizing the leadership of the Twelve and their relation to Paul, Luke stressed the sense of harmony that he thought prevailed in the early church.

The third tendency consisted of Luke's emphasis on the "political innocuousness" of the Christian movement. Its enemies are never responsible Roman officials but Jews, "false to the true meaning of their own faith and culture" (1950a:28). Knox observed that the fact that Luke ended his book without a narrative describing the final outcome of Paul's trial at Rome is "a consequence of his unwillingness to conclude his book with the story of its failure" (1950a:28).

The tendencies that Knox delineated are fairly standard in the critical literature on Luke-Acts. A recognition of their importance led Knox to reaffirm the priority of Paul's letters for the student of Paul, for the letters are "obviously and incomparably the more trustworthy" (1950a:31). Despite the obviousness of this assertion, there is insufficient clarity in regard to the way in which it might affect the actual study:

"The truth in principle of this last statement no serious student of Paul's life is likely to deny, but its meaning in practice is not so widely or so clearly seen" (1950a:31). Therefore, Knox next turned from the "meaning in principle" to the "meaning in practice" of his observations about sources.

He began the chapter on "The Use of Our Sources" with a distinction between internal and external spheres of Paul's life. The internal sphere is concerned with ideas and beliefs, while the external one consists of the chronological and geographical circumstances, the observable course of his career. It is typical of Pauline studies to draw on the letters for the internal facts and to consult Acts for the external: "The consequence is that while we tend to harmonize Acts with the letters as regards the inner facts of Paul's life, we tend to harmonize the letters with Acts as regards the outer" (1950a:32). But this procedure, though common even for perceptive and informed scholars, cannot be justified: "Whereas the first is relatively innocuous, since the letters are given their true importance in the process, the second is seriously distorting" (1950a:32). The letters are primary sources not only for the internal but also for the external details of Paul's life, even though Acts gives fuller information about the latter. This led Knox to state the principle, "A fact only suggested in the letters has a status which even the most unequivocal statement of Acts, if not otherwise supported, cannot confer. We may, with proper caution, use Acts to supplement the autobiographical data of the letters, but never to correct them" (1950a:33).

To show how this principle should work, Knox next examined the major external facts that come from Acts. Some of these "facts" may be reasonably accepted. For example, although only Acts refers to Paul's Jewish name, Saul, there is no reason to doubt it. Paul had no occasion to use it in his letters, and no alternative tradition is known. Likewise, the reference to Tarsus as his place of birth causes little trouble since Paul's own letters suggest that he was a Jew of the Diaspora, some of whose early Christian missionary work was carried on in Cilicia. His arrest in Jerusalem, his trials, and his trip to Rome seem plausible. Nothing in Paul's letters can conflict with these points, since all of the letters were written before the events in question.

But grave doubts must be expressed about several of the external "facts" found in Acts. Paul's training in Jerusalem under Gamaliel is one such "fact." Here, Paul's silence in the letters is important, and the connection of Paul with Jerusalem and with a leading Rabbi served to reinforce Luke's sense of the linkage between Christianity and Judaism.

The circumstances surrounding Paul's conversion must be rejected, because they conflict directly with the testimony in the letters. There is, of course, fundamental agreement on the fact that Paul was a persecutor of the Christian movement, but Luke set the scene of the persecution in Jerusalem and Judea, while Paul claimed not to be known to the Christians there (Gal 1:22-23). These Christians had heard about his earlier persecuting activity and about his conversion, but they did not know Paul first-hand. Likewise, there is disagreement on Paul's actions following his conversion. "Paul says, 'I did not...go up to Jerusalem to those who were apostles before me'; Acts says that he did precisely that" (1950a: 37). Knox concluded that the story in Acts 9:1-2, "while not incredible, is improbable" (1950a:39). The conception of Paul as engaged on three great missionary journeys likewise "represents a later way of seeing and interpreting a career which originally did not appear so at all" (1950a:41).

After this preliminary study, Knox turned to a more detailed application of his principles and attempted to lay out the chronology of Paul's career by drawing on the letters alone. This chronology differed from that derived from Acts in major respects. For one thing, Paul himself referred to only three visits to Jerusalem, visits that Knox designated "acquaintance," "conference," and "offering." Acts, however, has five such visits: 9:26-27; 11:29-30; 15:1-29; 18:22; and 21:15. Knox showed that the second visit has been confused with Paul's final "offering" visit and that the fourth in Acts is the result of some confusion about the real location of the third, the "conference" visit. But the key to Knox's treatment of these differences between Acts and the letters was his identification of the third visit in Acts with the "conference" visit in Galatians and his claim that Acts has located this visit earlier in Paul's career than it really belongs. Knox returned to his earlier work, "Fourteen Years Later," and repeated his contention that the conference between Paul and the Jerusalem pillar-apostles occurred at the peak of Paul's career rather than earlier. He thought that Luke had a source for the report about this visit but intentionally altered the chronology in order to avoid any implication of a long-standing disharmony between Paul and the Jerusalem apostles. In actual fact, the conference visit occurred in close proximity to the time when the letter to the Galatians and the letter to the Romans reflected Paul's great concern with the issues discussed at this meeting. Similarly, Luke did not understand Paul's last visit to Jerusalem as the "offering" visit but moved it to an earlier point and changed it from a peace offering to a famine relief offering in order to avoid any implications of disharmony.

Knox's fundamental principle for using Acts in the study of Paul, in its theoretical formulation, is clear: Acts is a secondary source. It must be used cautiously, the intentions of its author must be considered, and its tendentiousness must be carefully weighed. The letters are the primary sources. The impact of this principle on the actual study of the external sphere of Paul's life, its "meaning in practice," must be more carefully nuanced. If there is disagreement between a point made in a letter and a point made in Acts, we must reject Acts, but if the question regards a point made in Acts on which the letters are silent, then the situation appears to be more difficult. In these cases Knox wanted to examine the significance of the silence in the letters and the relationship of the point in Acts to the tendentiousness of Luke. Although Tarsus as Paul's birthplace is not confirmed in the letters, it may be accepted. But the concept of the three missionary journeys, likewise not confirmed in the letters, must be rejected.

In his article on "The Pauline Chronology," Knox was cautious, even suspicious, about any move to reject Acts (1939a:15-29). He observed that there would be something problematic about a historical construction that goes against Acts on several major points. He did not repeat this observation in *Chapters*. Indeed, he seemed prepared to reject Acts on a number of points important to the scheme of that book, especially those points that are useful to the author in developing his basic conceptions of things. Knox was here less apologetic about his treatment of Acts as a source for Paul's external sphere. But his method still did not involve the wholesale rejection of Acts. Rather, Knox's intent was similar to that of Riddle, namely, to treat Acts as a secondary source, a source limited in usefulness not only by the fact that it came from an "outsider" but also by the fact that the author was committed to certain principles for conceiving Paul and making him available to a later generation.

The early reviews of Knox's *Chapters* were mixed. Some reviewers were offended by any suggestion that there were inaccuracies in Acts. The editor of *Expository Times* said that the author of Acts, identified as Paul's traveling companion, must have known more about Paul than any American professor.[5] Others expressed a decided preference for harmonistic methods. D. G. Miller preferred the methods of W. Ramsay,

---

[5]*ExpTim* 66 (1954/55) 129-30.

A. von Harnack, and W. L. Knox, "of seeking to reconcile differences between Acts and Paul's Letters wherever possible, and of admitting that where a reconciliation is impossible it may be due to the limitations of our knowledge."[6] J. W. Beardslee thought that Knox was too rigorous in distinguishing the letters from Acts. He wrote: "Paul, of course, at one time and in some moods knew much more about his movements and their purpose than did the author of Acts. But Paul wrote Galatians in a burst of anger, which climaxed his usual deeply emotional temperament. Cannot his statements—still more the implications of these statements—be too literalistically accepted?"[7] F. Filson was not convinced by Knox's reconstruction of Pauline chronology and thought that Knox was too skeptical of the historical value of Acts, but he agreed with his basic methodological principle.[8]

Other reviewers, however, were clearly supportive of Knox's position. H. J. Cadbury commended not only the methodology employed in *Chapters* but also agreed with the reconstructed chronology. He wrote: "But undoubtedly the usual arrangement, with its unbalance of too little record for many years before the Jerusalem council and too much activity for the few available years after it, must be corrected somehow, and that at the expense of Acts."[9] Although she had strongly negative criticisms of some late chapters, M. E. Andrews gave the historical section of *Chapters* a ringing endorsement: "This reviewer has never seen a better demonstration of the value of a rigidly historical approach to a New Testament problem than is here presented. It ought to be a deterrent to the continued employment of harmonistic method which so often has added only confusion."[10] R. T. Stamm defended the book against fundamentalist critics, who might prefer harmonistic approaches: "Yet we have to recognize that *any* harmonization of Acts with Paul is a *human* construction, and hence can lay no claim to infallibility, however much it may satisfy the minds of its advocates."[11]

A more substantial and more recent appraisal of Knox's contributions to the study of Acts and Pauline chronology was provided by J. C. Hurd

---

[6]*Int* 6 (1952) 373.

[7]*JR* 30 (1950) 275.

[8]*Religion in Life* 19 (1949/50) 632-33.

[9]*Christian Century* 67 (1950) 560.

[10]*JBR* 18 (1950) 197.

[11]*LQ* 2 (1950) 345. For additional appraisals see the Preface to the second edition of *Chapters* by D. R. A. Hare (1987a:x-xiii).

in the Knox *Festschrift* of 1967.[12] Hurd began by calling attention to the distinction Knox had made between principle and practice, where principle refers to the basic methodology proposed by Knox (and Riddle) and practice refers to the ways in which the methodology is used, in this case in the study of Paul. On the matter of principle, Hurd distinguished three groups of scholars. A very few have adopted the methodology and consistently applied it, among them F. R. Crownfield[13] and M. J. Suggs.[14] In this connection one should also call attention to an article by D. T. Rowlingson,[15] who accepted Knox's methodology and attempted to find support for its application from another direction. A second group of scholars, Hurd said, "have responded to the proposals of Riddle and Knox merely by becoming more guarded in their statements about the dates and sequence of events in Paul's life."[16] He referred to the work of D. J. Selby as an example of this tendency.[17] The largest group of scholars included D. Georgi,[18] G. B. Caird,[19] and W. G. Kümmel, [20] all of whom rejected Knox's chronological conclusions on the grounds that they depend on a devaluation of the historical accuracy of Acts. Hurd also treated the work of T. H. Campbell,[21] who dealt specifically with the matter of principle and attempted to show that, in respect to the number of missionary journeys and the general course of Paul's ministry, there are significant correspondences between the letters and Acts. W. D. Davies has also faced the methodological problems directly. He outlined three ways in which the book of Acts may be assessed. This outline, quoted by Hurd, bears repetition here:

---

[12]J. C. Hurd, "Pauline Chronology and Pauline Theology," in *Christian History and Interpretation*, ed. by Farmer *et al*, 225-48.

[13]F. R. Crownfield, *A Historical Approach to the New Testament* (New York: Harper and Brothers, 1960).

[14]M. J. Suggs, "Concerning the Date of Paul's Macedonian Ministry," *NovT* 4 (1960) 60-68.

[15]D. T. Rowlingson, "The Jerusalem Conference and Jesus' Nazareth Visit: A Study in Pauline Chronology," *JBL* 71 (1952) 69-74.

[16]Hurd, "Pauline Chronology," 227.

[17]D. J. Selby, *Toward the Understanding of St. Paul* (Englewood Cliffs: Prentice Hall, 1962).

[18]D. Georgi, *Die Geschichte der Kollekte des Paulus für Jerusalem* (Hamburg-Bergstedt: Herbert Reich, 1965).

[19]G. B. Caird, "The Chronology of the New Testament," in *IDB* (Nashville: Abingdon, 1962) 1:599-607.

[20]W. G. Kümmel, *Introduction to the New Testament*, trans. by A. J. Mattill, Jr. (Nashville: Abingdon, 1966).

[21]T. H. Campbell, "Paul's 'Missionary Journeys' as Reflected in His Letters," *JBL* 74 (1955) 80-87.

Three positions can be taken: (1) We may regard Acts as so unreliable historically that we have to depend entirely, or almost entirely, on the Epistles. (2) We may take the Epistles as primary but take Acts with utmost seriousness as containing reliable information which must be reconciled with the Epistles. This is the position taken by British scholars usually. (3) We may take a mediating position. The Epistles are primary, but while we should not twist their evidence to fit that of Acts, Acts does provide valuable information which deserves to be considered as historically significant. This position is held by J. Munck.[22]

Hurd claimed that Knox and Riddle belong in the third category, and that it is difficult to find scholars in the first. Although Davies was not explicit in the quotation, it is probable that he thought of Knox as the chief representative of the view that Acts is not reliable.

At this point Hurd made an important clarification that called attention to the deficiencies in almost all of the previous responses to Knox's work on Acts and Paul. The distinction between primary and secondary sources "means not just a difference in the degree of reliance that is to be placed on each type of source, but also involves necessarily the order in which these sources are to be consulted. Thus the basic first step in the reconstruction of Paul's career is the examination of his letters entirely apart from Acts."[23]

In turning to the second major section of his paper on "the meaning in practice," Hurd illustrated how Knox and Riddle applied their basic principle in studying the biography and theology of Paul. Hurd was able to show that, despite claims to the contrary from the majority of scholars, one aspect of the historical reconstruction of Knox and Riddle is quite close to traditional views. Hurd claimed that this was due to a failure on the part of both Riddle and Knox to connect the analysis of Paul's thought with the order in which the letters were written. This point, surely of great significance for the study of Pauline thought and chronology, goes beyond our current interest in Knox's contribution to the study of Acts and so may be noted only in passing.[24]

---

[22]W. D. Davies, *Invitation to the New Testament* (Garden City: Doubleday, 1966) 240.

[23]Hurd, "Pauline Chronology," 233.

[24]Cf. C. Buck and G. Taylor, *Saint Paul: A Study of the Development of his Thought* (New York: Charles Scribner's Sons, 1969). These authors have accepted Knox's principle but also recognize the problem for Pauline chronology. "If the chronology of Paul's life is to be based on the evidence of the letters, it is necessary to know beforehand the order in which the letters were written, and once the framework of Acts is dispensed with, some of the letters are extremely difficult to

In my judgment, Hurd's major contribution to the assessment of Knox's work was in rigidly stressing the distinction between primary and secondary sources and in drawing out the implication that primary sources must be analyzed first and in their entirety before secondary sources are consulted. But in so stating the matter, Hurd also showed that Knox and Riddle have had far fewer followers than they deserve.

The Knox *Festschrift* appeared in 1967. By 1980, the influence of Knox's work on Pauline chronology appeared to have strengthened considerably. Knox was honored and his influence assessed in a seminar held in Fort Worth, TX, in November, 1980.[25] Here again, Hurd was a moving force, but the seminar was also connected with the publication of two recent books dealing with Pauline chronology, one by R. Jewett,[26] and the other by G. Luedemann.[27] Jewett and Luedemann each presented papers at the seminar, for which Hurd acted as moderator. The published proceedings include not only papers by Luedemann and Jewett and a transcript of the discussion, but also a response from John Knox.

Both Luedemann and Jewett were engaged in the attempt to establish the chronology of Paul's life and letters. Luedemann appeared to follow Knox's method with consistency and fully recognized his indebtedness to him. He attempted to reconstruct the chronology of Paul by a critical use of the letters that examines such things as the genre of the individual sections of the letters and their historical background. Then he turned to Acts and isolated some of the traditions that Luke used. He was able to identify these traditions by a redactional study of Acts that makes use of the indications provided in Paul's letters. Luedemann's work may thus be regarded as a genuine advance on Knox's. As Knox stated in the foreword to the English edition of the book: "The extraordinary significance of Gerd Luedemann's book lies in its being the first full-length, full-bodied, and fully documented study of Paul's apostolic

---

date even relatively" (p. 9). Buck and Taylor propose to establish the sequence of the letters by means of an analysis of the development in Paul's thought.

[25]The seminar was one of three that met at that time, the other two being on the Synoptic problem and the question of gospel genre. The papers, together with transcripts of the seminar dialogues, have been published in *Colloquy on New Testament Studies: A Time for Reappraisal and Fresh Approaches*, ed. B. Corley (Macon, GA: Mercer University, 1983).

[26]R. Jewett, *A Chronology of Paul's Life* (Philadelphia: Fortress, 1979).

[27]G. Luedemann, *Paulus, der Heidenapostel*, vol. 1: *Studien zur Chronologie* (Göttingen: Vandenhoeck & Ruprecht, 1980); E. T.: *Paul, Apostle to the Gentiles: Studies in Chronology* (Philadelphia: Fortress, 1984).

career which is based solely on the letters. It is the author's aim to use material from Acts only when it supports what the letters either state or suggest."[28]

Jewett also affirmed the superior value of Paul's letters in establishing a chronology. After a discussion of the possible source material that may be useful, he wrote:

> The result is that the general outline of Paul's life must be worked out on the basis of the evidence from the letters and these alone. This means one must break with Luke's framework of five different trips to Jerusalem after Paul's conversion, and one must seriously investigate the possibility of articulating Pauline chronology on the basis of the three Jerusalem journeys and the various phases of missionary activity reflected in the letters. To compromise between Luke's general outline and that reflected in the Pauline letters is to open the door to a subjective chaos that can never be tamed by the whim of the scholar. A general rule therefore is that material from Acts is usable in the chronological experiment only when it does not conflict with evidence in the letters.[29]

Jewett's application of the principle allowed him to sift the book of Acts for chronological suggestions and other details. Those details that are useful are those that seem to be irrelevant to Luke's overall theological or chronological framework and that do not conflict with the evidence in Paul's letters. In his paper for the Fort Worth colloquy, Jewett emphasized his indebtedness to Knox and described his work as an effort to expand on and sustain Knox's hypothesis. He also indicated that the reviews of his own book have given "the impression that the Knox hypothesis is gaining decisive headway."[30]

In his introduction to the seminar papers, Hurd questioned Jewett's adherence to the Knox hypothesis. Hurd claimed that Jewett had misunderstood the real force of Knox's work. Jewett was able to locate his work as an advance upon the Knox hypothesis by defining it as a claim that Paul paid only three trips to Jerusalem instead of the five reported in Acts. Jewett claimed that his work was an advance, since he started with a three-journey structure and filled in details drawn from a data-base that, in turn, drew on Paul's letters, Acts (as critically qualified), and other relevant sources. Hurd affirmed that this was a misunderstanding of Knox's contribution, which is totally in the area of method. The concept that Paul paid only three trips to Jerusalem is a

---

[28]Ibid., p. xiii.

[29]Jewett, *Chronology*, 23f.

[30]Jewett, "Chronology and Methodology: Reflections on the Debate Over Chapters in a Life of Paul," in *Colloquy*, 276.

result of the application of the method, to which Jewett did not fully adhere. The same point was made within the seminar discussion. Indeed, Knox himself was perplexed by Jewett's claim (1983:339-64; esp. pp. 361-64). He stated that in reading Jewett's book, he was led to believe that Jewett did not consider himself to be an adherent of the method Knox had earlier outlined and that Jewett had come to his views more or less independently. In describing the differences between himself and Jewett, Knox called attention to Jewett's disposition to accept material in Acts that is not contradicted in Paul's letters. Knox wrote: "But, one might ask, if Acts can be shown to be wrong at so many points where the letters happen to provide a 'check,' what assurance can one have that it is right when the letters do not provide a 'check'?" (1983:363).

An analysis of the work of Luedemann and Jewett helps us to sharpen our perception of Knox's contribution to the study of Acts. Clearly, the work of Luedemann is very close to that of Knox in terms of both methodology and substantive result. He has, however, developed a more sophisticated way of sifting Acts for authentic historical traditions. Whereas Knox was willing to accept certain minor details that were not contradicted by Paul's letters, Luedemann used the letters as control documents in his redaction-critical study of Acts. Knox's comments on Luedemann's work indicate that he found himself in agreement with the younger scholar's position.

The discussion at the Fort Worth colloquy showed that the real force of Knox's work was not to commend any particular Pauline chronology, not even a particular structuring of Pauline chronology along a three-journey hypothesis. Rather, his major contribution is in the area of methodology and in his strictures about the relative use of Acts and Paul's letters in the study of Paul's internal and external life. As Knox himself said in commenting on his own work and that of Hurd, Suggs, H. L. Ramsey, C. H. Buck, P. Minear, and E. P. Sanders: "There has never been complete agreement within this group on chronological details, but we have all agreed on methodology, which is the principal thing" (1983:345). Hurd echoed this judgment: "But for Knox 'method is everything.'"[31]

In summary, one may say that, with respect to methodology, Knox has presented a hypothesis about the use of Acts for Pauline studies that is irrefutable. The fact that those who embrace his hypothesis may still

---

[31]Hurd, "Introduction," in *Colloquy*, 266f.

be in the minority is not due to any lack of clarity in the presentation of the hypothesis. The future for scholarship in this area probably lies with those who, like Luedemann, take the hypothesis seriously and attempt to apply it rigorously.

Marcion and the Acts of the Apostles

If Knox's work on Acts as a source for Pauline biography has met with moderate success, his work on Marcion and Acts has been almost totally ignored. Although treated here as the second of two foci, the work on Marcion appeared in an earlier, more general work, *Marcion and the New Testament*, published in 1942 (1942a).

Knox's argument about the relationship of Acts and Marcion can only be understood in the larger context of his analysis of the relationship of Marcion to Luke-Acts and indeed, to the NT as a whole. The usual view about Marcion, based on patristic statements, is that his scriptures consisted of an abbreviated version of canonical Luke and certain letters of Paul. These scriptures would have provided the authority for Marcion's theology of two Gods and for his rejection of scriptures and theology associated with Judaism. But Knox raised a serious question about this viewpoint. If Marcion was intent on stressing the discontinuity between Judaism and Christianity, then, Knox claimed, his alleged choice of Luke is incomprehensible: "Why did he select a book [the Gospel of Luke] from which he was forced to delete so large a portion—a book so steeped, especially in its opening chapters, in Jewish lore?" (1942a:163) Considering Luke-Acts as a whole, Knox commented: "That the one work among early Christian documents whose primary purpose was to demonstrate the continuity of Christianity with Judaism should have been deliberately selected and adopted by the one church leader whose primary interest was to deny that continuity is to me almost incredible" (1942a:139).

Knox not only rejected the traditional view of the relationship of Marcion to Luke, he reversed it. In his theory, canonical Luke was written, in part, as a reaction against Marcionism. Marcion had a slightly abbreviated form of a proto-Luke (not to be confused with the proto-Luke of B. H. Streeter) which contained approximately the same Markan and Matthean materials that canonical Luke contains. But canonical Luke is an expansion of the more primitive gospel by the addition of peculiar Lukan material. Knox wrote:

This would mean that the relation between Marcion's Gospel and the canonical Gospel of Luke is not accurately described either by the simple statement that Marcion abridged Luke or by the assertion that Luke enlarged Marcion. The position would rather be that a primitive Gospel, containing approximately the same Markan and Matthean elements which our Luke contains and some of its peculiar materials, was somewhat shortened by Marcion or some predecessor and rather considerably enlarged by the writer of our Gospel, who was also the maker of Luke-Acts (1942a:110).

According to Knox, then, one of the important purposes of the book of Acts was to counteract Marcionite theology, which it does in two major ways. First, it emphasizes the relationship of Christianity to Judaism—indeed the continuity of the two; and second, it places Paul among the apostles and emphasizes the harmony between him and the others. Acts was written by one who was fully informed about the use that Marcion was making of Paul, and his solution to the problem was not to attack Paul but to neutralize him. So Knox saw Luke-Acts as, at least in part, an early apologetic response to Marcionism and an attempt "to reclaim both a Gospel and Paul from the Marcionites" (1942a:139). Knox also maintained that the Marcionite canon of gospel and apostle served as a model for Luke-Acts and subsequently for the orthodox canon.

A major part of Knox's argument about Luke is a linguistic one. He divided the gospel material into three categories: (a) material in Luke that certainly was in Marcion's gospel; (b) material that certainly was not in Marcion's gospel; and (c) material about which there is substantial uncertainty. This categorization, largely based on Harnack's analyses, was used by Knox for linguistic and theological comparisons. In making the linguistic comparisons, his main purpose was to call into question the argument of W. Sanday, who had claimed that characteristic Lukan terms are found both in the materials that Marcion included and in those he did not have.[32] Knox readily conceded that Sanday's thesis, if true, had the effect of settling the question about priority in favor of the traditional view. If it can be proven that there is homogeneity of vocabulary between the text of those parts of canonical Luke which Marcion's gospel did *not* contain and the Marcionite text of those parts of Luke which Marcion's gospel *did* contain, the view that Marcion abbreviated the canonical Luke would almost be required. But Knox sought to demonstrate that Sanday's thesis was not established by his argument because he did not take into any account the actual text of

---

[32]W. Sanday, "Marcion's Gospel," *Fortnightly Review* 23 [17n.s.] (1875) 855-75. Cf. also *idem., The Gospels in the Second Century* (London: Macmillan, 1876).

Marcion's gospel, which is known to be significantly different from the
text of our Luke. Knox attempted, by examining Harnack's
reconstruction of that text, to demonstrate this. In *Marcion*, he made
some attempt not only to discredit Sanday's thesis but also to build upon
the textual data a positive argument for his own case. In later writings,
he expressed the wish that he had not made this latter attempt but had
instead been content with the more modest endeavor, concluding finally
that we simply do not know enough about the text of Marcion's gospel
to make confident judgments on the basis of merely linguistic evidence
either confirming or rejecting the traditional view (1980a:v-vi). He
nevertheless claimed that much of this evidence points away from it.

Knox then turned to considerations of a more general nature
affecting the content of Luke. Drawing mainly on Cadbury, he studied
the special features of Luke's writing, such as the concern for local color,
interest in soldiers, cities, lodging and entertainment, emphasis on joy,
grace, divine guidance and control, interest in Gentiles, women, and
Samaritans, and the stress on Jerusalem. By use of the three categories
mentioned above, Knox was able to show that, while some of the
features are certainly present in Marcion's gospel, none of them is
stressed, and most are altogether absent. This observation is consistent
with the view that these features were added to Marcion's gospel in the
process of producing canonical Luke.

Knox pointed out that many of these features are to be found in
passages peculiar to Luke and provided statistical observations worth
quoting:

> It will be apparent at once that verses lacking in Marcion are
> predominantly from among the peculiarly Lukan materials in the Gospel.
> Although 50.4 per cent of the verses of the Gospel of Luke are peculiar to
> that Gospel, only 38.5 per cent of the verses which there is even the
> slightest positive reason to believe belonged to Marcion's Gospel fall
> within that category. In Luke as a whole there are 1.4 per cent more
> peculiar verses than common verses, but in "A" [Knox's category of
> materials certainly in Marcion] there are 60 per cent more common verses
> than peculiar. And of the verses which there is positive evidence to show
> did *not* belong to Marcion, 79.7 per cent are peculiar to Luke. Of all the
> verses of Luke which are peculiar to Luke, 39 per cent are known to be
> missing in Marcion, whereas of verses of Luke paralleled in Matthew or
> Mark or both, only 10 per cent are known to be missing from Marcion
> (1942a:108).

These observations demonstrate that, on the traditional view,
Marcion omitted a much higher proportion of material peculiar to

canonical Luke than he did of material common to the three Synoptic Gospels. Knox asked: "Why should he have done this? If he did not like what was distinctively Lukan, why did he choose this gospel, when, according to the usual view, he had all the Gospels at hand, including Mark and John? On the other hand, if our Luke is a later composition than Marcion's gospel, the peculiarly Lukan character of the material in it which is not also in Marcion is precisely what we would expect" (1942a:110). Thus, in Knox's judgment, Marcion's version of Luke was an abbreviated proto-Luke that contained most of the material common to Luke and either Matt or Mark or both; whereas canonical Luke is an expansion of this material by a second-century author who added mostly Lukan *Sondergut*—the material that makes the Third Gospel distinctive.

In Chap. IV, "Marcion's 'Gospel-Apostle' and Luke-Acts," Knox made the point that the arrangement of Marcion's canon—the short Gospel of Luke and letters of Paul—was a model for Luke-Acts, i.e., an expanded Luke and a narrative of the apostles and Paul. The chapter begins with a question about the place of Paul's letters in the NT canon. By their very nature, letters are not especially suited for inclusion in a religious canon. Even if the letters of Paul were widely read, a conclusion that Knox questioned, it was not inevitable that they would have been included in the Christian Bible, unless there were some compelling reason for doing so. Further, given the conservatism of churches such as that at Rome, the letters of Paul would constitute problems. Knox suggested that the factor that impelled the acceptance of Paul's letters was their use by heretics, especially Marcion. Recognizing the heretical and partisan use of Paul's letters, the "orthodox" church was faced with two choices: either to accept Paul or to repudiate him. But repudiation was not a viable choice in view of Paul's general reputation and the respect that adhered to his martyrdom. Although the "orthodox" church opted to accept Paul and to do so wholeheartedly, the letters by themselves still constituted problems. For one thing, they might suggest, as Marcion claimed, that Paul was the only apostle, or that he was completely independent of the group in Jerusalem. Here is where the book of Acts came in. At precisely the point at which there was a need for "catholicizing" Paul, the book of Acts appeared and provided the basis for doing so. Here Paul was not independent, for he was clearly subject to the Jerusalem apostles to whom he reported on a regular basis. The book of Acts, together with other apostolic letters and the Pastorals, allowed for the acceptance of

Paul as one among the apostles. Knox noted that in the Muratorian canon, Acts is called, "The Acts of All the Apostles."

Knox, therefore, dated the writing of Luke-Acts in the first half of the second century, favoring the latter part of that period because it is early enough to account for external references to both documents. The first clear use of the Gospel of Luke in its present form was Justin's, and the first reference to Acts was Irenaeus. There is no reason to think that Marcion was aware of Acts. The alleged connection between Luke and Josephus does not rule out a date as late as 150 for Luke-Acts in its present form. The author's knowledge of letters of Paul, if indeed he knew them, likewise does not preclude this date. In concluding this chapter, Knox declared: "The author of Luke-Acts sought to reclaim both a Gospel and Paul from the Marcionites" (1942a:139).

Knox returned to the question of the connection between Acts and the Pauline letter corpus in his contribution to the *Festschrift* for Paul Schubert, published in 1966 (1966d:279-87). In this article, he confronted an apparent impasse. First, in agreement with Edgar Goodspeed, he recognized that Luke made no use of Paul's letters. Second, he agreed with Morton S. Enslin,[33] that Luke must have been acquainted with at least some of the letters. Knox wrote:

> This impasse should lead us to examine the hidden major premise of both sides, namely: If Luke knew the letters of Paul, he must have used them. I believe we are forced by the literary evidence (or rather, by the lack of it), on the one hand, and by the a priori probabilities, on the other, to question this premise and to consider seriously the possibility that Luke knew, or at least knew of, letters of Paul—even *the* (collected) letters of Paul—and quite consciously and deliberately made little or no use of them (1966d:284).

So Knox was able to return to his earlier suggestion that Acts was prompted in part by the heretical use of Paul's letters. It is worth observing, however, that here Knox allowed this stimulus to come either from a pre-Marcionite or a Marcionite source, and he allowed the date of the finished product, Luke-Acts, to be no earlier than 125 CE.

The early reviews of Knox's *Marcion*, while sometimes appreciative of the treatment of the role of Marcion in respect to the development of the NT canon, were almost totally negative in respect to the date of Luke-Acts. Harvie Branscomb maintained that much of the material in the Lukan *Sondergut* was irrelevant to the Marcionite problem.[34]

---

[33]"'Luke' and Paul," *JAOS* 58 (1938) 81-91.
[34]*Christendom* 8 (1943) 408-10.

Similarly, the structure of Acts and much of its material do not seem to apply. Carl Kraeling objected to a literary analysis of Luke that involved several precanonical stages.[35] He wrote: "Like all other arguments that posit several stages in the development of a document without the support of a careful literary analysis of the document itself, it hangs in the air and is hard to answer but still harder to maintain. The burden of proof lies with the proponent."[36] Notably, Kraeling proposed an alternative in which there are several versions of Luke. Morton S. Enslin called attention to the linguistic homogeneity of Luke-Acts and wondered how a second-century author could have used an earlier source and produced an expanded version with such homogeneity.[37] Others, such as Otto Piper, doubted that the sources for Acts would only have become available in the middle of the second century.[38] Many objected to a second-century date for the "finished" product, Luke-Acts, and emphasized the Tübingen pedigree for Knox's hypothesis. Henry Cadbury found himself unimpressed with Knox's argument and continued to incline toward a first-century date.[39]

In his review, W. F. Howard predicted that Knox's book would show "the direction which the debate is likely to take in the next few years."[40] It is difficult to account for the failure of this prediction. Indeed, a search of the NT literature from 1942 to the present has shown that Knox's theory about the relationship of Acts to the Marcionite controversy has been virtually ignored, a fact that has recently been confirmed by John T. Townsend.[41] Townsend has called attention to some evidence that tends to confirm the Knox hypothesis, namely linguistic and ideological similarities between Acts and the Clementine Homilies and Recognitions. His point was that a second-century date for Luke-Acts is more likely than a first-century date in view of (a) the absence of any

---

[35]*Crozer Quarterly* 20 (1943) 159-61.
[36]Ibid., 160.
[37]*JR* 23 (1943) 140-42.
[38]*Princeton Seminary Bulletin* 36 (1943) 41. Cf. also the review by S. Johnson in *ATR* 25 (1943) 228-33.
[39]*JBL* 62 (1943) 123-27.
[40]*JTS* 44 (1943) 224.
[41]Cf. J. T. Townsend, "The Date of Luke-Acts," in *Luke-Acts: New Perspectives from the Society of Biblical Literature Seminar*, ed. by C. H. Talbert (New York: Crossroad, 1984) 47-62. See especially n. 6 on p. 59. But see also L. E. Wilshire, "Was Canonical Luke Written in the Second Century?—A Continuing Discussion," *NTS* 20 (1974) 246-53. Wilshire pays particular attention to Knox's linguistic arguments against the use of canonical Luke by Marcion, and he finds the arguments wanting.

references to either document prior to 170 CE; and (b) the similarities in Luke-Acts to the second-century sources for the Clementine literature. Although he explicitly rejected Knox's linking of Luke-Acts with Marcion, Charles Talbert claimed that it was a response to Gnostic, specifically docetic, versions of Christianity.[42] But I should avoid any treatment of either Townsend or Talbert in view of the fact that both will speak for themselves in this volume.

There is a striking contrast between the two foci of Knox's work on Acts. Substantial discussion followed the publication of his *Chapters*, and his hypothesis worked out there has not been without adherents. But there has been little comparable discussion or critical assessment of *Marcion*. If a review of this work, coming fifty years after its publication, should serve to generate such discussion, then the community of NT scholarship will be well served.

There are grounds for making a very positive assessment of Knox's 1942 work. In the first place, the argument itself has been persuasively presented, as is characteristic of Knox. It is a model of clarity and precision. He wrote me to say that he would like to rework the material in the chapter on Marcion and Luke, where he dealt with William Sanday's work on the linguistic data, and he was probably correct in perceiving that this chapter falls short of his usual clarity. But, as for the rest, he cannot be faulted for haziness or lack of precision.

In the second place, Knox's study has posited for Luke-Acts a *Sitz im Leben* that comes out of known historical situations, and this is a decided advantage for his hypothesis. The *Sitz im Leben* for Luke-Acts has always been a difficult problem in NT scholarship, and many plausible representations have been drawn. Most call on us to imagine a particular Lukan community dominated by Gentile Christians who needed to understand their place vis-a-vis their foundation and their connection with the scriptures. But it has been difficult to find a historical community that meets this description. Knox, however, has found a plausible location for Luke-Acts in the history of the second century. Further, he has been able to situate Luke-Acts against the background of events in which it is known that at least one component of it, the Marcionite version of Luke, was a point of controversy.

Thirdly, Knox has shown why it was a necessity for Luke to write a life of Paul and why that life differed from the Paul that might be known in the letters. Here Knox's work on Marcion connects with the work on

---

[42]Cf. C. H. Talbert, *Luke and the Gnostics* (Nashville: Abingdon, 1966).

Pauline chronology. If the contention is valid that the image of Paul in Acts is not the same as the one in the letters, one is led to question why this is the case. Virtually all who understand these differences say that the author of Acts was interested in de-emphasizing any problems that may have occurred in the early church and in harmonizing Paul with the apostles. So, Knox has taken this answer and pressed it one more step to show why Luke felt it necessary to write things in this way. Naturally, any individual during the late first or second century may have had an interest in an unproblematic harmonization of the early church. But the situation in the middle of the second century is known to be a time during which diversity was seen by many to be a particularly serious problem and unity was seen to be a pressing need. If some second-century Christians were using an understanding of Paul, based on his letters, to bolster factional purposes, then the need for a life of Paul that would undermine these purposes is manifest.

If there are grounds for a positive assessment, there are also questions that should be faced by anyone who wishes to take Knox's work seriously. One obvious question is, given the situation that called forth Luke-Acts and the primary purpose it was intended to serve, why is there nothing more explicit that points to Marcion, or Marcion's theology, or the misuse of Paul's letters or the Hebrew scriptures? To be sure, we should not expect Luke to have made a gross anachronism, such as mentioning Marcion by name. But the author of 1 Tim seems to have been able to make an allusion to *The Antitheses* (1 Tim 6:20), and the author of 2 Pet commented on the misuse of Paul's letters (2 Pet 3:16). There is nothing comparable in Acts, unless 16:7 may be understood as an allusion to the region of Marcion's initial influence. Here we read that Paul and his missionary party "attempted to go into Bithynia, but the Spirit of Jesus did not allow them." Is this, perhaps, Luke's way of severing any perceived relationship between Paul and Marcion? The verse has the effect of leaving Bithynia untouched by Paul, so one may ask how Marcion was able to learn of him. Acts 16:7 might lead to the conclusion that, however Marcion came to embrace his theological concepts, his faith could not be compared for validity with that found in those communities established by Paul himself. But this is precious little to find in a document supposedly aimed to rescue Paul from Marcionite Christianity.[43]

---

[43]References to "fierce wolves" and "men speaking perverse things" in Acts 20:29-30 are not sufficiently precise to suggest that Marcionites are in view.

A second question has to do with the portrait of Paul that is found in canonical Acts. Knox called attention to the fact that Paul is pictured here in harmony with the Jerusalem apostles and, indeed, subordinate to them. Luke signified this subordination by denying to him the title apostle (except in Acts 14:14 and, by implication, 14:4). All this, of course, is correct and constitutes a major difference between Acts and Paul's letters. But the picture of Paul in Acts is more complex than Knox has suggested. Simply from a literary perspective, Paul is the hero of Acts 12-28. In more than half the book, he is on stage, and all other characters are secondary at best. Despite the fact that Peter is instrumental in converting the first Gentile, it is Paul who brings the gospel to the Gentile world—Asia, Macedonia, and Achaia. No reader who gets to the end of Acts 28 is likely to be greatly concerned about the fate of Peter, or Philip, or James, although he or she may not be satisfied about what happened to Paul. No doubt, Paul is shown to be subordinate to James in the apostolic conference described in Acts 15, but he is still the central character. He may not be an apostle, but he is led by God's word to him. Several scholars have observed the parallels between the life of Jesus in Luke and the life of Paul in Acts. Such parallelism is a literary device that cannot fail to suggest to the reader that the two most important characters in Luke-Acts are Jesus and Paul. These considerations suggest that the matter is not so simple as Knox has imagined, that Paul is harmonized with the others. He is, but he also outstrips them. There is a tension in the way in which Luke presents Paul—Paul is a kind of superapostle and a missionary of the second generation, one of heroic stature who is nevertheless subordinate to other leaders, one who is led by the Spirit and is, thus, independent of human supervision but who nevertheless needs to report to the apostles in Jerusalem. To relieve the tension in Acts by overlooking either side of Luke's portrayal may lead to a misapprehension about the author's intent.

A third question has to do with the attitude toward Judaism and the Hebrew scriptures in Luke-Acts. A significant part of Knox's argument is based on the supposition that one intention of Acts is to link Christianity with Judaism. Knox had asked why anyone would think that Marcion would have chosen the one NT book that forges this link, when he could have chosen others in which the connection is denied or at least seriously qualified. There is, however, a possible problem at this point. In the traditional view, Marcion was not required to separate Luke and Acts. It is only stated that he excised from his copy of the Gospel of Luke those sections in which the continuity between Judaism and Christianity might appear to be affirmed, such as Luke 1-2. It is uncertain that a second-century reader of canonical Luke (not Luke-Acts) would be so impressed with this sense of continuity that he would be led to conclude that it could not be purged by use of prudent excisions. A reader of Luke, together with Acts, might judge that the concept of continuity belongs to the very warp and woof of these texts. But even here some recent studies of Luke-Acts have raised serious questions about Luke's attitude toward Judaism and the Jewish people.[44] My own studies have led me to come to the tentative conclusion that Luke's attitude toward Judaism and the Hebrew scriptures displayed a good deal of ambivalence and tension. In neither Luke nor Acts do the Hebrew scriptures hold the position of authority that one might expect if a primary intention of the final editor of these texts was to counteract Marcionite theology.[45]

Conclusion

Although other questions might be raised, I should like to conclude with some suggestions for future discussion. If Knox's work on Marcion and Acts is to be taken seriously, there are certain kinds of studies that will be required. Two come readily to mind.

Although Knox has proposed that a primary purpose lying behind the writing of Acts was to counteract Marcionite Christianity, he was convinced that Luke did not write this book *de novo*. He worked with traditions about the early church and Paul. NT scholars have probably had difficulty with this understanding of Acts partly because Knox's hypothesis was not accompanied by an attempt to distinguish between tradition and redaction (to use more recent language) in Acts. The hypothesis therefore would be aided by a new source analysis that would show what Luke had at his disposal and what he did with his materials. With that information in hand, scholars could then see if there were sufficient signs of anti-Marcionite polemic in that work that came from the hand of the final redactor. Of course, no confidence can be placed in a source analysis that uses a hypothesis to demonstrate itself,

---

[44]Cf. the several essays in *Luke-Acts and the Jewish People: Eight Critical Perspectives*, ed. J. B. Tyson (Minneapolis: Augsburg Fortress, 1988).

[45]Cf. Tyson, "The Gentile Mission and the Authority of Scripture in Acts," *NTS* 33 (1987) 619-31; and "Scripture, Torah, and Sabbath in Luke-Acts," in *Jesus, the Gospels, and the Church: Essays in Honor of William R. Farmer*, E. P. Sanders, ed. (Macon, GA: Mercer University, 1987) 89-104.

and previous attempts at a source analysis of Acts have foundered. G. Luedemann has claimed that there are ways of separating tradition and redaction in Acts, and perhaps his method can be extended to produce a comprehensive treatment.[46]

There is probably even greater need for comprehensive literary studies of Luke-Acts. Such studies may have the value of being independent of hypotheses about authorship, date, *Sitz im Leben*, literary development, and sources. They could provide a check on Knox's effort to determine the character of Luke-Acts. Thus, studies that concentrate on the treatment of the Hebrew scriptures in Luke-Acts, the attitude toward Judaism in Luke-Acts, the picture of Paul in Acts, and any number of additional relevant topics would improve our ability to assess the value of Knox's work in this area.

In conclusion, I want to affirm that John Knox belongs in that small group of twentieth-century American scholars who have contributed mightily to the study of Acts. His contention about the way in which it should be used in the study of the life of Paul is beginning to produce positive results. My hope is that, at long last, his hypothesis about the historical situation that lay behind the writing of Acts will have a similar salutary effect.

---

[46]Leudemann displays the results of his study of Acts in *Early Christianity According to the Traditions in Acts*, trans. John Bowden (Minneapolis: Fortress, 1987). Luedemann also includes here his judgments about the historicity of the traditional material. Unfortunately, this volume lacks a comprehensive discussion of the methods actually employed in the study.

THE CONTRIBUTIONS OF JOHN KNOX
TO THE STUDY OF ACTS:
SOME FURTHER NOTATIONS

John T. Townsend

Introduction

Joseph Tyson has given an accurate and reliable account of John Knox's contributions to the study of Acts and Paul in two major areas: (a) Acts as a source for Pauline biography and, (b) the relation of Acts to Marcion. In addition, he has shown to what extent Knox's views have been accepted in the world of NT scholarship. It would be difficult to improve on what he has done. What is surprising, as Tyson rightly suggests, is that Knox's views were not too widely accepted, even regarding Pauline chronology. Knox's logic has always seemed unassailable: where Paul and Acts disagree on what Paul did, the presumption of error must lie in Acts. The conclusion seemed obvious when I first read Knox, and it seemed obvious to my teachers, including two of Knox's contemporaries, H. J. Cadbury and A. D. Nock. Cadbury, as Tyson points out, agreed with Knox's presumption and chronology (although not with his late dating of Acts)[1] from the beginning. What is more surprising is that even Nock, whose own earlier book on Paul had made great use of Acts, treated Knox's views with great respect. Nock also introduced me to Knox's book on Marcion. My essay, then, does not challenge Knox or Tyson on major issues. Rather, it offers some

---

[1] Cadbury always believed that the author of Luke-Acts claimed first-hand knowledge of some of the events he was describing in Acts. See "The Knowledge Claimed in Luke's Preface," *Expositor*, ser. 8, vol. 24 (Dec., 1922) 401-20. Although I have never read a satisfactory rebuttal of his arguments here, I find Knox's reasons for a late dating more persuasive.

notations and suggestions for pursuing Knox's arguments somewhat further.

The Priority of Paul's Epistles

The first point is quite general and concerns Knox's views on the Pauline letters as a whole. As part of that corpus, he accepted Colossians and 2 Thessalonians, letters whose Pauline authorship has become increasingly questionable in recent years. Still, Knox's actual chronological arguments did not depend on these two letters. Moreover, although Knox included Colossians and 2 Thessalonians among the "presumably authentic letters of Paul, coming to us substantially as they left their author's hand" (1950a:20f.), he certainly recognized that the whole Pauline corpus had undergone revision at the hands of those who had collected and edited it (1950a:16-20; 1942a:39-76; 1966d:279-87). There is also another caution for any who would blindly accept the Pauline witness as unassailable. Did Paul always give, or even intend to give, his readers the full and unbiased truth about his actions? While he was certainly in a position to know more about his own life and teaching than the author of Luke-Acts, Paul's personal biases were at least as strong as the biases of that author.[2]

In spite of such cautions, however, Knox's logic still stands. Where Paul and Acts disagree about events in Paul's life, the weight of evidence must lie with the witness of Paul.[3] Moreover, since Knox has shown that Acts is incorrect again and again against the measure of the Pauline Epistles, we should be wary of Acts, even where the Pauline measure is absent. If that dictum means we can know less about the apostolic age than was once assumed, then our true knowledge of that age has in fact advanced. Awareness of ignorance is better than acceptance of what is likely untrue. Knox's assessment, however, did not entirely rule out Acts as an historical source for the life of Paul. Knox always recognized that Acts might be helpful if properly used, and he affirmed, for example, that "we have good reason to trust the Acts account of the general order in which this work [Paul's earlier missionary work] was done," because

---

[2]"See H. D. Betz, *Galatians* (Hermeneia; Philadelphia: Fortress, 1979) 60. For a questioning of Paul's accuracy apart from rhetorical considerations, see Jack T. Sanders, "Paul's 'Autobiographical' Statements in Galatians 1-2," *JBL* 85 (1966) 335-43; see also the preceeding essay by Tyson.

[3]For a study of how the narrative in Acts 9 arose, see my "Acts 9:1-29 and early Church Tradition," *Society of Biblical Literature 1988 Seminar Papers*, ed. David J. Lull (Atlanta: Scholars Press, 1988) 119-31.

"the letters nowhere contradict, and often confirm, this story" (1950a:79).

Paul's Visits to Jerusalem

The next notation concerns the number of visits the Lukan Paul makes to Jerusalem. Knox wisely chose to count visits and not missionary journeys. He recognized that this invention had little to do with what Paul actually did. In fact, he could have gone further and recognized that our concept of numbered missionary journeys is not even found in the book of Acts. The concept was simply read into the book with the rise of modern missionary societies, which themselves sent out missionaries from a home base.[4]

In *Chapters in a Life of Paul* (1950a), Knox reconstructed the three Jerusalem visits from Paul's letters and compared them with the five visits in Acts. Knox's count is correct, however, only if we ignore the readings from two of the earliest NT mss. According to most translations of Acts 12:25, Barnabas and Saul returned "from Jerusalem." Such a reading fits in well with the fact that the last mention of the two evangelists (in Acts 11:30) has them being sent off to Jerusalem. But mss S and B, along with the majority of later mss, all read "to Jerusalem." According to this reading, Barnabas and Saul would necessarily have left Jerusalem before returning there for an extra visit. While P[74] reads "out of (*ex*) Jerusalem" and the so-called "Western Text" reads "from (*apo*) Jerusalem," the mss support for the more difficult reading, namely, "to Jerusalem," is strong.[5] It is not remarkable, therefore, that the twenty-sixth edition of the Nestle-Aland NT has adopted it.[6] Thus, in order to harmonize the three Jerusalem visits of the Epistles with the visits in Acts, one needs to recognize that Acts probably has not five visits, but six.

---

[4]The earliest use of this interpretation is found in the first edition of Johann Albrecht Bengel's *Gnomon Novi Testamenti* (Tübingen: J. A. Philippus Schrammius, 1742) 410f. See my "Missionary Journeys in Acts and European Missionary Societies," *ATR* 68 (1986) 99-104.

[5]Charles H. Buck once suggested orally that the difficult reading "to Jerusalem" is an inconsistency, which reflects the forced joining of two sources.

[6]The reading is also accepted by Ernst Haenchen, *The Acts of the Apostles: A Commentary.* (Philadelphia: Westminster, 1971) 387; S. Giet, "Les trois premiers voyages des saint Paul à Jerusalem," *RSR* 41 (1953) 321.

Contradictions Between the Epistles and Acts

The third notation concerns Knox's listing of contradictions between the Epistles and Acts. They may be somewhat more significant than even he believed, if one makes a detailed comparison of Galatians 1-2 and 2 Cor 11:32-33 with Acts 9. Some years ago, O. Linton[7] made a study, not of what Paul affirmed about himself in Galatians 1-2, but of what the Apostle was denying, i.e., the views of those opposing him. What is especially interesting is that Acts 9 agrees with the views of Paul's opponents. In fact, the agreement is so striking that one could make a case for the source behind Acts 9 actually coming from these opponents.[8] Although the author of Luke-Acts probably regarded himself as pro-Paul, one of his sources may well have stemmed from those who opposed the Apostle.[9]

The Translation of Gal 2:1

The fourth notation concerns the translation of Gal 2:1. With few exceptions,[10] the Greek *dia* is translated "after," i.e., "after fourteen years," even though the interpretation poses a problem for Pauline chronology. Why not translate the *dia* as "during," so that the text reads: "Then, during [the] fourteen years (i.e., the years between the conversion and the writing of Galatians)[11] I again went up to Jerusalem...." This translation fits a more general interpretation of the whole of Gal 1:16-2:10, according to which Paul was arguing that he had visited Jerusalem only twice since his conversion. He was concerned about minimizing his contacts with Jerusalem and needed to account for the whole period, not just the first fourteen years of it. The translation finds additional support in the fact that throughout this section, Paul was consciously repeating his language, as in the threefold use of the adverb, *epeita* ("then"). Now Paul had already used *meta* with the

[7]O. Linton, "The Third Aspect; A Neglected Point of View: A Study in Gal. i-ii and Acts ix and xv," *ST* 3 (1949) 79-95.

[8]Linton himself concludes cautiously (ibid, 95): "It is therefore very probable that the account of Acts derives from older sources, surely not identical with those current in Galatia but akin to them."

[9]See my "Acts 9:1-29 and Early Church Tradition," 125-26. Note also that Paul's opponents may not have regarded themselves as such.

[10]E.g., Joseph A. Fitzmyer, "The Letter to the Galatians," *Jerome Biblical Commentary* eds. Raymond E. Brown, Joseph A. Fitzmyer, and Roland E. Murphy (Engelwood Cliffs, NJ: Prentice Hall, 1968) 2:239, following Giet, 321-47.

[11]Fitzmyer (ibid.) translates the verse, "Once again in fourteen years."

accusative for the "then-after-three-years" visit in Gal 1:18. In a passage where he was consciously using repetitious vocabulary, why would he have changed prepositions for the visit in Gal 2:1, unless he had a different meaning in mind?

One reason that the suggested translation has not found greater favor is that all the ancient Greek exegetes understood the relevant phrase in this verse to mean "after fourteen years." Since they probably knew the language better than we do, we cannot dismiss their interpretation unless we can find some ulterior motive for their exegesis. Such a motive is their well-known embarrassment over Paul's non-Classical Greek.[12] This bias caused them to interpret Paul's Greek in the classical idiom wherever possible. Since *dia* with the genitive in reference to time must mean "after" in classical Greek, the ancient Greek exegetes understood Gal 2:1 in this sense. However, while *dia* with the genitive cannot express duration of time in classical Greek, it is a common usage in the *Koine* and as such appears several times in the NT, for example, in Acts 1:3 with reference to the risen Jesus appearing to the Apostles "during forty days" (RSV) before his ascension.[13] In addition, Paul himself, in Rom 11:10 (citing Ps 69:24 [LXX 68:24]), used *dia* with the genitive in the sense of "during" (i.e., "for all time") to translate the Hebrew *tamid*.[14] Apart from the verse under discussion (Gal 2:1), he never used *dia* with the accusative in the sense of "after." Against this position, Friedrich Sieffert[15] pointed out that *dia* is never used to mean "during" except in the case of continuous (as in Mark 14:58) or repeated action (as in Acts 1:3). But does not the *palin* ("again") in Gal 2:1 refer to the repetition of a visit to Jerusalem?

---

[12]See Tatian, *Oratio ad Graecos*, 26-30; Origen, J. Scherer edition of *Le commentaire d'Origene sur Rom. 3:5-5:7* (Cairo: L'institut francais d'archéologie orientale, 1957) 218f. on Rom. 4:23; Jerome, *Ep.* 22. 30. In the fourth century Apollinarius the Elder rewrote the Bible in suitable literary forms and style. See my "Ancient Education in the Time of the Early Roman Empire," in *The Catacombs and the Colosseum*, eds. Stephen Benko and John J. O'Rourke (Valley Forge, PA: Judson, 1971) 148, and nn. 50-51.

[13]Also in Matt 26:61 // Mark 14:58 ("Within three days," where John 2:19 has *en* with the dative. For other examples, see F. Blass, A. Debrunner, and R. W. Funk, *A Greek Grammar of the New Testament and Other Early Christian Literature* (Chicago: University Press, 1961) 119. See also K. Hauser, *Grammatik der griechischen Inscriften Lykiens* (Diss. Zurich & Basel, 1916) 27f.

[14]Cf. 2 Thess 3:16, where the expression is used apart from a quotation.

[15]*Comm. Gal.* (Krit. Exeg. Kom. über. d. NT; Göttingen: Vandenhoeck & Ruprecht, 1899), ad. loc.

This interpretation of Gal 2:1 has implications for more than mere chronology. Since Knox has shown that Paul's collection for the Jerusalem church was a onetime effort (1950a:51-57), those Epistles which mention the collection (i.e., Romans, 1-2 Corinthians, and Galatians) must have come from the same period. If one then interprets the fourteen years of Gal 2:1 as beginning with Paul's Damascus experience and ending with the writing of Galatians, the religious experience "fourteen years ago" in 2 Cor 12:1-5 tends to coincide with that Damascus experience. If so, we have a description of Paul's so-called "conversion"[16] from the Apostle himself. This position has been accepted by a few, including C. Buck and G. Taylor.[17]

Knox has shifted his own position over the years. He accepted the identification of 2 Corinthians with the Damascus experience in 1936 (1936c:341-49) and in 1939 (1939a:16f., 22), but by the time he wrote *Chapters* in 1950, he regarded his former position as doubtful. Some years after he wrote *Chapters*, Knox told me in a private conversation that his doubt had only increased. Still, an interpretation of Gal 2:1 which places the writing of Galatians fourteen years after the conversion removes any chronological objections to equating 2 Cor 12:1-5 with that conversion.[18] In fact, if 2 Cor 12:1-5 is not a depiction of the conversion, then it is a depiction of a "revelation" which Paul places about the time of the conversion.[19]

Paul of Tarsus

The next notation concerns Tarsus as Paul's origin. Knox accepted that Paul was from Tarsus, an assertion found only in Acts, because "there is no obvious reason why Paul should have mentioned it and no plausible reason why Luke should have invented it" (1950a:34; cf. 43).

---

[16]Krister Stendahl (*Paul Among Jews and Gentiles* [Philadelphia: Fortress, 1976] 7-23) shows convincingly that Paul's conversion had more the nature of a calling in that Paul never thought of himself as converting to a new religion.

[17]C. Buck and G. Taylor, *St. Paul: A Study of the Development of His Thought* (New York: Schribner's, 1969) 104, 220-26.

[18]For a sample posing of this chronological objection, see E.-B. Allo, *Comm. 2 Cor.* (Paris: Gabalda, 1956); cf. Buck and Taylor, *St. Paul*, 221-22.

[19]For an excellent study of the meaning of 2 Cor 12:1-5, see James D. Tabor, *Things Unutterable: Paul's Ascent to Paradise in its Greco-Roman, Judaic, and Early Christian Contexts* (Studies in Judaism; New York: University Press of America, 1986). Although Tabor does not consider the possibility of this epiphany being the conversion, his interpretation of the epiphany could fit such a consideration.

Robert Kraft has maintained for many years that Luke may indeed have believed that Paul came from Tarsus because of a mistranslation. Luke simply misunderstood the expression, "Saul the Tarsian," which in Aramaic reads *Sha'ul Tarsaya* (Hebrew: *Sha'ul haTarsi*) and can mean "Saul the weaver," as a designation of his native city.[20] The result was a transformation of "Paul" or "Saul the weaver" into "Saul, the man from Tarsus." Knox, writing in 1950, assumed that Paul's Tarsian birth was "in line with the general impression the letters give that their author was an extra-Palestinian Jew" (1950a:34). But might not Paul's supposed Tarsian birth have overinfluenced exegetes like Knox in determining just how Palestinian the Apostle was? In any case, there was enough Hellenism in the land of Israel to account for a considerable degree of Greek influence upon anyone from there.

Marcion and the Date of Acts

Now let me turn to Knox's 1942 book, *Marcion and the New Testament* (1942a).[21] Knox concluded that canonical Luke derives from Marcion's gospel rather than the other way around. Those who criticize Knox's view have argued that we do not know enough about Marcion's gospel to make any comparison. They maintain that, since Knox used Adolf von Harnack's reconstruction, Knox's argument shares all its uncertainties. But Knox's major conclusions need not depend on a reconstruction of Marcion's gospel. It is enough to have Tertullian's witness that Marcion's gospel contained matter that contradicted Marcion's own views.[22] If Marcion were rewriting our Luke, he would certainly have made the gospel agree with what he believed. Since he did not do so, it is doubtful that he rewrote his gospel source to any great extent.[23] Thus, there is little reason to believe that Marcion edited his version of Luke more radically than he did the Pauline Epistles.

I have recently added supporting material to Knox's arguments, showing that his late dating of Luke-Acts has much to commend it.[24] In

---

[20]Kraft has presented this interpretation in various oral papers, but to my knowledge he has not yet published it.

[21]See also the rev. ed. (1980a).

[22] Tertullian, *Marc.* 4:43.

[23]Tertullian tried to explain the inconsistency of a radically censored work not agreeing with the censor by claiming that Marcion deliberately left material with which he disagreed in his gospel in order to fool his opponents into thinking that he had not tampered with the work.

[24]"The Date of Luke-Acts," in *Luke-Acts: New Perspectives from the Society of Biblical Literature Seminar.* ed. Charles Talbert (New York: Crossroad, 1984) 47-62.

the first place, no definite citation of Acts exists before the last quarter of the second century. There seemed to be little reason, therefore, to reject Knox's late dating out of hand. Indeed, several aspects of Acts, many of which exegetes accept as "primitive theology,"[25] fit in well with a second-century dating. Unusual Christian titles for God, like "the God of Abraham, Isaac, and Jacob" or "the God of our ancestors (*pateron*)"; and unusual titles for Jesus, like "author of life," "servant (*pais*)," "the Holy One," and "the Just One," all appear in second-century Christian writings, and occur rarely or never in Christian writings before that time. There is also a special affinity between Acts and the Pseudo-Clementine literature, especially the second-century *Kerygma-Petrou* (=*KP*) source. Points in common include the "Apostolic Decree," the sacramental use of salt,[26] the importance of the apostles other than Paul, the designation of Jesus as the Deuteronomic Prophet like Moses (Deut 18:15-18),[27] the importance of baptism,[28] and the total rejection of the Jerusalem Temple with its cult. Such evidence tends to confirm Knox's dating of Acts in the second century. This evidence also explains another objection to Knox, namely, that much of the material in Acts is irrelevant to the Marcionite problem.[29] Acts does indeed contain much that was irrelevant to the Marcionite problem, but what was irrelevant to this problem was very relevant to other second-century problems, such as Church-Synagogue relations, Jewish Christianity of the Pseudo-Clementine type, and the continuing concern about political relations with the empire.

Conclusion

Once we accept that Knox's late dating of Acts is possible, the rest of his arguments concerning Marcion and Luke-Acts fall into place. The fact that Acts ignored the Pauline Epistles, for example, is not a valid

---

[25]E.g., Richard F. Zehnle, *Peter's Pentecost Discourse* (SBLMS 15; Nashville: Abingdon, 1971).

[26]*Synalizomenos* in Acts 1:4; Hom. 13:4:3 (not *KP*); the Epistle of Clement to James 15:4.

[27]Acts 3:22, 7:37; Recog. 1:43 (*KP*) et passim; cf. *Barn* 12:1-7. Apart from Acts there is no specific use of this designation for Jesus in the NT.

[28]The only NT works which specifically mention baptism as a necessary requirement for salvation are Acts (2:3 8) and I Pet (3:21). Surprisingly, in the Pseudo-Clementine literature, it is baptism, not circumcision, which God requires. See Hom. 11:26-27 and Recog. 5:34:2 (both *KP*).

[29]Harvie Branscomb, "Second Sentury Christianity Re-Examined," *Christendom* 8 (1943) 408-410.

argument against a late dating. Knox himself pointed out the hidden assumption here: that "if Luke knew the letters of Paul, he must have used them" (1966d:284). But is such an assumption valid? After all, Justin Martyr managed to ignore Paul altogether throughout a corpus much larger than Luke-Acts!

Acts represents an attempt to treat various second-century problems. One such problem was Marcion. The solution was to keep Paul the great missionary while rejecting Paul the Apostle, along with the distinctive theology of his Epistles. Paul's reaction, had he lived long enough, might have been: "With friends like this, who needs enemies?"

A SOCIO-RHETORICAL LOOK AT THE WORK
OF JOHN KNOX ON LUKE-ACTS

Vernon K. Robbins

The Position of John Knox on the Date for Luke-Acts

In his contribution to this volume, Joseph Tyson has outlined Knox's proposal about the stages of composition of Luke and Acts. One of the keys for understanding Knox's position is, as Tyson says, that Knox proposed neither that Marcion's gospel was an abridgement of canonical Luke nor that canonical Luke is an expanded version of Marcion's Luke. Rather, Knox's position is that a primitive gospel containing the same Markan and Matthean elements as canonical Luke, plus some special Lukan materials, was (a) *somewhat shortened* by Marcion, and (b) *considerably expanded* by the author who rewrote it as the first volume of the two-volume work, Luke-Acts. This means that an early edition of the Gospel of Luke, which is no longer available to us, was extant by ca. 125-135 CE. Marcion produced a shorter edition of it by excluding quotations from OT scriptures, and the author of Acts produced a longer edition of it ca. 150 CE by re-writing it as the first volume of Luke-Acts.

There is a second key for understanding the proposal by Knox. The primary data Knox uses to establish his hypothesis is Christian literature about which an historian can know the date of composition within approximately a decade of accuracy. The first clear use of the Gospel of Luke in its present form is not earlier than the writings of Justin Martyr, which can be dated 155-165 CE,[1] and the first clear evidence of Acts is in

---

[1] "Not earlier," because even Justin's citations would not have had to be from a document containing everything in the Gospel of Luke "as we currently have it."

Irenaeus (175-200 CE). Polycarp (145-55 CE), the earliest writer to tell us
about Marcion's production of one authoritative gospel (135-145 CE),
does not identify Marcion's source as the Gospel of Luke, but simply says
that Marcion tampered with "the sayings of the Lord." It is only
beginning with the last quarter of the second century that Irenaeus and
Tertullian (190-225 CE), who had copies of canonical Luke, said that
Marcion's gospel was an abridgment of "the Gospel of Luke." In other
words, they simply saw that Marcion's version was shorter than
canonical Luke, but they were not in a position to know what source
Marcion had used. Thus, Knox observes, it is possible that an early
edition of the gospel we call Luke was the text Marcion "somewhat
shortened" and the author of Luke-Acts "considerably enlarged." This
means that "historical data" that explicitly exhibit the existence of our
Gospel of Luke require a date no earlier that Justin Martyr (155-165 CE).
Beginning with this explicit information available in datable Christian
literature, Knox formulated an hypothesis that correlated other known
data about Marcion and the establishment of the NT canon with data
internal to Luke-Acts.

The Major Alternatives to Knox's Date for Luke-Acts

People who react against Knox's hypothesis work from the other end
of the possibilities, namely from the earliest possible date Luke-Acts
could have been written as a two-volume work. Luke and Acts could
have been completed as soon as Paul arrived in Rome ca. 61-63 CE. The
major reason most scholars think Luke and Acts were composed 80-85
CE is the conviction that Luke used the Gospel of Mark in very nearly
the form we have it and that both Luke and Acts reflect a situation after
the Jewish-Roman wars of 66-70 CE.[2]

If we ask why the earlier date for Luke-Acts is more attractive to a
majority of people, the reason appears to lie in a double principle: (a)
Luke and Acts are documents in the sacred canon of the Christian
community, and (b) it is considered best for a canonical document to
have been written as close to the origins of Christianity as possible.
Should a different form of reasoning begin to emerge in Christian

---

See Knox's reference in 1942a:126, n. 18 to Albrecht Ritschl, *Das Evangelium Marcions und das kanonische Evangelium des Lukas* (Tübingen: Osiander, 1846) 130ff.

[2]Joseph A. Fitzmyer, *The Gospel According to Luke* (I-IX) (AB 28; New York: Doubleday, 1981) 1.53-57.

belief—namely, that the later a document came to be accepted as canonical the better, since the truth of the document would have been tested among a variety of believers who had knowledge from the full range of early disciples—then the latest possible time for the composition of their final form might become more attractive. In other words, early dating is linked to a belief that the closer a document is to the origins of Christian belief, the better the document is; assuming that is, that the document was not produced by people who already were leading others astray.

In our interpretive environment, characterized as it is by significant pressure for canonical documents to be early, there has, nevertheless, been significant resistance to a proposal by John A. T. Robinson to date these texts "as early as possible." Reasoning from the evidence in Eusebius about John Mark, Robinson argued for the possibility that Mark "put pen to paper after the first preaching mission of Peter in Rome (c. 45), gave it limited circulation as what we called 'P', and subsequently put it out in more ordered form as 'proto-Mark'." The first drafts of Matthew and Luke were produced soon after this. Then, "[t]he final stages of the three synoptic gospels as we have them would then have occupied the latter 50s or early 60s." This sequence clears the way for "the writing of Acts in 62+."[3]

Neither Robinson's argument for the earliest date nor Knox's argument for the latest date has attracted significant scholarly consensus. In the heat of the debate, however, it is usually not noticed that the scholarly consensus is much closer to Robinson's position than Knox's, since a date of 62 CE is less than two decades earlier than 80 CE, while 150 CE is seven decades later. This means that the general scholarly consensus is an "early dating" based on a desire to have the canonical form of Luke and Acts produced during the first century, as soon after the Gospel of Mark (and for some, after the Gospel of Matthew) as appears to be feasible.

It is informative to observe that both the late date proposed by Knox and the early date proposed by Robinson presuppose that the NT gospels grew in stages of editorial composition. In other words, both of these positions reveal an awareness of the nature of text production in antiquity that many, perhaps most, adherents to an 80-85 CE date for Luke and Acts appear not to have. The weight of evidence for texts not

---

[3]John A. T. Robinson, *Redating the New Testament* (Philadelphia: Westminster, 1976) 116.

considered to be sacred scripture—i.e., the multiple manuscripts among the Dead Sea Scrolls, the variations among the Oxyrynchus Papyri and the Coptic Gospel of Thomas, and the letter attributed to Clement of Alexandria that cites data from three editions of the Gospel of Mark— lies on the side of substantive editorial rearrangement, addition, and omission as documents were copied and recopied during the last centuries BCE and the first two centuries CE. Put simply, the greatest likelihood is that the gospels and Acts were written and rewritten in various editions until ca. 150-200 CE, when they began to be considered part of the "New Covenant" alongside the "Old Covenant."

The sad result, in my view, of a "categorical defense" of the 80-85 CE date for Luke and Acts is the support it lends to interpretation of this two-volume work in isolation from the Mediterranean social and literary world matrix in which various people nurtured it into existence and used it for their purposes. After a quarter of a century of notable presence of the Nag Hammadi literature in the study of early Christianity, it has become obvious that certain early Christians used Luke and Acts to consolidate streams of Pauline Christianity with groups that presented Peter, James, John, Stephen, Philip, and Barnabas as the major heirs of the wisdom and work of Jesus of Nazareth. Fashioned within this matrix, Luke and Acts functioned as a social and political tool to gather Christian groups together into a socio-political agglomerate with boundaries and inner principles of congruence. Above all Thomas, who figures prominently in circles in Eastern Syria and Egypt, is not a significant figure in Luke and Acts. Such findings should issue a call to probe the social location of Luke and Acts in relation to other early Christian literature.

A Mood for Reassessment

There are some signs of interest in taking a new look at the process of composition of Luke and Acts. Three arenas of activity are worth discussing briefly. First, in 1979, M.-E. Boismard gave a general call to NT scholars in 1979 to move beyond the two-source theory and Griesbach's theory, because both are too simple to explain the data in the Synoptic Gospels.[4] His proposal is to consider Mark to be the product of two distinct sources he calls Document A and Document B, Matthew to be the result of two stages of composition, and Luke to be a

---

[4]M.-E. Boismard, "The Two Source Theory at an Impasse," *NTS* 26 (1979) 1-17.

document that results from an author's use of sources and stages detectable in Mark and Matthew as well as other sources.[5]

During the last few years, Boismard and A. Lamouille have extended this approach to the Acts of the Apostles.[6] Through detailed comparison of the Alexandrian and Western texts of Acts, they have distinguished three successive editions of Acts. In the first edition, a proto-Luke existed as the initial part of a single work that concluded with a version of the Book of Acts. In the second edition, the author divided the gospel and Acts into two works and composed a prologue for each. A version of the gospel close to our canonical Luke (perhaps a pre-Alexandrian "Western" text of Luke[7]) plus the Western text of Acts represent this edition. In the third edition, the author revised the Western text of Acts with independent access to the first edition, producing our canonical Alexandrian version of Acts.[8] At this time, the author also may have produced our canonical Alexandrian text of Luke by revising an earlier edition.[9]

Many NT interpreters will reject the work of Boismard and Lamouille because it carries forward an approach characteristic of a previous era in which hypothetical sources are reconstructed on the basis of an interpreter's assertion of disjunctures, incongruities, and gaps in the text. Their work, however, has two undeniable strengths. Above all, the authors make it clear that any truly responsible interpretation of Acts will give close attention to both the Western and Alexandrian texts. If Knox's theory about the date of Luke and Acts had included data from a detailed comparison of the Alexandrian and Western texts of Acts, it may have been much less easy to disregard. In addition, Boismard and Lamouille treat each edition as a coherent literary work, in contrast to a previous era in which every text was considered to be an assemblage of pre-existing sources. As a result, many of the observations about the text transcend any particular theory about stages of composition of Luke and Acts. Knox's work on the date

---

[5]Further data for these conclusions are present in *Synopse des quatre évangiles en francais*, tomes i-iii (Paris, 1972); *La vie des évangiles. Initiation à la critique des textes* (Paris: Editions du Cerf, 1980).

[6]M.-E. Boismard and A. Lamouille, *Les Actes des deux Apôtres*. Vol. I: Introduction—Textes; Vol. II; Le sense des récits; Vol. III: Analyses littéraires (Études Bibliques, Nouvelle Série 12-14; Paris: Gabalda, 1990).

[7]Based on a letter from Justin Taylor, S.M., May 25, 1990.

[8]Taken from Justin Taylor, "The Making of Acts: A New Account," *RevBib* 97 (1990) 504-24.

[9]Again, based on Taylor's letter, May 25, 1990.

of Luke and Acts, however, may suggest that Boismard and Lamouille could strengthen their work by addressing data that emerge from Marcion's activity on Luke. As of now, their work avoids Marcion's activity by dating the composition of the Western text ca. 80 CE and the Alexandrian text in the 90's.

A second arena of activity points specifically to a new look at the relation of the Synoptic Gospels to one another. In a recent work, Bruce Chilton takes issue with a "genetic" approach to synoptic relationships, since the relationships among the synoptic texts are so varied. In place of a genetic two or four-source theory, he would distinguish performances, construals, and transformations.[10] He understands a performance as "a distinctive, autonomous conveyance of meaning with the language of early Judaism" attributed to creative people like Jesus and Hillel.[11] Construals and transformations, in contrast, are simply "greater or lesser degrees of congruence in that promulgation of performance which is known as tradition."[12]

Chilton makes advances in his work which cannot be pursued in this context. Two limitations are noticeable at the outset. One is the attention to rabbinic sources without the aid of insights from rhetorical activities in Graeco-Roman culture within which both Christian and rabbinic literature were produced.[13] The other is the misguided distinction which makes "performances" a different category from "construals" and "transformations." With this move, Chilton constructs an "original oral source" behind certain sayings in our extant texts, and it is likely that this introduces as many problems as it solves.

From my perspective, every instance on a written page or in a reconstructed oral medium is a performance somewhere on a spectrum in which performed speech is interacting with traditional speech. Using this approach, we could establish definitions that describe the dynamics of interaction we want to delineate at any place in the spectrum. Chilton's statement that performances use "the language of early Judaism" is the Achilles' heel of the special place he gives to "performances," since it assumes the presence of traditions with which the performances are in dialogue. But his method is so concerned to

[10]Bruce Chilton, *Profiles of a Rabbi: Synoptic Opportunities in Reading About Jesus* (Brown Judaic Studies, 177; Atlanta: Scholars Press, 1989) 137-182.

[11]Ibid., p. 97.

[12]Ibid.

[13]Burton L. Mack and Vernon K. Robbins, *Patterns of Persuasion in the Gospels* (Sonoma: Polebridge Press, 1989).

emphasize "individual creativity" that it makes a special maneuver around analysis of the performances' relation to those traditions. Performances, as he discusses them, are either "construals" or "transformations" of tradition that can be analyzed perceptively only if one understands the nature of the rhetorical chreia in late Mediterranean antiquity.[14]

There is a third area of activity which exhibits a mood for reassessment. The clearest representative is Burton L. Mack's *A Myth of Innocence: Mark and Christian Origins*.[15] This work, like the work of Boismard and Lamouille, perceives our canonical texts to be the result of an author's dialogue with documents that we usually refer to as sources. Mack is not interested, however, in reconstructing the wording of these previous documents. Rather, he is interested in the potential of these earlier documents to reveal socio-religious dynamics within spheres of Christianity prior to and contemporary with the composition of our canonical texts. In short, Mack is interested in uncovering layers of knowledge about socio-political interaction in the mode of Michel Foucault's archaeology of knowledge.[16]

My own interest is to integrate aspects of these new activities in an approach I call socio-rhetorical criticism.[17] I think we should use insights about synoptic relationships related to those of Chilton, but supplemented by insights from Graeco-Roman rhetoric in a context of interpretation informed by an awareness that language is a social possession. In my view, M. M. Bakhtin's strategies for exhibiting the dialogical nature of language, again supplemented by insights from

---

[14]Ronald F. Hock and Edward N. O'Neil, *The Chreia in Ancient Rhetoric. Volume I. The Progymnasmata* (Atlanta: Scholars Press, 1986); Vernon K. Robbins, "The Chreia," in *Greco-Roman Literature and the New Testament*, ed. David E. Aune (Atlanta: Scholars Press, 1988) 1-23; Mack and Robbins, *Patterns of Persuasion*.

[15]Burton L. Mack, *A Myth of Innocence: Mark and Christian Origins* (Philadelphia: Fortress Press, 1988).

[16]Michel Foucault, *The Order of Things: An Archaeology of the Human Sciences* (New York: Random House, 1970); *The Archaeology of Knowledge* (New York: Pantheon Books, 1972).

[17]Vernon K. Robbins, *Jesus the Teacher: A Socio-Rhetorical Interpretation of Mark* (Philadelphia: Fortress Press, 1984); "Picking up the Fragments: From Crossan's Analysis to Rhetorical Analysis," *Foundations & Facets Forum* 1.2 (1985) 31-64; "Pragmatic Relations as a Criterion for Authentic Sayings," *Foundations & Facets Forum* 1.3 (1985) 35-63; "Rhetorical Argument about Lamps and Light in Early Christian Gospels," *Context, Festskrift til Peder Johan Borgen*, ed. Peter Wilhelm Bøckman and Roald E. Kristiansen, *Relieff* 24 (Trondheim: Tapir, 1987) 177-95.

Graeco-Roman rhetoric, can introduce a program of analysis that bridges a gap that Foucault's approach leaves when it bypasses a close reading of texts.[18] Such an approach to the text brings a broad context of interpretation similar to that which Knox brings to Luke and Acts. Yet it moves beyond literary-historical issues to social and rhetorical issues and strategies of analysis.

Roman Officials in Luke-Acts

Socio-rhetorical analysis is grounded in the insight that language is a social possession.[19] One basic result of this perception is an awareness that everyone speaks through the language of other people. This means that Luke and Acts are constituted by a wide range of "socio-ideological conversations."[20] This also means that language always presents an interplay of "openness" and "closedness"—in other words, the only way for language to create "its own world" is through conversation with language in socio-ideological situations "outside its world." Thus, any suggestion that a text can be read "simply on its own terms" is illusory. Every text is read in terms of socio-ideological situations outside itself, because every reader is dependent on real or imagined social situations to give meaning to the patterned signs in the text.

One major characteristic of Luke-Acts is its presentation of language through portrayal of a significant range of characters. This range of characters reveals a social location of thought significantly different from the gospels of Mark, Matthew, and John.[21] In addition to a wide variety of Jewish people—yet a variety that does not include Essenes, Hillel, Shammai, and many other Jews—Lukan language speaks through *prosōpopoiia* of a fascinating spectrum of Roman administrative and military personnel.[22] The first Roman military person to whom speech is attributed is the centurion at Capernaum (Luke 7:1-10). The second centurion who comes to speech "glorifies God"

---

[18]M. M. Bakhtin, *The Dialogic Imagination* (Austin: University of Texas Press, 1981) 259-422.

[19]Michael A. K. Halliday, *Language as Social Semiotic: The Social Interpretation of Language and Meaning* (Baltimore: University Park Press, 1978).

[20]Bakhtin, *The Dialogic Imagination*, provides the best techniques for this kind of analysis.

[21]Richard Rohrbaugh, "'Social Location of Thought' as a Heuristic Construct in New Testament Study," *JSNT* 30 (1987) 103-119.

[22]For a discussion of *prosōpopoiia*, see Mack and Robbins, *Patterns of Persuasion*, 44.

at the foot of the cross and declares that Jesus was innocent of wrongdoing (Luke 23:47). The third centurion is Cornelius who, with his entire household, converts to Christianity (Acts 10:1-11:18). The last centurion is Julius, of the Augustan Cohort, who treats Paul kindly, letting him go to his friends to be cared for (Acts 27:3), and who saves Paul from being thrown overboard by the ship's crew (27:42-43).

In addition to centurions, Roman administrative and military personnel of higher status appear. Asiarchs, who are priests of the Roman imperial cult in Ephesus, act as Paul's friends (Acts 19:31); Lysias, a Roman tribune in Jerusalem, protects Paul from Jews (Acts 21-23); and Sergius Paulus, the proconsul of Cyprus, converts to Christianity (Acts 13:6-12). Other ruling elites also appear in Luke-Acts: Joanna, wife of Herod's steward Chuza (Luke 8:3); the Ethiopian eunuch (Acts 8:26-39); Manaen, who was raised with Herod the tetrarch (Acts 13:1); and the Greek women and men of noble birth from Beroea (Acts 17:12). The socio-ideological implications of the portrayal of these people in Luke's account of early Christianity are more important, I would submit, than whether the final form of Luke and Acts was produced in 62 CE, 80 CE, or 150 CE. It would be good if we could date the production of the final literary form within a decade, but since we cannot secure such a date with any reliability, it would be much better to go on to other issues in a context of knowledge that Luke and Acts were produced sometime between 62 and 150 CE.

The implications of Luke's attribution of action and speech to Roman administrative and military personnel begin to appear when we know the basic nature of social stratification in the provincial cities of the Greek East during the first and second centuries CE. In Rome itself, there were two social categories with official definition: (a) the senatorial *ordo*; and (b) the equestrian *ordo*. Membership in these *ordines* was based on property qualification. In order to be a member of the senatorial order, one needed to possess property valued at 250,000 denarii; and to be a member of the equestrian order required less than half this much property. Since the daily wage of a laborer was usually 1 denarius, an enormous chasm existed between the elite and the majority of people. The ability to support this kind of affluence in Mediterranean society was limited by a low level of technology to produce surpluses. Therefore, in Tacitus' day, it is estimated that two thousandths of 1% of the population were members of the senatorial order and less than one-tenth of 1% of the equestrian order.[23]

The provincial cities of the eastern Roman empire, however, created the environment for another class of citizen: the decurion. A provincial city was governed by a council, called a *curia* or *boulē*. Members of the council were decurions or *bouleutai*. In order to be a decurion, one had to have a property value of 25,000 denarii and the "mustering-out pay" of a centurion when he had finished his time of duty, was sufficient for him to enter the order of decurions. While councils in the West usually were limited to 100 members, councils in the East could have as many as 600 members. The magistrates in an eastern provincial city, the local aristocracy, were elected from the decurions.[24]

Among the people in Luke-Acts listed above, Sergius Paulus would have been a member of senatorial rank; the centurions would have had access to the rank of decurion when they received their mustering-out pay, or they already would be decurions, and the remainder would have a status equal to decurions.[25] Thus, the language in Luke-Acts dialogues with a particular socio-ideological arena of Roman society in such a manner that it evokes a conclusion that a significant number of Roman administrative and military personnel either are members of Christianity or have a readiness to accept membership in it.

In order to see what the significance of such an insight might be, let us look briefly at the first episode in Luke that features a centurion in Capernaum. All the gospels suggest that Capernaum, a village on the north shore of the Sea of Galilee about three miles west of the Jordan river, was a place where Jesus lived for a period of time and performed a number of memorable deeds.[26] Matthew, Luke, and John present a story about an official in Capernaum—a centurion (Matthew 8:5, 8, 13; Luke 7:2, 6) or simply a royal official (John 4:46)—who has either a son or a slave[27] who was ill, and Jesus heals him simply by his word rather than by going to where the sick person is. In both Matthew and John, the official goes to Jesus and requests the healing of his son or slave. The

[23]Philip Francis Esler, *Community and Gospel in Luke-Acts* (Cambridge: Cambridge University Press, 1987) 171.

[24]Ibid., 171-72.

[25]Ibid.

[26]Matt 4:13; 8:5-17; 17:24-18:35; Mark 1:21-34; 2:1-3:6; 9:33-50; Luke 4:23, 31-41; 7:1-10; John 2:12; 4:46-53; 6:17-21, 24-65.

[27]Matt 8:6-13: *pais*; Luke 7:1-10: *doulos/pais*; John 4:46-53: *huios/paidion/pais*. *Huios* means son, *doulos* means slave, *paidion* means little or dear child, and *pais* means either son or servant.

Lukan account differs from the other accounts by having the centurion send people to Jesus rather than by going himself to Jesus. As the story unfolds, the centurion's act of sending first Jewish elders and then friends to Jesus enacts the authority which the centurion attributes to himself and which the centurion attributes to Jesus—namely, both speak a word and things happen. When Jesus' positive response to the centurion heals the slave, the reader not only sees that the centurion is right about Jesus but also sees how close a centurion may be to perceiving "the ways of God."

The Lukan account also contains an assertion, unparalleled in any other account, that the centurion built the synagogue for the Jews in Capernaum (Luke 7:5). The material reality of such a claim during the lifetime of Jesus is an interesting issue. On the one hand, evidence from the excavated synagogue at Capernaum shows that it did not exist before the second or third centuries CE.[28] On the other hand, the very concept of synagogue as a meeting place for Jews could point to a space made available by a centurion that is not architecturally identifiable as a synagogue in modern excavations.

The interesting feature for our discussion is that the Gospel of Luke gives the impression that a centurion possessing sufficient wealth to function as a patron of Jews at Capernaum now turns to Jesus for help with his slave. When he receives this help, he owes a debt to Jesus and his followers. In other words, the power and wealth of this centurion, which was oriented toward the Jews in Capernaum, has taken a significant turn toward Jesus and his followers. From this time forward, Christians have a right of access to the centurion's power and wealth if he is the honorable man the narrative portrays him to be.

Jesus as a Reader of Scripture

Given a social location in which Luke and Acts are engaged in energetic dialogue with the socio-ideological arena occupied by Roman military and administrative personnel in the Greek East, it is informative to see that the Gospel of Luke presents Jesus as a "lettered" person, one who can read with rhetorical grace. In contrast to Mark, who describes Jesus as a carpenter or builder (6:3: *tektōn*) and Matthew, who describes Jesus as a son of a carpenter (13:55), neither Luke nor Acts refer to Jesus or his father as a *tektōn*. Rather, Jesus' father, Joseph, has

---

[28]Lee I. Levine, ed., *Ancient Synagogues Revealed* (Jerusalem: Israel Exploration Society, 1982) 42-62, esp. 42-43.

royal lineage "of the house of David" (Luke 1:27; 2:4). At twelve years of age, Jesus sits among the teachers in the Temple and amazes them with his understanding and answers (Luke 2:46-47). After he is filled with holy spirit, he cites passages from written scripture in a contest with the Devil (Luke 4:4, 8, 12). Then, in his home town in Nazareth, he reads from the book of Isaiah in the synagogue on the Sabbath day (Luke 4:16-22). A reader of the Gospel of Luke has the right to presuppose that Jesus is "lettered" — he can read with rhetorical grace—and one might suppose he can also write.

It is surprising that no discussion, to my knowledge, of the portrayal of Jesus' ability to read in Luke has led to detailed analysis of the Infancy Gospel of Thomas. Scholars have had in their possession manuscripts of Infancy Thomas for many years, and Tischendorf made a good edition of the Greek manuscripts available during the last half of the nineteenth century. The final story in Infancy Thomas, as many know, recounts the Lukan scene of Jesus in the Temple at twelve years of age. Ron Cameron states that Infancy Thomas "appropriated this story from Luke, retaining the language, structure, and distinctively Lukan redactional features in the narrative,"[29] but not all this is true. The account in Infancy Thomas varies considerably from the account in Luke.

A considerable amount of wording in the account of Jesus in the Temple is closely related in Luke and Infancy Thomas. There are, however, important variations. The version in Luke emphasizes the role of the parents who go each year to Jerusalem for the Passover feast, who are not aware that Jesus remains in Jerusalem but suppose that he is with the company of travelers, who seek him among his kinsfolk and acquaintances, who return to Jerusalem seeking him, who find him after three days in the Temple and are amazed, and who do not understand when Jesus tells them that he must be about the business of his father. In contrast, the version in Infancy Thomas emphasizes the role of Jesus, who leaves the company of his parents and goes up to Jerusalem after the feast when he is twelve years old, who silences the elders and teachers of the people as he expounds the law and the prophets, and who arises and follows his mother when she confronts him. It also emphasizes the role of Mary, who is praised by the scribes and Pharisees for bearing such a son. In the midst of these differences, the narrator claims that Jesus has knowledge of the scriptures at a level of rhetorical

---

[29]Ron Cameron, ed., *The Other Gospels* (Philadelphia: Westminster Press, 1982) 123-24.

competence (beyond the elementary and grammatical levels),[30] since he expounds the main topics (*kephalaia*) of the law and the similes (*parabolas*) of the prophets. The special interest of Infancy Thomas is to claim that Jesus has attained the abilities of a lettered person without submitting to the social environment of *paideia* training through which people regularly become lettered. While Luke and Acts are opening doors toward Roman administrative and military personnel, Infancy Thomas is closing doors toward Hellenistic teachers. The author of the narrative purports to be Thomas "the Israelite," who is communicating to "brethren among the Gentiles" (1.1), and the major dialogue is with *paideia* training in Greco-Roman culture. The author also is writing in Greek, and he presupposes that *paideia* training occurs through teaching Jesus Greek. When Jesus is five years old (2.1), the teacher Zacchaeus announces the training he will pass on to Jesus (6.2):

> You have a clever (*phronimos*) child, and he has understanding (*nous*). Come, hand him over (*parados*) to me that he may learn letters (*mathē grammata*), and I will teach him with the letters all knowledge (*epistēmē*), and to salute (*prosagoreuein*) all the older people and honour (*timan*) them as grandfathers and fathers, and to love (*agapan*) those of his own age.

Jesus, of course, is smarter than this teacher; so Jesus teaches him and drives him to shame. After Jesus is eight years old (12.2), a second teacher practices the letters with Jesus a long time before Jesus gets angry with him and curses him so that the teacher faints and falls to the ground (14.1-2). Finally a third teacher, who is a good friend of Joseph, suggests that perhaps he can teach Jesus the letters "by persuasion" (*meta kolakias*). Jesus goes with him and finds a book, and, without reading the letters in it, "opened his mouth and spoke by the Holy Spirit and taught the law to those that stood by" (15.2). After this, all of Jesus' actions are benevolent, in contrast to the intermixture of benevolent and violent actions during his earlier childhood.

There is interesting dialogue with *paideia* training in this text. On the one hand, when Jesus is eight years of age he practices letters a long time with a teacher. On the other hand, he rejects his first teacher as incompetent and bypasses his teacher at the rhetorical level by showing that he already has attained the competence of rhetorical delivery "without reading." The socio-ideological implications seem clear. The

---

[30]Stanley F. Bonner, *Education in Ancient Rome* (Berkeley and Los Angeles: University of California Press, 1977).

implied author wants to claim the major achievements of *paideia* training—namely prudence, benevolence, and rhetorical grace—with assistance only for a time on writing the letters. In other words, the eye of the author is on the achievements of Hellenistic education, but he wants to claim an avenue toward these achievements that only involves a modicum of work with Hellenistic tutors. This points to a highly Hellenized Christian environment in which leaders are interested in maintaining an alternative culture they call "Israelite."

What questions does this raise about the story of Jesus in the Temple at twelve years of age? In what environment, we may ask, was the story of Jesus in the Temple formulated and transmitted? Raymond E. Brown remarks that while he is reluctant to talk about earlier sources for most of the units in Luke 1-2, this is one of the stories of the hidden life for which there is a serious possibility of a pre-Lukan source.[31] He explores, in a very suggestive manner, the possibility that this story came from an environment that also nurtured the story of Jesus' changing of water to wine at Cana (John 2:1-12).[32] The role of Mary, which presupposes that Jesus still has not moved away from the family, supports this suggestion.

When would it be likely that Luke 2:41-52 became part of the Gospel of Luke? Perhaps the story of Jesus at twelve years of age was added by an author who rewrote Luke and Acts as a two-volume work to counter Marcion's emphases (Knox). Perhaps it was added to Luke when an author separated Luke from an earlier version of Acts to make it a two-volume work (Boismard). Perhaps Infancy Thomas was composed in the environment in which the Western text of Acts also was produced. Perhaps the story was present in the earliest version of Luke (Knox; Boismard). Infancy Thomas was a response to its beginning point, and Luke 1:1-2:40 were prefixed to address the relation of Jesus to John the Baptist. At some point in time someone also wrote a version of the Protevangelium of James as a response to the beginning point of Luke, ending with a reference to Simeon who would not die until he had seen the Messiah in the flesh (fulfilled in Luke 2:25-35).

The Gain from Socio-Rhetorical Analysis of Luke-Acts

How, then, is it best to address these issues? My major point is that it is important for us to follow an "open poetics" that establishes dialogue

---

[31]Raymond E. Brown, *The Birth of the Messiah* (Garden City, NY: Doubleday, 1977) 480.
[32]Ibid., 487-89.

with other documents and social locations of thought. An insistence on early dating for Luke and Acts, in contrast, easily nurtures a "closed poetics," a poetics that presupposes that someone succeeded in molding stories, sayings, and speeches into a closed, autonomous system of discourse, a monologue that should not be contaminated by dialogical analysis that sees it as part of a lively conversation within early Christianity. The challenge must be to introduce this lively conversation into interpretation that also is interested in the inner conversations the document is having with itself, that is, within its story world. Closer reading of our texts in the manner of recent literary interpretations should go hand in hand with analysis of our texts that sets them in lively dialogue with other texts and socio-ideological environments in the Mediterranean world during the first centuries of early Christianity.

If interpretation of Luke and Acts would focus on dialogues occuring among these two volumes and various socio-ideological environments in first- and second-century Christianity, aspects of early Christianity would begin to appear with a richness not experienced since the nineteenth century, when most NT interpreters not only knew second- and third-century Christian literature but also knew Greek and Roman literature. When the Gospel of Luke presents Jesus as a lettered person in an environment that is inviting Romans of higher social status into Christianity, one could presume that Christians also are inviting traditional *paideia* training into Christian communities. The Western text of Acts may further encourage such a presupposition with its intensified portrayal of rejection of Paul by Jews. Infancy Thomas and the Protevangelium of James may show circles in early Christianity where people are very much against the wholesale invitation of Hellenistic training and ideology into Christianity.

Since we probably never will have data that allow us to know when canonical Luke and Acts were composed within the span of 62-150 CE, we should seek the social location of its thought as it dialogues with other first- and second-century documents and social locations. If we would group Christian, Jewish, and perhaps other Mediterranean literature according to their socio-ideological locations, we could gain quite new insights into early Christianity. I would recommend that such an approach be accompanied by honesty and humility about the limits of our knowledge concerning the date of composition of the edition of the canonical text with which we are working.

REFLECTIONS

John Knox

The editors of this volume have generously requested me to make some response to it, especially perhaps to the essay of Joseph Tyson, which treats the contribution I am presumed to have made to the study of the book of Acts, but also, if I wish and have opportunity, to the papers of other participants in this book's discussion. This "response" may take either of two forms: 1) it may be simply a critical review in some detail of Professor Tyson's article and possibly of that of others; or 2) I may use it as offering an opportunity of saying whatever I should like to say on the general subject of this volume. Of these two options I definitely choose the second. My references to Professor Tyson's essay will be occasional and incidental, appreciative of it as I am.

Let me begin my response by disclaiming most emphatically any expertise in Acts studies. I am honored by being "bracketed" in this connection with Cadbury and Talbert, but also embarrassed because it is an honor far beyond my deserving. Such attention to Acts as I have paid in the course of my New Testament work has been strictly *ad hoc*—incidental to work on other themes, only two of which are relevant, namely, Paul's life and thought and the beginnings of the New Testament canon. But such forays, so to speak, into Acts territory have not yielded results extensive enough and, for Acts studies, significant enough, to justify the distinction this book and particularly Professor Tyson's paper confer on me.

But evidently he graciously does not agree, and I must make some fuller and more detailed response to his generous appraisal than this disclaimer. So far as his general representation of my conclusions on the two relevant areas is concerned, I should say it is as accurate and adequate as I have any right to expect. Therefore, my comments will deal only with a few selected subjects where, it seems to me, I may possibly have something useful to say.

Any reader of either of the articles of 1936 and 1939, to which Tyson makes reference, as well as of my book, *Chapters in a Life of Paul* (1950a), will know that I accord to Acts a strictly secondary role as a source for the life of Paul. This Tyson clearly recognizes and affirms. But I have never denied to Acts any role at all. This also Tyson recognizes equally clearly. Beyond this point, however, I seem to detect, possibly mistakenly, a certain wavering, an uncertainty about my position, for which I believe my writings provide no ground. He appears to find changes from time to time in my estimate of the kind and degree of dependence on the book of Acts a biographer of Paul can properly have, and sometimes he suggests some progressive development in my thinking on this point. Once or twice he seems to suggest that Donald Riddle's work on the chronology made advances on and in some unexplained way affected my thinking in this regard. Any such alteration, not to say development, I would deny. From the time of my first article in 1936 through the revised edition of my book, just 50 years later, and in every writing touching on this subject during that half-century, I have been aware of no changes in my thinking on this particular point, although I may have "spelled it out" more clearly and fully later than earlier. Although it is possible that in various contexts I have laid more stress upon the negative implications of my position as regards the use of Acts than upon the positive, and *vice versa*, but the position itself, so far as I am aware, has not altered.

The brief and passing reference to Donald Riddle in the preceding paragraph leads me next to comment on a matter of which, I had hoped, I should never find it necessary to speak—namely, the question of priority between Riddle's work on the Pauline chronology and mine. I had hoped that the suspicion that my work rested on his had finally been entirely dispelled. But Tyson's paper brings it again to mind. Not that he himself entertains this suspicion! He rejects it. But he does more than tell of an original "confusion" on this matter; he at least hints that the suspicion still persists to some extent. Thus far I have refrained from any attempt to refute it except in the indirect way of referring on occasion to Riddle's book of 1940, *Paul: Man of Conflict*, as representing the first published reaction to my articles. But I have made no direct denial of the suspicion of Riddle's priority, regarding it as too obviously false to merit even mention. But I was evidently mistaken as to how others might regard it. The question, it would seem, refuses to die.

Since this paper is, in all probability, the last piece of writing for publication I shall ever do, I trust I may be forgiven if I now make the explicit denial from which I have hitherto refrained, and make it with some detail. My doing this will involve some inevitable repetition, but it will also involve some previously unpublished history which may be of interest to some readers, especially to those who have made the Pauline chronology an object of special study.

My first article was written not long after my graduation from the University of Chicago and while I was living in Nashville, Tenn., and was published in April of 1936. In the summer of that year I moved back to Chicago to serve as the editorial staff of *The Christian Century*. I well remember the evening, either in the autumn of 1936 or early in 1937, when my friend and former teacher, Donald Riddle, telephoned me at my home to say that, having been abroad for some months, he had only now read my article, that he was convinced of its truth, that he was greatly excited by it, and that he was going to write a book about Paul on the basis of it. In my article I had briefly, but strongly, defended the idea that the letters of Paul were, not only our only entirely reliable source for the life of Paul, but also were able, without any help at all from Acts, to provide us with a complete sketch of its basic structure. The article also defended, as had several other biographers, that the key to the chronology of Paul's career as an apostle lay in the recognition that his visit to Jerusalem referred to in Gal 2:1-10 should be thought of as occurring, not before his work in western Asia Minor, Macedonia, and Achaia had been begun, but at a time when that work was far advanced, indeed nearing completion. Needless to say, Don's praise greatly cheered me; he was going to give much needed and distinguished support to my idea. Meantime, I busied myself with a second article published in 1939, in which my idea was reaffirmed and further defended, and the structure of the emerging chronology and some of its implications were clearly adumbrated. These publications elicited not a little discussion, much of which had occurred before I incorporated the substance of the articles with some elaboration and at least one correction in the earlier part of a book, *Chapters in a Life of Paul*, published in 1950.

The one correction of which I have spoken just now was not an unimportant one. In both of the two articles, I had advanced as an additional, and really clinching argument for the position I was defending, the rather curious repetition of an interval of 14 years in Gal 2:1 and 2 Cor 12:2. I argued, I think with not a little plausibility, that in both of these passages the same "revelation" was being referred to and that therefore approximately 14 years after his conversion, when, according to the traditional chronology, he would not even have begun his Macedonian mission, Paul had in actual fact reached Ephesus, where 2 Corinthians was presumably written. I thought of the several serious objections to this identification of the two "revelations" of which Luedemann much later reminds us and which, in his opinion, renders it impossible. But I believed (and still do) that these could have been satisfactorily met. Martin Dibelius, however, whose opinion I had the opportunity of asking soon after the first article was published, raised an objection which I found more recalcitrant. He made the point that the two "revelations" could hardly be the same because the first of them Paul boldly proclaims; the second he feels somewhat guilty even to mention. The first was, for him, a "public" fact, an important item in the apostolic preaching, the culminating proof of the resurrection, whereas the second was a most secret experience of his very own, of which he is almost ashamed to speak. I resisted this objection at first, as witness my second article of 1939 (1939a), but by the time my book was published in 1950, I had come to feel it was too strong to be rejected; and attractive as my earlier view had been, I had abandoned it. But this change in my thinking took place well after Riddle's book had been written. In that book, he had adopted my original view on this point, as I recall, without any question.

My gratification at the news that Riddle was writing in support of my position was not shared by everyone. I recall that some months or maybe a year or so later, Ernest ("Pomp") Colwell, a close friend of mine and a friend and colleague of Don in the New Testament department of the University, said to me with an indignation I did not feel: "He is writing *your* book!" I did not feel the same way because, for one thing, I felt no need to write a book; the second article would suffice to say all that was essential in what I had to say—as in fact, I think it did. Indeed, at no later time have I seen my way to devoting a whole book to the Pauline chronology, only a few "chapters." My principal interest soon turned to problems in New Testament theology, particularly Christology. The important task of a full exposition of the proposed chronology devolved much later in Luedemann, who was far better qualified than I to accomplish it.

But this lack of motivation was not the chief reason for my not sharing Pomp's attitude. The decisive considerations were, first, the fact that I knew Don would acknowledge his dependence on my work, as indeed he does, very clearly and comprehensively, in the Preface of his book, and secondly, the fact that the dates of my articles as compared with the date of his book would put beyond question the truth about precedence in any case.

But, strangely enough, this did not prove to be true. On the basis of absolutely no evidence at all, but solely because this projected book of Don Riddle, *Paul: Man of Conflict*, was published 10 years earlier than my book, *Chapters in a Life of Paul*, a number of influential scholars decided that I had received the chronological idea and the chronology which followed from it, basic to Riddle's book and to the first few chapters of mine—that I had got these from Riddle. These scholars either did not know my two earlier articles or decided to ignore their decisive significance as well as the clear and full acknowledgement of his dependence upon my work by Riddle himself in the Preface of his book, also ignoring the absence of even a hint in any of my writings of the slightest dependence on my part upon *his* work. Even among some scholars, who did know the articles and did recognize that they fully revealed the proposed chronological scheme and the method I followed in arriving at it, I was at that time sometimes made aware of a suspicion, perhaps very vague, that although I *published* these views before Riddle, I had got the ideas from him, in his lectures or in conversations.

To cite one case: A friend, a most competent and highly esteemed New Testament scholar, in an influential article showed—with some ambiguity, it is true, but still especially if the article is read to its end, quite unmistakably, that he was inclined to regard Riddle as the true originator, my earlier work providing only the "stimulus" for his book. This article was published more than 20 years ago—and, ironically enough, in a *Festschrift* honoring me—and I have reason for believing that his position on this point may have shifted to some extent in the interval since, but the fact that he has never, so far as I know, retracted or modified what is clearly indicated as to his thinking at that time leaves me and others with the impression that, at the very least, he still regards the question of priority as an open one.

As a matter of simple fact, although I learned much from Dr. Riddle, he had absolutely nothing to do with the forming of any of my judgments about the Pauline chronology which are expressed in either of my two articles or in any of the "chapters" of my book, or indeed in anything else I may have written about that subject. On the contrary, while making his own significant contribution to the subsequent discussion, he based his work *as regards this chronology and its implications* entirely on mine, although he reached some conclusions in detail which I think are mistaken. Even the theme "man of conflict" (namely, the idea that conflict with a Judaizing faction within the Church, far from ending early in Paul's career as an apostle, dominated it almost from the beginning and grew more bitter as it proceeded)—even this idea is pointed to in my first article and emphasized in my second. At the end of Chapter IV of my book I recognized Don's contribution in further emphasizing and developing it.

I have in mind two other topics supplied by Professor Tyson's paper on which I should like to comment, but the fact that, as of this date, I have not received copies of Professor Townsend's, Robbins', and other papers to be included in this volume prevents my doing so except in a very limited way, for these writers will have important things to say on both of these topics, of which I should want to take account. The topics are, first, the possible contribution my book on Marcion may make to discussions of the purpose of Acts and its date, and, secondly, the judgment of Professor Henry J. Cadbury on Acts-related work I may have done.

As to my hypothesis about Marcion and about its bearing on the purpose of Acts and its date, Tyson has again presented, I should say, as accurate and full a statement of it as I have the right to expect from even so friendly a critic as he is. And although he finds some mistakes and lacks (and I know the book contains not a few of both), on the whole he insists that my hypothesis deserves to be taken more seriously than has so far been the case; and *that* is all I would ask. He also suggests some interesting additional work which could be done in this area.

As to my own appraisal of the hypothesis, I repeat what I have said several times before, that I find the basic and central thesis, namely, that Marcion's gospel-Apostle was prior to Luke-Acts and provided the immediate occasion for the latter, as it did also for the very idea of a distinctly Christian scripture and for the basic structure of the New Testament canon—that I find this central thesis fully true. If I were writing the book again, I should want to make only one substantial change in it, and that would be in the radical reduction of its discussion of the vocabulary and literary style of the Marcionite gospel as found in a reconstructed text. I built much too large and elaborate a superstructure, often weak and sometimes demonstrably faulty, on much too shaky a foundation. I should have depended upon the little we can *surely* know of that text to refute Sanday's presumably final demonstration of Luke's priority to Marcion, but should have depended on it no further. The vindication of the hypothesis required no more than this. The strength of the argument for its truth consists, not altogether but largely, in its inner consistency, each element in it supporting and being supported by every other; and although this argument would to a small degree be weakened by the removal of the purely linguistic evidence, it would by no means be invalidated, and the remaining evidence would be rendered more secure.

As for Professor Cadbury's estimate of my Acts-related writings, I shall leave to others any analysis and appraisal of his comments in published reviews, etc. (and I know they were sometimes, perhaps often, adversely critical), and shall do no more than add to the evidence three items, all of them unpublished so far as I know, which lie in my memory of conversations or in letters. 1) In a letter written soon after my *Chapters in a Life of Paul* appeared, he thanked me for "the clearest possible analysis of the difference in character and usefulness of the dual set of sources" and told me he was sure I was "right in putting the Judaizing crisis nearer the end than the beginning of Paul's work in the 4 provinces and much of the 14 years in that work, too." 2) He expressed in conversation not long after my *Marcion* was published the judgment that, in that book, I should, in effect, have followed the advice I have just now given to myself about the textual evidence adduced in that book and have depended upon it only to refute Sanday's argument. 3) In a letter written soon after his retirement at Harvard, or possibly in a conversation at about that time, he told me that he had decided I was right about the comparatively late date of Acts, although, as I recall, he gave me no reason to conclude that it was my arguments alone which had convinced him.

BIBLIOGRAPHY OF JOHN KNOX*

Mikeal C. Parsons

1929   "'He Shall Be Like a Tree.'" *Christian Century* 46:680-81.
1930   "Why the Revival Did Not Come." *Christian Century* 47:1415-16.
1932a   *"He Whom a Dream Hath Possessed": Some Aspects of Religious Living.* New York: R. Long and R. R. Smith.
Reviewed:
    Crozer Quarterly 9 (1932) 242. (W. S. Sheriff)
    Pulpit 3 (1932) 23. (C. C. Morrison)
1932b   "God Is Still Building His World." *Christian Advocate* 93:1128-30.
1932c   "'...When There is No Peace.'" *Christian Advocate* 93:1576-77.
1934   "'Ugly Ducklings.'" *Christian Advocate* 95:744-45.
1935a   *Philemon Among the Letters of Paul: A New View of Its Place and Importance.* (University of Chicago: A Dissertation Submitted to the Faculty of the Division of the Humanities in Candidacy for the Degree of Doctor of Philosophy, Department of New Testament and Early Christian Literature) Chicago/London: University of Chicago/Cambridge University.
Reviewed:
    ATR 18 (1936) 42-43. (B. S. Easton)
    Christian Century 53 (1936) 466. (W. E. Garrison)
    Crozer Quarterly 13 (1936) 127-28. (M. S. Enslin)
    JBR 4 (1936) 50. (H. J. Cadbury)
    JR 16 (1936) 114-15. (A. M. Perry)
    JTS 37 (1936) 414-16. (H. Burnaby)
    LCQ 9 (1936) 225-26. (R. T. Stamm)

See also:

E. J. Goodspeed. *Christianity Goes to Press* (New York: Macmillan, 1940) esp. 8, 12, 57, 83.

P. N. Harrison. "Onesimus and Philemon." *ATR* 32 (1950) 268-94.

H. Greeven. "Prüfung der Thesen von J. Knox zum Philemonbrief." *TLZ* 79 (1954) 373-78.

C. L. Mitton. *The Formation of the Pauline Corpus of Letters* (London: Epworth, 1955) *passim*.

C. F. D. Moule. *The Epistles of Paul the Apostle to the Colossians and to Philemon* (CGTC; ed. C. F. D. Moule; Cambridge: Cambridge University, 1957) 14-18.

S. B. C. Winter. "Methodological Observations on a New Interpretation of Paul's Letter to Philemon." *USQR* 39 (1984) 203-12.

L. Cope. "On Rethinking the Philemon-Colossians Connection." *BR* 30 (1985) 45-50.

1935b   "Are the Gospels History?" (Review of R. H. Lightfoot, *History and Interpretation in the Gospels*). *Christendom* 1:205-7.

1936a   "A Note on II Thessalonians 2:2." *ATR* 18:72-73.

1936b   "A Conjecture as to the Original Status of II Corinthians and II Thessalonians in the Pauline Corpus." *JBL* 55:145-53.

1936c   "'Fourteen Years Later': A Note on the Pauline Chronology." *JR* 16:341-49.

1936d   "The Preaching Mission Starts." *Christian Century* 53:1288-90.

1936e   "Christianity Reinterpreted" (Review of I. Edman, *The Mind of Paul*; P. B. Kern, *The Basic Beliefs of Jesus*; W. R. Bowie, *The Renewing Gospel*; H. Carrington, *Loaves and Fishes*). *Christendom* 1:535-38.

1936f   Review of C. R. Bowen, *Studies in the New Testament: Collected Papers of Clayton R. Bowen*. *Christian Century* 53:1394.

1937   Review of E. F. Scott, *The Pastoral Epistles*. *Christian Century* 54:619-20.

1938a   "The Bible in College." *Christian Century* 55:47-49.

See also:

C. W. Quimby. "Letter to the Editor." *Christian Century* 55 (1938) 117.

A. R. King. "Religion in the Colleges." *Christian Century* 55 (1938) 206-8.

C. W. Quimby. "Teach the Bible as Religion." *JBR* 6 (1938) 70-72.

1938b "'As Religion'—But in What Sense?" *JBR* 6:72-74 [in reply to C. W. Quimby above].

See also:

A. R. King. "Religion a By-Product in Education" *JBR* 6 (1938) 74-76.

C. W. Quimby. "Mr. Quimby Comments." *JBR* 6 (1938) 76.

1938c "Our Knowledge of Jesus." *Christendom* 3:44-54.

1938d "Philemon and the Authenticity of Colossians." *JR* 18:144-60.

1938e "A Pastoral Prayer." *The Christian Century Pulpit* 9:139.

1938f Review of M. S. Enslin, *Christian Beginnings. Christian Century* 55:561.

1938g Review of R. Otto, *The Kingdom of God and the Son of Man. Christian Century* 55:699.

1938h Review of H. J. Cadbury, *The Peril of Modernizing Jesus. JBL* 57:351-52.

1939a "The Pauline Chronology." *JBL* 58:15-29.

See also:

W. G. Kümmel. "Das Urchristentum." *TRu* 17 (1948/49) 4, 48-49.

1939b "On the Vocabulary of Marcion's Gospel." *JBL* 58:193-201.

1939c "'They Suffer from a Nothingness.'" *Christian Century* 56:1303-4.

1939d "New Testament History and Interpretation" (Review of F. V. Filson, *Origins of the Gospels*; H. G. Wood, *Did Christ Really Live?*; W. W. Fenn, *The Theological Method of Jesus*; R. N. Flew, *Jesus and His Church*; J. Moffatt, *The First Epistle of Paul to the Corinthians*). *Christendom* 4:147-50.

1939e "Recent Studies in Christian Historical Sources" (Review of A. N. Wilder, *Eschatology and Ethics in the Teaching of Jesus*; E. W. Parsons, *The Religion of the New Testament*). *Christendom* 4:593-95.

1940a Review of J. Baillie, *Our Knowledge of God. JR* 20:191-92.

1940b Review of E. J. Goodspeed, *Christianity Goes to Press. JR* 20:304-5.

1941a   *The Man Christ Jesus.* Chicago: Willett, Clark & Company.
Reviewed:
>*Christendom* 6 (1941) 441-43. (A. N. Wilder)
>*Christian Century* 58 (1941) 752-53. (C. T. Craig)
>*Churchman* 155 (1941) 34. (W. L. Caswell)
>*Crozer Quarterly* 18 (1941) 259-60. (M. S. Enslin)
>*Expositor and Homiletic Review* 43 (1941) 483. (P. D. Leedy)
>*JBR* 9 (1941) 257. (J. P. Deane)
>*JR* 21 (1941) 486. (F. C. Grant)
>*Kirch Zeit* 65(1941) 752-53. (Mattes)
>*LCQ* 14 (1941) 343-44. (W. C. Waltemyer)
>*Pulpit* 12 (1941) 71. (C. C. Morrison)
>*RevExp* 38 (1941) 454-55. (H. W. Tribble)
>*Scroll* 42 (1944) 27-28. (E. S. Ames)

1941b   Review of F. C. Grant, *The Gospel of the Kingdom.* JBL 60:74-75.

1941c   Review of A. W. Blackwood, *Preaching from the Bible.* *Christian Century* 58:322.

1941d   Review of C. Seidenspinner, *Form and Freedom in Worship.* Eds. G. A. Buttrick *et al*, *Preaching in These Times.* JR 21:207-9.

1941e   "Contemporary Study of the Gospel" (Review of M. Dibelius, *The Sermon on the Mount*; J. Moffatt, *Jesus Christ the Same*). *Christendom* 6:269-72.

1942a   *Marcion and the New Testament: An Essay in the Early History of the Canon.* Chicago/London: University of Chicago/Cambridge University.
Reviewed:
>*Alumni Review (Chicago)* 19 (1943) 38. (A. A. Hays)
>*ATR* 25 (1943) 228-33. (S. E. Johnson)
>*BullThéolAncMéd* 5 (1947) 196-97. (C. Van Puyvelde)
>*ChicagoTheolSemReg* 33 (1943) 25. (M. Spinka)
>*Christendom* 8 (1943) 408-10. (H. Branscomb)
>*The Christian Advocate (Chicago)* 118 (1943) 380. (R. W. Goodloe)
>*Christian Century* 60 (1943) 14-15. (C. T. Craig)
>*CH* 12 (1943) 64. (E. F. Scott)
>*Churchman* 157 (1943) 15. (B. S. Easton)
>*Crozer Quarterly* 20 (1943) 159-61. (C. H. Kraeling)

ExpTim 54 (1942/43) 151-52. (W. Fulton)

JQR 34 (1943/44) 385-86. (F. V. Filson)

JBR 11 (1943) 54-56. (M. E. Andrews)

JBL 62 (1943) 123-27. (H. J. Cadbury)

JR 23 (1943) 140-42. (M. S. Enslin)

JTS 44 (1943) 220-24. (W. F. Howard)

Kirch Zeit 67 (1943) 240. (S. Zwemer)

London Quarterly and Holborn Review 168 (1943) 90-91. (F. B. Clogg)

LQR 18 (1945) 210-11. (M. L. Stirewalt, Jr.)

PSB 34 (1943) 41. (O. A. Piper)

RL 12 (1942/43) 308-9. (D. T. Rowlingson)

TS 4 (1943) 287-91. (J. E. Steinmueller)

TRu 17 (1948/49) 147. (K. Grobel)

Nouvelle Revue Théologique 69 (1947) 1109. (J. Levie)

Watchman-Examiner 31 (1943) 633. (editor)

WTJ 6 (1943/44) 86-98. (N. B. Stonehouse)

See also:

C. L. Mitton. *The Formation of the Pauline Corpus of Letters*. London: Epworth, 1955.

C. F. D. Moule. *The Epistles of Paul the Apostle to the Colossians and to Philemon*. CGTC; Ed. C. F. D. Moule. Cambridge: Cambridge University, 1957, 14-18.

1942b Editor. *Religion and the Present Crisis*. (Lectures under the Charles R. Walgreen Foundation for the Study of American Institutions, University of Chicago, 1941). Chicago: University of Chicago.

Reviewed:

ATR 24 (1942) 275. (L. M. Hammond)

Christendom 7 (1942) 573-74. (H. T. Kerr, Jr.)

Crozer Quarterly 19 (1942), 241-42. (H. C. Newell)

JBR 10 (1942) 229-30. (C. S. Braden)

JR 22 (1942) 319-21. (J. C. Bennett)

LCQ 15 (1942) 314-16. (D. F. Putman)

TRu 17 (1948/49) 181-82, 190. (F. C. Sell)

1942c "Re-examining Pacificism." Pp. 30-47 in 1942b.

1942d Review of E. F. Scott, *The Nature of the Early Church. JR* 22:107-9.

1942e Review of G. A. Buttrick, *Prayer. JR* 22:205-6.

1942f   Review of H. T. Kerr, *Preaching in the Early Church*. *Christian Century* 59:957-58.

1943a   "We Are Divided." *Christian Century* 60:13-14.

1943b   "Can Evil Always Be Overcome With Good?" *Christianity and Crisis* 3:2-4.

1944a   "The Beginnings of Christianity." Pp. 36-53 in *The Vitality of the Christian Tradition*. Ed. G. F. Thomas. New York/London: Harper & Brothers.
         Reviewed:
         Religious Book Club Bulletin 17 (1944) 1-2. (editors)

1944b   Review of W. Kirkland, *Discovering the Boy of Nazareth*. *RL* 13:631.

1944c   Review of H. B. Sharman, *Son of Man and Kingdom of God*. "Did Jesus Use Technicalities?" *Christendom* 9:111-12.

1945a   *Christ the Lord: The Meaning of Jesus in the Early Church*. (The Ayer Lectures of the Colgate-Rochester Divinity School, 1944). Chicago: Willett, Clark & Company.
         Reviewed:
         ATR 28 (1946) 170-71. (S. E. Johnson)
         CBQ 9 (1947) 372-73. (R. Kugelman)
         Crozer Quarterly 23 (1946) 284-85. (P. S. Minear)
         JBR 14 (1946) 120-21. (E. W. K. Mould)
         JR 27 (1947) 57-58. (R. M. Grant)
         LCQ 19 (1946) 208-9. (R. T. Stamm)
         Pulpit 17 (1946) 23. (C. C. Morrison)
         RL 15 (1945/46) 460-61. (B. M. Metzger)
         USQR 1 (1946) 29. (C. T. Craig)
         WTJ 9 (1946/47) 105-10. (N. B. Stonehouse)

1945b   *The Fourth Gospel and the Later Epistles*. A Guide for Bible Readers. Ed. H. F. Rall; NT IV. New York: Abingdon-Cokesbury.

1945c   "Christianity and the Christian." Pp. 160-90 in *The Christian Answer*. Ed. H. P. Van Dusen. New York: Charles Scribner's Sons.

1946a   "The Revelation of God in Christ." Pp. 3-26 in *The Gospel, the Church and the World*. Interseminary Series, Vol. III. Ed. K. S. LaTourette. New York: Harper & Brothers.

1946b   "A Survey of Recent Theological Literature." *USQR* 2:26-27.

1947a *On the Meaning of Christ.* (The William Belden Noble Lectures, Harvard University, 1947). New York: Charles Scribner's Sons.
Reviewed:
ATR 30 (1948) 170-72. (S. E. Johnson).
ATR 31 (1949) 40-42. (O. J. F. Seitz)
Christendom 13 (1948) 239-40. (R. M. Grant)
Christian Century 64 (1947) 1584-85. (A. N. Wilder)
Crozer Quarterly 25 (1948) 176-77. (F. M. Derwacter)
LCQ 21 (1948) 82-85. (R. T. Stamm)
Pulpit 18 (1947) 287. (C. C. Morrison)
RL 17 (1947/48) 312-13. (E. T. Thompson)
TToday 5 (1948/49) 451-53. (O. A. Piper)
WTJ 11 (1948/49) 94-97. (J. H. Skilton)

1947b Review of A. M. Ramsey, *The Resurrection of Christ. TToday* 4:156-57.

1947c Review of C. H. Dodd, *The Johannine Epistles. Christian Century* 64:1366.

1948 "Modern Biblical Research Summarized" (Review of H. R. Willoughby, ed., *The Study of the Bible Today and Tomorrow). Christendom* 13:247-49.

1949 Review of G. S. Duncan, *Jesus. Son of Man. Christian Century* 66:560-61.

1950a *Chapters in a Life of Paul.* (An expansion of The Quillian Lectures, Emory University, 1949). New York: Abingdon-Cokesbury.
Reviewed:
ATR 33 (1951) 109-10. (J. L. Moreau)
Christian Century 67 (1950) 560. (H. J. Cadbury)
ExpTim 66 (1954/55) 129-30. (editor)
Int 6 (1952) 372-73. (D. G. Miller)
JBL 69 (1950) 281-83. (C. F. Nesbitt)
JBR 18 (1950) 197-98. (M. E. Andrews)
JR 30 (1950) 275-76. (J. W. Beardslee, Jr.)
LQ 2 (1950) 343-49. (R. T. Stamm)
Religious Book Club Bulletin 23 (1950) 1-2. (editors: "The March Selection")
RL 19 (1949/50) 632-33. (F. V. Filson)
RB 59 (1952) 126-27. (P. Benoit)
Theologia 23 (1952) 633-34. (S. Agouridis)

Theology 53 (1950) 305-7. (C. F. Evans)

WTJ 13 (1950/51) 69-73. (N. B. Stonehouse)

See also:

D. T. Rowlingson, "The Jerusalem Conference and Jesus' Nazareth Visit: A Study in Pauline Chronology." *JBL* 71 (1952) 69-74.

G. Ogg, "A New Chronology of Saint Paul's Life." *ExpTim* 64 (1952/53) 120-23.

S. Agouridis. "St. Paul after 1900 Years." *Ecumenical Review* 5 (1952/53) 309-12.

M. J. Suggs. "Concerning the Date of Paul's Macedonian Ministry." *NovT* 4 (1960) 60-68.

J. C. Hurd, Jr. *The Origin of 1 Corinthians.* London: S.P.C.K. New York: Seabury, 1965, 6-42, 296.

1950b   "The Peril in Thanksgiving." *USQR* 5:3-5.

1950c   Review of E. C. Blackman, *Marcion and His Influence. CH* 19:95.

1951   "A Note on Mark 14:51-52." Pp. 27-30 in *The Joy of Study: Papers on the New Testament and Related Subjects Presented to Honor Frederick Clifton Grant.* Ed. S. E. Johnson, New York: Macmillan.

Reviewed:

Crozer Ouarterly 29 (1952) 195-97. (D. M. Beck)

1952a   *Criticism and Faith.* (The Jackson Lectures, Southern Methodist University, 1950; and The McFadin Lectures, Texas Christian University, 1952). NewYork: Abingdon-Cokesbury.

Reviewed:

ATR 35 (1953) 283. (F. C. Grant)

Christian Century 70 (1953) 108-9. (W. E. Garrison)

ExpTim 64 (1952/53) 66. (editor)

Int 7 (1953) 96-97. (D. G. Miller)

JBL 73 (1954) 53-54. (F. W. Beare)

JBR 21 (1953) 38-39. (F. V. Filson)

JR 33 (1953) 239-40. (J. C. Rylaarsdam)

LQ 5 (1953) 210-11. (E. E. Flack)

RL 22 (1952/53) 472. (C. F. Nesbitt)

SJT 8 (1955) 85-87. (W. Lillie)

TToday 10 (1953/54) 259-61. (L. Mowry)

WTJ 16 (1953/54) 116-22. (W. E. Welmers)

1952b "The Gospel According to St. Luke: Exposition of Chapters 7-
12." *IB*. Ed. G. A. Buttrick *et al.* 12 vols.; New York:
Abingdon, 1951-57, 8:128-239.
Reviewed:
Int 6 (1952) 350-52. (D. G. Miller)
JBR 20 (1952) 268-69. (J. W. Bailey)

1952c "Christian Hope." *Christianity and Crisis* 12:33-34.

1953a "Pliny and I Peter: A Note on I Peter 4:14-16 and 3:15." *JBL*
72:187-89.

1953b "Authenticity and Relevance." *USQR* 9:3-9.

1954a "The Epistle to the Romans: Introduction and Exegesis." *IB*.
Ed. G. A. Buttrick *et al.* 12 vols.; New York: Abingdon,
1951-57, 9:353-668.
Reviewed:
Int 8 (1954) 479-81. (L. O. Bristol)
JBR 23 (1955) 52-54. (L. P. Pherigo)
South East Asia Journal of Theology 20 (1955) 72-76. (K.
Stendahl)

1954b "Ethical Obligations in the Realm of Grace." (Lectures
delivered at the Butler University School of Religion).
The Shane Quarterly 15:53-93.

1955a *The Early Church and the Coming Great Church.* (Several
chapters formed The William Henry Hoover Lectureship
on Christian Unity, The Disciples Divinity House of the
University of Chicago, 1955). New York: Abingdon.
Reviewed:
ATR 38 (1956) 102-3. (F. W. Beare)
Christianity Today 1 (1957) 17-18. (J. M. Kik)
CQR 159 (1958) 584-85. (L. W. Grensted)
Ecumenical Review 8 (1956) 339-42. (J. R. Nelson)
Encounter 17 (1956) 187-90. (R. E. Osborn)
ExpTim 66 (1954/55) 257-58. (editor)
Int 10 (1956) 116. (E. T. Thompson)
JBL 75 (1956) 240-41. (H. R. Willoughby)
JBR 24 (1956) 50, 52. (R. W. Battenhouse)
JR 35 (1955) 257. (P. H. Igarashi)
RL 25 (1955/56) 144-45. (G. Harkness)
South East Asia Journal of Theology 2 (1961) 62-63. (E. A.
Hessel)
Theology 59 (1956) 36. (V. de Waal)

TToday 12 (1955) 532-34. (S. de Dietrich)
USQR 11 (1956) 45-46. (G. Florovsky)

1955b "The Epistle to Philemon: Introduction and Exegesis." IB Ed. G. A. Buttrick et al. 12 vols.; New York: Abingdon, 1951-57, 11:553-73.
Reviewed:
JBR 24 (1956) 120-21. (J. W. Bowman)

1955c Review of B. S. Easton, The Purpose of Acts and Other Papers. RL 24:461.

1956a "The Ministry in the Primitive Church." Pp. 1-26 in The Ministry in Historical Perspectives. Ed. H. R. Niebuhr and D. D. Williams. New York: Harper and Brothers.

1956b "A Note on the Text of Romans." NTS 2:191-93.

1957a The Integrity of Preaching. (The James A. Gray Lectures, The Divinity School of Duke University, 1956). New York: Abingdon.
Reviewed:
USQR 12 (1957) 106-7. (D. H. C. Read)
WTJ 20 (1957/58) 109-11. (J. W. Sanderson, Jr.)

1957b "Literary Chronology: The New Testament." IB. Ed. G. A. Buttrick et al. 12 vols.: New York: Abingdon, 1951-57, 12:669-72.

1957c "A Note on the Format of the Pauline Corpus." HTR 50:311-14 [A reply to J. Finegan, "The Original Form of the Pauline Collection." HTR 49 (1956), 85-103, which commented upon "The Epistle to the Romans: Introduction" (1954a), and Marcion and the New Testament (1942a)].

1957d Review of O. Cullmann, The State in the New Testament. JBL 76:70, 72.

1958a The Death of Christ: The Cross in New Testament History and Faith. (Contains material from The Shaffer Lectures, Yale Divinity School, 1956; The Carew Lectures, The Hartford Theological Seminary, 1957; and The Convocation Lectures, Eden Theological Seminary, 1957). New York: Abingdon.
Reviewed:
CBQ 21 (1959) 107-9. (J. J. Davis)
CQR 161 (1960) 253-54. (C. F. D. Moule)
CTM 30 (1959) 314. (H. W. Reimann)
Encounter 19 (1958) 214-18. (L. B. Gilkey)

ExpTim 69 (1957/58) 161-62. (editor)
ExpTim 70 (1958/59) 290-92. (editor)
Int 12 (1958) 321-23. (L. O. Bristol)
JBL 77 (1958), 165-67. (H. C. Kee)
JBR 26 (1958) 254. (T. S. Kepler)
RSR 48 (1960) 489, 506-7. (X. Léon-Dufour)
RL 27 (1957/58) 610-11. (P. S. Minear)
RevExp 55 (1958) 447. (H. F. Peacock)
South East Asia Journal of Theology 1 (1960) 86. (R. Alm)
Theology 62 (1959) 372-74. (J. Montague)
USQR 14 (1958) 75-79. (A. T. Mollegen)
WTJ 21 (1958/59) 234-39. (N. B. Stonehouse)
See also:
F. H. Cleobury, "Jesus or Christ?" *Modern Churchman* n.s. 2 (1958/59) 200-204.
P. C. Hodgson, "The Son of Man and the Problem of Historical Knowledge." *JR* 41 (1961) 91-108.

1958b *Jesus: Lord and Christ—A Trilogy Comprising "The Man Christ Jesus," "Christ the Lord," "On the Meaning of Christ."* New York: Harper & Brothers. (See 1941a, 1945a, and 1947a above.)
Reviewed:
Christian Century 75 (1958) 1378-79. (R. M. Grant)
JBL 78 (1959) 94-96. (E. C. Blackman)
SJT 14 (1961) 81-87. (D. Deegan)

1958c "The Church Is Christ's Body." *RL* 27:54-62.

1959a *Philemon Among the Letters of Paul: A New View of Its Place and Importance.* Revised edition. New York: Abingdon. (See 1935a above.)
Reviewed:
CBQ 21 (1959) 538-40. (N. M. Flanagan)
ExpTim 70 (1958/59) 353-54. (editor)
Int 14 (1960) 110. (S. A. Cartledge)
JBL 78 (1959) 277-78. (W. G. Rollins)
Pulpit 30 (1959) 380. (L. P. Smith)
RB 67 (1960) 456-57. (P. Benoit)
Theology 63 (1960) 345, 347. (E. M. Sidebottom)

1959b With J. C. Beker "Bibliography for Ministers: The New Testament." *USQR* 14:51-57.

1960a   With J. C. Beker, NT eds. *A Basic Bibliography for Ministers Selected & Annotated by the Faculty of Union Theological Seminary, New York City.* 2d ed. New York: Union Theological Seminary Book Service, 1960. (See 1959b above.)

1960b   *Christ and the Hope of Glory.* (Essay written in preparation for The Ingersoll Lecture on the "Immortality of Man," Harvard University, 1960). New York: Abingdon.
Reviewed:
ExpTim 72 (1960/61) 162-63. (editor)
USQR 16 (1960/61) 224-25. (J. D. Smart)

1960c   "The Hope of Glory: The Ingersoll Lecture 1960." *Harvard Divinity Bulletin* 24:9-19.

1961a   *The Ethic of Jesus in the Teaching of the Church: Its Authority and Its Relevance.* (Draws on The Willson Lectures on Christian Education, Nashville, 1960; and on addresses delivered at the United Theological Seminary, and the Wesley Theological Seminary; The C. I. Jones Memorial Lectures, Rayne Memorial Methodist Church, New Orleans; and "Ethical Obligations in the Realm of Grace" [see 1954b above]) New York: Abingdon.
Reviewed:
Chicago Theological Seminary Register 52 (1962) 35-36. (V. Obenhaus)
Christian Century 78 (1961) 1304. (R. V. Moss, Jr.)
ExpTim 73 (1961/62) 289-90. (editor)
HeyJ 4 (1963) 293-95. (J. Bligh)
JBR 30 (1962) 64-65. (M. S. Enslin)
RL 31 (1961/62) 136-37. (J. R. Branton)
RevExp 58 (1961) 515-16. (N. P. Howington)
Theology 65 (1962) 469-71. (C. F. D. Moule)
TToday 18 (1961/62) 377-79. (H. Anderson)
USQR 17 (1961/62) 254-56. (H. C. Kee)

1961b   *Life in Christ Jesus: Reflections on Romans 5-8.* Greenwich, CT: Seabury.
Reviewed:
SJT 16 (1963) 214-15. (J. W. Fraser)
Theology 66 (1963) 435-36. (F. H. Borsch)

1962a   *The Church and the Reality of Christ.* (Contains The Bohlen
        Lectures, Philadelphia Divinity School, 1962). New York:
        Harper & Row.
        Reviewed:
        Christian Advocate 7 (1963) 17-18. (J. G. Williams)
        Christian Century 80 (1963) 1241-42. (R. H. Fuller)
        Christianity Today 7 (1962) 298. (L. B. Smedes)
        CQR 165 (1964) 356-57. (G. Leonard)
        ExpTim 74 (1962/63) 193-94. (editor)
        ExpTim 75 (1963/64) 233. (C. L. Mitton)
        JBL 82 (1963) 244-45. (G. Johnston)
        JBR 32 (1964) 76-78. (J. L. Price)
        JR 43 (1963) 159-60. (F. V. Filson)
        RL 32 (1962/63) 312-13. (C. M. Laymon)
        RevExp 60 (1963) 436. (R. B. Brown)
        Theology and Life 6 (1963) 76-78 (P. J. Achtemeier)
        TS 24 (1963) 132-34. (A. Dulles)
        Ttoday 20 (1963/64) 558-60. (H. T. Kuist)
        USQR 19 (1963/64) 57-58. (S. E. Johnson)
        See also:
        E. Tilson. "The Eclipse of Faith." *Int* 17 (1963) 466-78 [a review
        article].

1962b   "Introductions and Annotations to Romans, 1 and 2
        Corinthians, and Philippians." Pp. 1359-1407, 1421-25 in
        The Oxford Annotated Bible: Revised Standard Version.
        Eds. H. G. May and B. M. Metzger. New York: Oxford
        University.

1962c   "Letter to the Galatians." *IDB.* Ed. G. A. Buttrick *et al.* 4 vols.
        New York: Abingdon. 2:338-43.

1962d   "What I believe About the Activity of the Holy Spirit." *USQR*
        17:294-96.

1962e   Review of H. Rhys, *The Epistle to the Romans. JBL* 81:94, 96.

1963a   P. 39 in *A Guide for the Reader of the New Testament for Use
        with the New English Bible.* New York: Oxford
        University/Cambridge University, 1963.

1963b   "Archippus," "Epistle to the Colossians," "Demas," "Epistle to
        the Ephesians," "Onesimus," "Philemon," "Epistle to
        Philemon," "1 Thessalonians," "2 Thessalonians,"
        "Tychicus," in *Dictionary of the Bible.* Ed. J. Hastings.

Rev. ed. by F. C. Grant and H. H. Rowley. New York: Charles Scribner's Sons.

1963c   "The Foolishness of God." *USQR* 19:1-4.

1964a   *Myth and Truth: An Essay on the Language of Faith.* (The James Richard Lectures in Christian Religion, University of Virginia, 1963-64). Charlottesville: University of Virginia.

1964b   "Romans 15:14-33 and Paul's Conception of His Apostolic Mission." *JBL* 83:1-11. [Presidential Address, SBL, Jan. 1, 1964.]

1964c   "The Greatest Missionary: Paul." *Life* 57:112-25.

1964d   "Charles Clayton Morrison at Ninety." *Christian Century* 81:1487.

1965a   "The Humanity of Jesus in New Testament Thought." *The Alumni Bulletin of Bangor Theological Seminary.* [The first of The Francis B. Denio Lectures on the Bible, Bangor Theological Seminary, 1965.] 40:1-8.

1965b   *The Spirit in the Church.* [A lecture delivered at the Cathedral of St. John the Divine, New York.] "Cathedral Papers." Cincinnati: Forward Movement Publications: 19.

1966a   "Paul's Mission to the Nations." *Bible Today* 24:1571-77.

1966b   "A Few Memories and a Great Debt." *Criterion* 5:24-26.

1966c   "The 'Prophet' in New Testament Christology." Pp. 23-34 in *Lux in Lumine: Essays to Honor W. Norman W. Pittenger.* Ed. R.A. Norris, Jr. New York: Seabury.

1966d   "Acts and the Pauline Letter Corpus." Pp. 279-87 in *Studies in Luke-Acts: Essays Presented in Honor of Paul Schubert.* Ed. L. E. Keck and J. L. Martyn. New York/Nashville: Abingdon.
Reviewed:
W. O. Walker, Jr. "Acts and the Pauline Corpus Reconsidered." *JSNT* 1985:3-23.

1967a   *The Humanity and Divinity of Christ: A Study of Pattern in Christology.* Cambridge/New York: Cambridge University Press.

1967b   "The Identifiability of the Church." Pp. 67-79 in *Theological Freedom and Social Responsibility.* Ed. S. F. Bayne, Jr. New York: Seabury.

1967c   "A Plea for a Wider Ecumenism." Pp. 25-29 in *Realistic Reflections on Church Union.* Ed. J. Macquarrie. New York: Consultation on Church Union.

1968   "The Problem of Faith in the Contemporary Church." *The Quarterly Bulletin of the Berkely Divinity School.* (additional bibliographical information was unavailable)

1970   *Limits of Unbelief.* London: Collins; New York: Seabury.

1971   "The Church and Higher Education." *RL* 40:489-99.

1975   *Never Far from Home.* Waco, TX: Word.

1980a   *Marcion and the New Testament.* Revised Edition. New York: AMS Press.

1980b   "Paul and the 'Liberals.'" *RL* 49:415-21.

1983   "*Chapters in a Life of Paul*—A Response to Robert Jewett and Gerd Luedemann." Pp. 339-64 in *Colloquy on New Testament Studies.* Ed. B. Corley. Macon, GA: Mercer University.

1985   *A Glory in It All: Reflections after Eighty.* Waco, TX: Word.
Reviewed:
Journal of Religion and Aging 3 (1987) 168-70. (V. L. Strempke)
Reformed Review 41 (1987) 69. (T. Bartha)
Churchman 101 (1987) 88. (G. Kirby)
RevExp 83 (1986) 657. (R. L. Omanson)

1987a   *Chapters in a Life of Paul.* Revised by the author and edited, with introduction, by D. R. A. Hare. Macon, GA: Mercer University
Reviewed:
RevExp 85 (1988) 565. (M. Marshall-Green)
SWJT 30 (1988) 46. (E. E. Ellis)

1987b   "Marcion's Gospel and the Synoptic Problem." Pp. 25-31 in *Jesus, the Gospels, and the Church.* Ed. E. P. Sanders. Macon, GA: Mercer University.

1987c   "A Note on Galatians 1:15." *JBL* 106:301-4.

1989   "John A. T. Robinson and the Nature of Biblical Scholarship." *Theology* 92:251-68.

1990   "On the Pauline Chronology: Buck-Taylor-Hurd Revisited." Pp. 258-274 in *The Conversation Continues: Studies in Paul and John In Honor of J. Louis Martyn* Eds. Robert T. Fortna and Beverly R. Gaventa. Nashville: Abingdon.

*Most of the material in this bibliography published between 1929 and 1967 was compiled by John Hurd, Jr. and published in *Christian History and Interpretation: Studies Presented to John Knox.* Eds. W. R. Farmer, C. F. D. Moule, and R. R. Niebuhr. Cambridge: Cambridge University Press, 1967, xxiii-xxxii. This bibliography has been expanded to include both reviews written by Professor Knox and reviews of his work by other scholars. This material was taken from a fuller version of the Hurd bibliography deposited by Hurd in the library of the Episcopal Theological Seminary of the Southwest, Austin, Texas. Before his death, Professor Knox generously provided an update of material he had published between 1967 and 1990. Appreciation is expressed to Professor Hurd and Cambridge University Press for permission to reproduce large portions of the bibliography published in the Knox *Festschrift*, to the library staff of the Episcopal Theological Seminary of the Southwest, Austin, Texas for making available the unpublished, fuller version of that bibliography, and to Professor Knox for providing the bibliographic data on material published since the Hurd bibliography was compiled.

THE FRUITFUL APPROACH
OF
CHARLES H. TALBERT

READING TALBERT:
NEW PERSPECTIVES ON LUKE AND ACTS

Mikeal C. Parsons

Introduction

Charles Harold Talbert was born in Jackson, Mississippi, to Carl E. and Audrey Hale Talbert in 1934. After finishing high school in Bessemer, Alabama, Talbert was graduated in 1956 from Howard College (now Samford University) in Birmingham, Alabama. Upon completing a Bachelor of Divinity degree in 1959 at The Southern Baptist Theological Seminary in Louisville, KY, he enrolled as a doctoral candidate in biblical studies at Vanderbilt University from 1959-63. During those years he received fellowships from the Lilly and Rockefeller Foundations. His doctoral dissertation, written under the supervision of Leander E. Keck, received an award from the Christian Research Foundation. Since 1963 Talbert has taught in the Department of Religion at Wake Forest University in Winston-Salem, NC. His wife, Betty, holds a Ph.D. from UNC-Chapel Hill in history and currently serves as Director of Spiritual Formation at Trinity Center in Winston-Salem. They have two children.

The son of a Baptist minister, Charles Talbert is a Southern Baptist by denominational confession and a NT scholar by vocation. To members of both his confessional and professional communities, such a statement may seem oxymoronic. Nonetheless, Talbert must be located as a leading figure within the small, but distinguished group of Southern Baptist NT scholars who have made significant contributions to the scholarly study of scripture.[1] Though far more will be said about

---

[1]This list includes among others, R. Alan Culpepper, Edgar V. McKnight, and Dan O. Via, Jr. Scholars from previous generations, e.g., A.T. Robertson and

Talbert's scholarly achievements than his confessional commitments, it is essential to locate Talbert in both of these communities to appreciate fully his work.

Talbert's work on the New Testament has been a part of his larger understanding of himself as a theologian of the church. At a conference held at Meredith College in 1981, he reflected on his understanding of this role:

> I learned what for me is the role of a theologian of the church years ago from Ernst Käsemann. One "becomes a theologian in the true sense by dint of that capacity which is called in Paul 'the distinguishing of true spirits from false'" (*N.T. Questions of Today*, p. 295). In order to do this task for the church one must not only be in touch with the living Lord and the historic tradition but also one must be exposed to the "spirits" in various positions. "It is not necessary for every Christian to expose himself voluntarily to their assaults, their seductions and their terrors. But it *is* necessary that some should do this in special measure on behalf of the rest of the community, and live and die on the job" (Käsemann, p. 296). With this conception of my calling before me, I have tried to come to terms with Bultmannian theology, the social action movement, the charismatic movement, and now the position of biblical inerrancy.[2]

Theologians of the church, Talbert pled, "...need to be heard, if for no other reason than to prevent those who are religiously zealous from expressing their devotion to the Lord in ways that run counter to what the Bible meant and means" (1987g:71).

The last two areas of discernment mentioned above, the charismatic movement and biblical inerrancy, serve as illustrations of his larger sense of vocation. In "The Bible as Spiritual Friend," originally delivered by Talbert as the Presidential Address to the National Association of Baptist Professors of Religion meeting in Anaheim, CA, in November, 1985 (see 1986b), we hear some of his criticisms of inerrancy and Pentecostalism.

Over against the position of the inerrantists who have difficulty fully affirming Jesus' humanity "because there is in biblical inerrancy a massive confusion about the relationship between finitude and sin" (1986b:63), Talbert argued: "For Jesus to have been a man of his own time in his knowledge of matters of fact would not have subverted either

---

Frank Stagg, were perhaps better known among their confessional constituency than their professional peers.

[2]Charles H. Talbert, "Biblical Inerrancy: Some Reservations," unpublished response delivered at the meeting of Teachers of Religion and Philosophy, Chaplains and Campus Ministers of North Carolina Baptist Colleges and Universities, 2-3 October 1981.

his divinity or his sinlessness but instead would have guaranteed his full humanity, including finitude, even the finitude of limited knowledge in matters of fact" (1986b:64). Such words have not endeared him to the fundamentalist group now in political control of much of the Southern Baptist Convention![3]

Despite his sympathy with much of charismatic experience like that of the felt presence of the God who indwells the believer, the expectation and experience of miracle, and answers to petitionary and intercessory prayer, Talbert denies most of the distinctive theology of Pentecostalism. This posture is not unexpected for one who describes himself as "a mystical Christian of the reformed tradition, not a charismatic/Pentecostal."[4] In "The Bible as Spiritual Friend," Talbert gave a typical reformed critique of the charismatic use of the Bible in his area of the country:

> ...a great majority of those who had rediscovered the presence of God within and were trying to live out of that presence were being taught a heteronomous view of Scripture that robbed them of what they had just experienced by putting a Law between them and God. It was in my study of Galatians during that period that I came to see that Galatians is not so much addressing how one becomes a Christian (justification) as how one who has experienced justification by grace through faith moves on to maturity: not by works of law (Gal. 3:1-5). One moves to maturity the same

---

[3]See, for example, the review by Paige Patterson (*CTR* 3 [1988] 231-236) of *The Unfettered Word*, in which an abbreviated version of Talbert's essay appears. Patterson, President of Criswell College, is one of the architects of the inerrantist movement in the Southern Baptist Convention. While commending "the honesty and integrity of Talbert in telling us what he believes," Patterson argued that on the humanity of Jesus, "Talbert is either less candid or else confused" (232). Patterson concluded (ibid.): "Believing in the full humanity of Jesus no more necessitates error in Christ's sayings, thinking, or perception than acknowledging His full humanity necessitates sinfulness in Jesus." Elsewhere he commented (234): "While acknowledging that the presence of errors in the text of Scripture would not render its entire message invalid, inerrantists would raise the question as to how one is to differentiate between reliable and unreliable portions of Scripture without superimposing some human authority upon the authority of the Bible. Now we will want to reflect at this point on the fact that Charles Talbert has openly admitted that he does precisely that, looking to other sources to correct the inadequacies of the Bible."

[4]Charles H. Talbert, private correspondence, dated 18 August 1989. On spiritual formation, see also "The Way of the Lukan Jesus: Dimensions of Lukan Spirituality" (1982e), where Talbert examines "one facet of Lukan Christology to cast light on the current struggle to find an acceptable form of spirituality for our time" (237). This essay was originally presented as the President's Address at the Association of Baptist Professors or Religion, Southeast Region, in Gainesville, FL, on 18 March 1982.

way one comes to Jesus the first time, through faith. One is not justified
through faith and then comes to maturity through works (1986b:59).

Talbert's confessional perspective, however, has not made him
provincial. He and his wife have led numerous interdenominational
retreats on spiritual formation. He has also been intimately involved
with the Catholic community for the past several years and is an active
member of the Catholic Biblical Association. One colleague, Richard
Cassidy, recently expressed what is typical of the Catholic community's
appreciation for Talbert's confessional convictions: "Among other
aspects of his work that I admire is the fact that he takes Luke's works
seriously as a resource for the life of discipleship and for the area of
spiritual theology."[5] Talbert's ability to move comfortably among
diverse believing communities can only be applauded.

Talbert has likewise been active in several scholarly societies. In
addition to chairing the SBL Luke-Acts Group (1973-78) and Seminar
(1979-83), he served as vice-president and president of the Southeast
Region of the SBL (1975-76; 1976-77) and of the National Association of
Baptist Professors of Religion (1984; 1985). He also holds membership in
the *Studiorum Novi Testamenti Societas*, the international organization
of NT scholars. He has served on the editorial boards of *Perspectives in
Religious Studies* (1979-87) and the *Journal of Biblical Literature* (1981-
83). From 1981 to 1984, he was editor of the NABPR Dissertation Series,
and from 1984 to 1989, he served as the editor of the SBL Dissertation
Series.

Throughout his scholarly career, Talbert has been engaged in the
quest for an interpretive method with which to explicate the theological
message of the biblical material. In that pursuit he has employed several
different methodological tools. To sense the development and
transitions in his thought, his major scholarly publications will be
examined chronologically. For convenience, Talbert's academic
pilgrimage may be divided into three periods.

1) *1965-73*. Talbert 's initial work employed redaction criticism as he
learned it from German scholars and his *Doktorvater*, Leander Keck. In
this first period, Talbert was primarily in dialogue with the premier
Lukan scholar of that time, Hans Conzelmann. His dissertation, *Luke
and the Gnostics* (1966b) was published during this phase.

2) *1974-80*. After post-doctoral fellowships studying ancient art and
literary criticism at the University of North Carolina and Duke (1968-69)

---

[5]Richard J. Cassidy, private correspondence, dated 7 April 1989.

and ancient history, biography, and romance at the Vatican Library in Rome (1971-72), Talbert began applying "architecture analysis" to the biblical texts as he learned it from the classicists. The second period is marked by the publication of *Literary Patterns, Theological Themes, and the Genre of Luke-Acts* (1974d) and *What Is a Gospel?* (1977a), as well as the establishment of a Working Group on Luke-Acts in the Society of Biblical Literature in 1974 (see 1978e).

3) *1981-90.* In his most recent contributions, Talbert synthesized a close reading of the text with the use of parallels from the literary environment of Luke-Acts and a focus on the text's theological message. In this third period were published *Reading Luke* (1982b), *Acts* (1984a), *Reading Corinthians* (1987a), and the second of two edited volumes on Luke-Acts (1983f), as well as numerous essays and articles.

Several objections could be lodged against this particular approach to reading Talbert. First, these dates are arbitrary, since they are based on the appearance of a manuscript in print. That everything which Talbert wrote was published sequentially is unlikely. Nor does such an approach allow for the pinpointing of the germination and maturation of his ideas. Still, these dates are useful in delineating the overall ways in which Talbert's work has developed. Second, it may seem premature to assess the work of a person at the height of his intellectual prowess. We hope and expect that Talbert will continue to make significant, creative contributions to biblical scholarship. This essay, however, is concerned with his contributions to Lukan scholarship, and all the data—personal conversations, recent publications, and professional involvement—indicate that he has turned his attention from Luke-Acts to other parts of the NT. What follows can only be considered an interim assessment of the work of one who has already profoundly shaped his discipline of study.

My plan is to trace Talbert's scholarly contributions through the three periods identified above. The Lukan writings were the laboratory for methodological inquiry, and he often tested his tools on other NT writings. Hence, this survey may at times move slightly beyond the parameters of the Lukan writings. Cataloguing the immediate reactions by his colleagues to his major works will hopefully safeguard from hasty or anachronistic judgments. Following my survey of "peer evaluation," Talbert's overall contributions to Lukan scholarship will be assessed, probing some potential areas for further research.

Conversations with Conzelmann:
The Redaction Critical Quest for Luke the Theologian (1965-73)

Two articles on Hans Conzelmann's watershed work on Luke serve to frame the effort of Talbert during his early years of scholarly endeavor. These two essays, one a short review of *The Theology of St. Luke* (1965a) and the other a longer working paper prepared for the Pittsburgh Festival on the Gospels in 1970 (1970a), demonstrate the way in which Conzelmann set Talbert's agenda in this first period. Indeed, the work of the German redaction critics fell with sledge-hammer swiftness, forging the shape of the interpretive enterprise for most of the American scholarly community.

Accepting Conzelmann's method of *Redaktionsgeschichte*, Talbert maintained in this short review of *The Theology of St. Luke*: "Any adequate criticism of Conzelmann's effort must be directed against his presentation of the Lucan *tendency* and *occasion*" (1965a:97). According to Talbert, Conzelmann understood the Lukan tendency to be "the recasting of primitive Christian eschatology into a history of salvation, removing the *parousia* to a distant future" (1965a:97). Further, the delay of the parousia was the occasion which precipitated this Lukan tendency. The redaction-critical questions of tendency and occasion engaged Talbert for most of this first decade.

The Lukan Occasion

The question of the Lukan occasion was actually first addressed by Talbert in his 1963 dissertation, subsequently published as *Luke and the Gnostics* (1966b). Not surprisingly, he employed the method of redaction criticism, at that time barely a decade old:

> This work is largely an exercise in *Redaktionsgeschichte*. As such it assumes the priority of Mark; the existence of some source or sources, whether written or oral, common to Matthew and Luke, which will be designated "Q" according to scholarly custom; and the existence of oral tradition peculiar to Luke which according to custom will be designated "L" (1966b:15).

Method in hand, Talbert attempted to substantiate his thesis that, rather than being a reaction of the church to the delay of the parousia, "Luke-Acts was written to serve as a defense against Gnosticism" (1966b:115), with Gnosticism vaguely defined as "a Christian heresy" (1966b:16). Three Lukan motifs—authentic witness, legitimate exegesis, and the succession of tradition—served the Lukan purpose of anti-Docetism. Talbert acknowledged that the "most obvious difficulty standing in the way of the thesis that Luke-Acts was written to serve as a defense against Gnosticism is the striking absence of references to Gnosticism in Acts" (1966b:83). He sought to overcome this difficulty with an argument from silence: heresy is absent in the apostolic age depicted in Acts because of the early Christian belief that "truth precedes error" (1966b:83-97). Hence Gnosticism is a later distortion of the authoritative apostolic age. The conclusion which he urged on the reader is clear: "The purpose of Luke-Acts is anti-Gnostic" (1966b:115).

Judging from the dearth of reviews, Talbert's thesis made little immediate impact. Criticism by those who did review the work clustered at four points: 1) the importance of the anti-Gnostic tendency as the Lukan purpose is overemphasized;[6] 2) Gnosticism is loosely defined;[7] 3) the silence of Acts on Gnosticism is problematic for Talbert's thesis; 4) and using redaction criticism to determine the occasion of the writing is exceedingly difficult.[8] Only two years after the appearance of *Luke and the Gnostics*, Talbert published a short, but important essay, "An Anti-Gnostic Tendency in Lucan Christology" (1968a). This essay reveals that Talbert made several advances in his argument, most of which may be seen as indirect responses to the criticism of his published dissertation.

1) In this article, Talbert did not explicitly claim that the singular purpose of Luke-Acts was a defense against Gnosticism. Rather, he said: "*At least a major facet* of Lucan Christology is a way of saying to docetism that the church's Saviour was really human from first to last" (emphasis mine; 1968a:271).

2) For the first time, Talbert made some suggestions as to the specific identity of the Gnosticism against which Luke reacted. Appeal to Gnostic writings from Nag Hammadi was coupled with citations from Irenaeus to conclude that Luke was arguing against first-century Docetists, particularly of the brand of Cerinthus (1968a:270-71).

3) The question of the silence of Acts on the Gnostic issue was avoided since this essay mostly dealt with the Christology of the Gospel. Only the ascension narrative in Acts 1 played any significant role in Talbert's line of reasoning.

---

[6]See the review by Frank Stagg, *RevExp* 4 (1967) 537.
[7]See the reviews by Peter Kjesth, *JR* 47 (1967) 77-78; Edgar Krentz, *CTM* 39 (1968) 53-54; E. Earl Ellis, *JBL* 85 (1966) 264-266.
[8]Ellis, 265.

4) Talbert combined the accepted methodological tool of redaction criticism with a type of "audience criticism" to discern Luke's Christology. He remarked:

> When Luke-Acts was read aloud in the worship of the early church, its readers and hearers did not sit with copies of Luke's sources before them so that they could compare what they heard with Mark and Q.... Consequently, if an author wanted to be understood, he would write with this in mind. It would be through the overall structure of Jesus' career that he would seek to convey his Christology (1968a:260).

He then proposed: "Any attempt to speak of the Christology of Luke-Acts must take into account both the situation of Luke's audience and that of the modern scholar" (1968a:261).

In "An Anti-Gnostic Tendency," Talbert has presented his case more concisely and incisively than in the earlier monograph. While failing to convince colleagues that an anti-Gnostic polemic was the *primary* purpose behind the writing of Luke-Acts, Talbert did manage to raise a voice against the "new look" in Luke-Acts given by Conzelmann and others, a voice that would soon be joined by a chorus of others.

The Lukan Tendency

Not only did Talbert disagree with Conzelmann's evaluation of the occasion which gave rise to the Lukan writings, he also objected to Conzelmann's judgment that the Lukan tendency was consistently to substitute an imminent expectation of the parousia with a periodized salvation-history, removing the parousia to some point in the distant future. He first addressed this issue in *Luke and the Gnostics*. There he argued that 1) certain passages in Luke-Acts indicate an expectation of an imminent parousia; and 2) the post-apostolic evidence (especially of 2 Pet and John) points to something other than a readjustment to the delay of the parousia, as Conzelmann had argued. This second contention is more fully developed in "II Peter and the Delay of the Parousia" (1966d). The former thesis is argued extensively in "The Redaction Critical Quest for Luke the Theologian" (1970a:171-222).

The significance of this latter article has rarely been acknowledged. According to Talbert: "This programmatic paper has as its purpose the presentation of an alternative picture of the Lucan theological perspective to that proposed by Conzelmann" (1970a:171-72). The paper is divided into two parts: the first examined "certain key passages that are explicitly related to the question of Lucan eschatology"; the second treated "two Lucan traits related implicitly to the eschatological problem of Luke-Acts" (1970a:172). The passages considered in the first half of the essay are Luke 19:11-27; Acts 1:6ff.; Luke 17:20-37; Luke 21:5-36; and Luke 12:35-48. Following his analysis of these passages, Talbert observed:

> Exegesis has led to the conclusion that there are two dominant eschatological emphases in Luke-Acts. One is the proclamation that the End is near....The other...is the attempt to prevent a misinterpretation of the Jesus-tradition by someone in the Lucan sphere of influence to the effect that the eschaton had been and could be fully experienced in the present (1970a:191).

Further, salvation-history functioned in Luke not as a response to the delayed parousia, but instead addressed the issues raised by those who held to an overly-realized eschatology. In these claims, Talbert challenged the very heart of Conzelmann's redactional work, and especially his conclusions regarding the function of the salvation-history schema in the Lukan community.

Other Redactional Work

Despite these points of departure from Conzelmann's conclusions, Talbert continued to use redaction criticism as his basic methodological tool, soon turning his attention from Luke-Acts to the Pauline literature. In "A Non-Pauline Fragment at Romans 3:24-26?" he argued that a post-Pauline fragment has been interpolated into the text of Rom 3:25-26 (1966c). Using the now familiar twin concerns of tendency and occasion, he concluded: "If our theory of interpolation be true, then the phenomena presented in this article serve as a call for an application of 'redaction criticism' to Paul's letters corresponding to this type of approach in the study of the gospels and Acts" (1966c:296). Likewise, in "Tradition and Redaction in Romans XII.9-21" (1969a), he argued: "It is my suggestion that the problems...and the ensuing discussion of Rom. xii.9 ff. can be solved if we approach the section in tradition-redaction terms" (1969a:84). Both these articles show Talbert's commitment to the methodological tool of *Redaktionsgeschichte* and his conviction that the method would work equally well on the Pauline letters.

Emerging Interests in Style and Structure

From the beginning, Talbert displayed an interest in the literary style and structure of the biblical literature. This claim is substantiated by looking briefly at three articles published in 1967. Although these articles address three of the thorniest problems in NT scholarship—the question of the Apostolic Decree and the Jerusalem Council (1967a); the Christology of Phil 2:6-11 (1967b); and the speeches in Acts (1967c)—the conclusions in these studies are not so pertinent here as the methods involved in reaching them. In each article, Talbert revealed a deep interest in the structure of the text, based on the assumption that "a proper delineation of *form* leads to a correct interpretation of *meaning*" (1967b:141).[9]

Throughout this first decade, Talbert employed redaction criticism to respond to the work of Hans Conzelmann on Lukan tendency and occasion. But his research toward the end of this period definitely points toward new interests, especially in the relationship between literary patterns and theological themes.

Architecture Analysis and Genre Criticism:
Literary Patterns, Theological Themes and the Genre of Luke-Acts
(1974-80)

In a recent review of Joseph Fitzmyer's work on Luke, Talbert suggested: "At the risk of oversimplification, one may attempt a summary of two distinct approaches to Luke, with 1974 as roughly the dividing line" (1986a:337). Major commentaries like that of Fitzmyer which "traditionally have gathered up and evaluated the findings of research derived from the acknowledged methods of a specific period of time" in a sense "mark the end of an era" (1986a:3376-37). In order to justify choosing this particular date as the end of an era in Lukan scholarship, he wrote:

> I use 1974 as a watershed because in that year lectures by Paul Minear, later published as *To Heal and To Reveal*...signaled a new methodological departure, and because in that year the Luke-Acts Seminar of the SBL,

---

[9]One other work by Talbert in this period should be mentioned in passing. In 1970, Volume 1 of the "Lives of Jesus Series," *Reimarus: Fragments,* appeared (1970c). Editor Talbert provided a forty-three page historical introduction in addition to voluminous notes throughout the text. These notes are especially helpful in determining Talbert's assessment of current biblical scholarship. This volume is the first of five volumes edited by Talbert and demonstrates his continued indebtedness to his *Doktorvater*. Later Talbert would publish *Literary Patterns* in a series edited by Keck (SBL Monograph Series). See the reviews of *Reimarus* in *Encounter* 32 (1971) 247-48; *Int* 25 (1971) 530-31; *CBQ* 34 (1972) 119-21; *Dialog* 11 (1972) 308-09; *JBL* 91 (1972) 120-21; *Theology* 75 (1972) 211-13; and *RevExp* 71 (1974) 399-400.

which was to give expression to a new way of doing Lucan studies, began (1986a:337).

The year 1974 may be termed a "watershed" in Lukan studies, not because of Minear's lectures (heard by only a few and not published until 1976), but because the Luke-Acts Group which Talbert chaired was formally established (after two years of consultations) and because, in 1974, Talbert's monograph, *Literary Patterns* (1974d) appeared.

Architecture Analysis

Literary Patterns was a ground-breaking work because, for the first time, Talbert departed from the "acknowledged method" of redaction criticism to explore extensively the narrative of Luke-Acts in terms of literary style and patterns. Though redaction criticism and the two-source theory were still part of his methodological repertoire, his interpretive tools now included "architecture analysis." Hans Conzelmann had been his primary dialogue partner in the "first phase" of his research; now by examining the literary patterns and style of Luke-Acts, Talbert reclaimed his inheritance as a descendent of Henry J. Cadbury.

The first fruits of Talbert's 1968-69 research leave had actually appeared earlier in "Artistry and Theology: An Analysis of the Architecture of John 1,19-5,47" (1970b).[10] His purpose was "to uncover the architectural design by which the *present form* of the Fourth Gospel was constructed" (1970b:341). Talbert argued that John 1:19-5:47 was arranged in a chiastic pattern and, on the basis of redaction or compositional analysis, he concluded that the pattern is a "conscious effort on the part of the Evangelist (or Redactor)..." (1970b:356). He went on to suggest that John 12-16 and 13-17 also reflect a chiastic structure.

Talbert then shifted attention to literary patterns in Luke-Acts. After noting the hiatus in Lukan scholarship since Cadbury in terms of appreciating the style and literary method of Luke, he noted that even those studies which are interested in pursuing Cadbury's stylistic investigations "are limited by their failure to use comparative materials from the wider Mediterranean world of Luke's time" (1974d:3). "What is needed," he suggested, "is a method of operation which will allow us to

---

[10]That this article actually appeared during the "first" period of Talbert's research demonstrates the fluidity of the divisions, particularly at the "close" of the first two phases.

investigate certain of the formal patterns of Luke-Acts...in such a way as to see them within Luke-Acts as a whole and in the author's environment" (1974d:5). The methodological solution is a combination of architecture analysis and a redaction criticism based on the two-source hypothesis (see 1972).

The primary concern of architecture analysis "is to detect the formal patterns, rhythms, architectonic designs, or architecture of a writing. That is, this approach is concerned with style insofar as it shapes the final product by the arrangement of the larger units of material, especially the whole" (1974d:7). Assuming that architecture analysis and redaction criticism are "mutually enriching methods," Talbert argued that redaction criticism needs architecture analysis to "guard against scholarly subjectivity"; conversely, architecture analysis needs redaction criticism to "deal effectively with the relation of a formal pattern to meaning" (1974d:8).

Talbert's method was three-pronged. First, architecture analysis should demonstrate patterns which control large thought units throughout the narrative as well as units of all sizes. Second, redaction criticism should demonstrate that the discerned pattern is located in redactional rather than traditional material. Finally, any architectonic pattern detected in a NT writing should permit easy location within the literary, artistic, and cultural environment of the writing.

The structure of *Literary Patterns* follows the three major emphases of the method employed. Chapters 2-4 delineate the architectural patterns of Luke-Acts, with special attention given to locating these patterns in the redactional activity of the author. These patterns are conveniently diagrammed for the reader at the conclusion of Chap 4 (1974d:63). In Chap 5, Talbert attempted to situate Luke-Acts in the literary, artistic, and cultural milieu of first-century Greeks, Jews, and Christians. In so doing, he observed that "symmetrophobia"—an adversity to perfect symmetry—in Greco-Roman and Jewish literature and art explains the imperfections in architectonic patterns of Luke-Acts. The chapter ends by addressing questions raised by the survey (the same concerns as those found in 1970b).

Talbert then examined the theological significance of these parallels. In Chap 6, he suggested that five of the detected parallels (between Luke and Acts; between Acts 1-12 and 13-28; between Acts 1:12-4:23 and 4:24-5:42; those in Luke 1:5-2:52; and those in Luke 3:1-4:15) are shaped by the Lukan concern for salvation-history. In the process, he proposed to modify Conzelmann's *Heilsgeschichte*, suggesting that "it may very well be necessary to speak of a four phase salvation history" in which "the apostolic age must be separated from the post-apostolic church" (1974d:106). Chapter 7 accounts for three more sets of correspondences (Luke 9 and 22-23; Luke 9 and Acts 1; Luke 24 and Acts 1) in terms of Lukan Christology (see also 1968a). Three sets of correspondences (those in Luke 4-8; Luke 9-18; and Acts 15-21) do not readily serve Luke's theological interests and are best explained as existing "primarily for aesthetic reasons" (1974d:120).

In the last chapter of the book, Talbert turned to a consideration of the genre of Luke-Acts. Assuming that Luke-Acts is most closely related to ancient biography, he drew the bulk of his comparative material from Diogenes Laertius' *Lives of Eminent Philosophers*. He concluded: "Luke-Acts like Laertius' *Lives* has the life of a founder as the first structural unit, followed by a second, namely, the narrative of successors and selected other disciples" (1974d:130). Following this generic pattern allowed the Third Evangelist to address the problem of heresy in his community by showing that the life and teachings of the apostles were rooted in the life of the founder of the community, Jesus of Nazareth.[11]

The immediate reception of this book, like that of *Luke and the Gnostics*, was mixed. The evaluations may be conveniently considered under headings which correspond to the major divisions of Talbert's work: 1) literary patterns; 2) the Lukan milieu; and 3) and theological themes and the occasion of Luke-Acts.

1) The value of the literary patterns is variously reckoned. Donald Miesner found convincing Talbert's view that many correspondences promote the *imitatio Magistri* theme.[12] Paul Minear, on the other hand, criticized the preponderance of literary parallels: "I find the study to be an excellent example of industrious and ingenious parallelomania. So many instances are cited of the architectural symmetries that I became more skeptical of them all."[13]

2) The evaluation of Talbert's setting Luke-Acts in its larger literary and cultural milieu was almost uniformly affirming. David Reeves' comment is representative: "The book is worthwhile to read, especially

---

[11]Talbert addressed several problems with his thesis (1974d: 129-32). The most difficult is that Acts is more fully developed than any of the "succession narratives" in Laertius' *Lives*. This problem and Talbert's response will be discussed later.

[12]Donald Miesner, *CurTM* 3 (1976) 361.

[13]Paul S. Minear, *JAAR* 45 (1977) 85-86. See also Geoffrey Graystone, *CBQ* 38 (1976) 131.

for the sections which summarize Talbert's considerable study of literary matters in Greek and Roman classics."[14] Talbert's utilization of literary parallels, particularly Greco-Roman, became a hallmark of his work from this point on, and subsequent assessments of his work have tended to bear out these early positive impressions.

3) Evaluations of the occasion of Luke-Acts, e.g., defense against heresy, have been as uniformly negative as assessments of Talbert's use of Greco-Roman parallels were positive. To cite David Reeves again: "Arguments from silence rest at the base of the conception of Luke and Acts as compositions in opposition to Gnostic Christians. When one presumes the existence of an enemy, one finds telltale evidence with some regularity."[15] The thesis about the occasion of Luke-Acts fared no better in this outing than it did in *Luke and the Gnostics.*

Despite the shortcomings surfaced by these reviewers, Talbert's efforts did in many ways mark a "new era" in the way Lukan scholarship, at least in North America, would proceed. Donald Miesner's judgment was not be altogether off the mark when he suggested that *Literary Patterns"* may well become a milestone in Lucan studies, perhaps of the stature of the works of Conzelmann, Cadbury, and Haenchen."[16]

The Genre of the Canonical Gospels

Throughout his career, when experiments in methodology have rewarded Talbert with an interpretive tool which he could employ with confidence, he has ventured out of his laboratory of Luke-Acts to test his new method on some other part of the NT. After genre criticism proved to be a satisfying way of placing the Lukan writings in their literary milieu in *Literary Patterns* (esp. Chap 8), Talbert widened his scope to investigate the other gospels using this particular method. The result was one of his most noted and controversial studies, *What Is a Gospel?* (1977a; cf. also 1978a).

In *What Is a Gospel?* Talbert extended his argument that Luke-Acts shares remarkable generic similarities with the ancient Hellenistic biographies of philosophers and rulers to include the other canonical gospels. He challenged the "critical consensus" that the gospels are *sui generis.* This *opinio communis* rests on three pillars: "1) the gospels are

---

[14] David Reeves, *Int* 31 (1977) 94.
[15] Ibid.
[16] Miesner, 361.

mythical, the Graeco-Roman biographies are not; 2) the gospels are cultic, the Graeco-Roman biographies are not; and 3) while the gospels emerge from a community with a world-negating outlook, the literary biographies are produced by and for a world-affirming people" (1977a:2). These pillars correspond to 1) structure, 2) function, and 3) attitude, and are "the criteria assumed...to be necessary for establishing the genre of a document" (1977a:6). Talbert attempted to refute the majority position and argued that the canonical gospels were, in fact, very similar to the genre of the ancient biography. Having addressed these obstacles, he surmised: "The gospels are biographies, albeit ancient ones" (1977a:135).

This book received more immediate attention than either of Talbert's two previous studies. Again, as might be expected, reactions were mixed. Fellow genre critic, Philip Shuler, suggested: "The altering of mind-sets—like the slaying of giants—is a formidable undertaking, and Talbert's significant book on gospel genre represents just such a conquest.... It is the ambitious nature of the task that will leave Talbert open to criticism."[17] Talbert's knowledge of Greco-Roman sources was again extolled,[18] though several reviewers were dissatisfied with Talbert's explanation regarding the relationship between mythical structure and genre in John, since none of the parallel biographies of antiquity employed the myth of the descending/ascending redeemer.[19] Norman Petersen pointed out that Talbert had caught himself in a methodological crossfire: "Having wedded himself to the literary categories of the old literary history, which is now under siege, Talbert exposes himself to attack from both the old school, for contradicting it, and from the new criticism, for not having been critical enough."[20] Nevertheless, despite quibbles with this and that detail of the book, most of the early reviewers agreed with Philip Shuler's assessment: "Talbert's work presents the latest and, to date, most convincing case for the view that the gospels may be considered biographies...."[21]

Another indication that Talbert's work was well received was his invitation to serve as moderator of a Seminar on Gospel Genre which was part of a "Colloquy on New Testament Studies" held in Fort Worth,

---

[17]Philip R. Shuler, *JBL* 98 (1979) 439; 440.
[18]See Richard H. Hiers, *Int* 33 (1979) 215; Walter E. Pilgrim, *Dialog* 19 (1980) 72; Victor P. Furnish, *PSTJ* 31 (1978) 45.
[19]J. K. Riches, *Theology* 82 (1979) 301; Sakae Kubo, *AUSS* 17 (1979) 130.
[20]Norman R. Petersen, *JAAR* 47 (1979) 314.
[21]Shuler, 439.

TX, in November, 1980.[22] Talbert himself wrote in the Proceedings to that Conference:

> At the present moment, among those who are working with the problem most directly, the burden of proof seems to have shifted from those who wish to falsify the Schmidt-Bultmann hypothesis of the literary uniqueness of the Gospels to those who would deny that the canonical Gospels belong in some way to the biographical genre of Mediterranean antiquity (1983b:200).

The most notable exception to this positive reception of *What Is a Gospel?* was a review by David Aune.[23] This fifty-one page review of a one hundred and thirty-five page book could only be described as scathing. Aune asserted: "In spite of the generally positive tone of the reviews which have thus far appeared, it is my view that he has unwittingly misinterpreted the ancient evidence to such an extent that his book is unusable in its present state."[24] Though Aune brought numerous charges against Talbert, the failure to consult the major reference works and secondary literature of classical scholarship was, for Aune, the most serious flaw in the study. Aune concluded: "The general failure to draw on the achievements of modern classical philology is perhaps the main reason for the many false assumptions, misinterpretations and oversimplifications which permeate Talbert's work."[25]

The only direct, written response which Talbert has made to Aune's charges is found in a footnote to a paper in which he assessed recent contributions to studies in gospel genre. Aune, he claimed "has produced a confused and confusing essay that does nothing to advance research" (1983b:200). The last part of this statement, at least, has some truth in it.

---

[22]This seminar served as a sequel to several other colloquies and festivals on the Synoptic Gospels, so popular during the 1970s. Previous conferences were held at Pittsburgh (1970), Münster (1976), San Antonio (1977), and Cambridge (1979). Talbert participated as an invited principal in three of these conferences (Pittsburgh, San Antonio, and Fort Worth). For Talbert's contribution to these meetings, see 1970a; 1978b; and 1983b. He also provided a written response to Alan Dundes' "The Hero Pattern and the Life of Jesus," the main position paper presented at the Twenty-fifth Colloquy of the Center for Hermeneutical Studies in Hellenistic and Modern Culture, 12 December 1976 (1977b).
[23]David E. Aune, "The Problem of the Genre of the Gospels: A Critique of C. H. Talbert's *What Is a Gospel?*" in *Gospel Perspectives: Studies of History and Tradition in the Four Gospels* (ed. R. T. France and D. Wenham; Sheffield: JSOT, 1981) 2. 9-60.
[24]Ibid., 11.
[25]Ibid., 18.

After fifty pages of critique, one does not have a clue about what genre, if any, Aune thought the canonical gospels fit or about the method which he would employ to discern such generic features.[26]

Even those who are generally sympathetic with Talbert's argument often share a common question regarding the genre of the gospels: "So what?"[27] In an article on the opening chapters of Luke, Talbert addressed this question and concluded:

> The biographical tradition of the Greco-Roman world would have conditioned a person in the Mediterranean region at the end of the first century C.E. to expect an account of the hero's career before he embarked on his public activity....When the reader confronted Luke 1:5-4:15, this narrative unit fulfilled these expectations in a remarkable way (1980a:135).

More recently, Talbert has offered a more modest assessment of genre studies: "Like all studies of background, these generic studies' contribution is indirect. Do not expect a revolution in interpretation to result from genre criticism" (1987e:737). Still, for those willing to accept Talbert's presuppositions regarding genre, he has shown convincingly that generic studies can make a contribution to the interpretive task by clarifying reader expectations.

Perspectives From the SBL Luke-Acts Group

Before passing on to the next section, one other volume published during this period should be mentioned because of the significance of the context out of which it emerged. Talbert served as editor of *Perspectives*

---

[26] Aune has attempted to remove this deficiency in his most recent book, *The New Testament in Its Literary Environment*, Library of Early Christianity (ed. Wayne A. Meeks; Philadelphia: Westminster, 1987) 17-76. Ironically, Aune argued that the canonical gospels (with the notable exception of Luke) belong to the genre of ancient biography. He claimed (32): "the canonical Gospels constitute a distinctive type of ancient biography combining (to oversimplify slightly) Hellenistic form and function with Jewish content." Aune took Luke with Acts to argue that the two together represent ancient historiography (see ibid., 77-157). In his review of this work (1987e:737), Talbert disagreed with Aune's categorization of Luke-Acts and extended an invitation to the reader: "Let the reader compare Luke-Acts with Diogenes Laertius' *Life of Epicurus* and with Polybius and see if general history fits better than the life of a founder followed by a narrative of his successors." Talbert made no mention of their previous, sharp exchanges, but rather concluded on a graceful note: "Even if one disagrees with its interpretative judgments, one can be thankful for the labor lying behind its pages" (737).

[27] See Pilgrim, 72; see also 1983b:247-49.

on Luke-Acts (1978e) and made the following explanatory comments in the "Foreword":

> After consultations in 1972 and 1973, the Luke-Acts Group of the Society of Biblical Literature was formed in 1974 with a five year lifespan. This collection of essays is an attempt to bring together the results of some of the work that was undertaken between 1972 and 1978 by those related directly or indirectly to the Group…. It is hoped that this book will offer both assistance in and a stimulus to further study of the Third Gospel and Acts (1978e).

The articles by Horton, Mattill, S. Brown, Karris, R. E. Brown, Trites, Robbins, and Veltman, were originally presented in some form to the Luke-Acts Group (See Appendix One).[28] Already the influence of Talbert on his peers can be seen in some of the presentations to the Group. Krodel and Karris offered critiques of *Literary Patterns*, while S. Brown, Miesner, Robbins, Quinn, Tyson, and Veltman, to varying degrees, either assumed or extended the arguments found in *Literary Patterns* (See Appendix One).[29]

During this second period of his scholarship, Talbert emerged as a leading interpreter of Luke-Acts in North America. *Perspectives on Luke-Acts* provides a useful summary of the major issues in Lukan scholarship during the late '70s. Those issues—the genre, style, and literary milieu of Luke-Acts—reflect the shift, at least in American scholarship, away from the agenda set by Conzelmann and toward the questions raised by Talbert and his colleagues.

Close Readings:
At Home in the Biblical Text Itself (1981-90)

In the concluding footnote to "The Redaction Critical Quest for Luke the Theologian," Talbert wrote:

> Only if we solve the riddles of Luke the theologian and Luke the literary artist will we be able, with some degree of success, to resume the quest for Luke the historian. In the meantime one can hope that until research has

---

[28]The lists which appear in Appendixes One and Two were taken from the Annual Programs of the Society of Biblical Literature (1974-83). I have assumed that the printed programs are accurate, though such an assumption could be erroneous.

[29] For reviews of *Perspectives on Luke-Acts*, see those by Pierson Parker, *ATR* 61 (1979) 410-412; I. Howard Marshall in *ExpT* 90 (1979) 280; E. V. Hamrick in *PersRelSt* 6 (1979) 254-58; and especially those by Robert O'Toole in *TS* 40 (1979) 351-54; and Robert Maddox in *RTR* 38 (1979) 88-89.

had time to deal with the items on these two agendas, a moratorium may be declared on the production of further commentaries on Luke and Acts which add nothing material to the discussion (1970a:222).

With *Reading Luke,* Talbert has broken his own self-imposed moratorium. This important volume should be understood both as a new methodological venture as well as a summary of Talbert's scholarship to this point. Both points are examined below.

A Literary and Theological Commentary on the Third Gospel

Joseph Tyson lamented that in *Reading Luke* Talbert had made "no attempt to...set forth the methods he intends to pursue."[30] In a previously noted review, however, Talbert did distinguish between the earlier redactional approach to Luke-Acts and a "new way of doing Lucan studies" (1986a:337). His remarks there serve as a convenient summary of Talbert's methodology adopted in *Reading Luke.*

New Perspectives. If *Literary Patterns* in 1974 contributed to the inauguration of a new era in Lukan scholarship, particularly in North America, then this "new look" burst into full flower with the publication of a spate of studies in the early 1980s, not the least of which was *Reading Luke.*

1) Talbert claimed: "Prior to 1974 the units studied are roughly equivalent to the pericopes of a traditional Gospel Parallels. After 1974 there is a concern to examine larger thought units within the Gospel, as these can be discerned from indications within the Gospel text and from analogies from the milieu" (1986a:337). This latter procedure is carefully followed in *Reading Luke*: "The thrust of this approach is on understanding large thought units and their relationship to Lukan thought as a whole rather than focusing on the individual pieces of the narrative" (1982d:2). Talbert divided his commentary into four major sections and dealt with these divisions in thirty-three segments, focusing on the heart of each thought unit. In so doing, he effectively captured the broader strokes on the Gospel canvas, which are often overlooked by those who are intent on examining the evangelist's portrait in minute detail.

2) On the use of sources, Talbert proposed:

The earlier approach, using a synopsis, involved careful scrutiny of every variant between the Lucan text and an alleged earlier source. The later

---

[30]Joseph Tyson, *JBL* 104 (1985) 341.

tendency has been to start with the continuous text of the Gospel and to do a close reading of it as a finished product by either rhetorical criticism or modern narrative criticism. Then a synopsis is used to compare Luke with the other Gospels, which are viewed not as alleged sources but as independent developments of the same basic tradition (1986a:337).

In a major methodological departure from most previous studies on Luke-Acts (including his own), Talbert discarded the two-source theory as "a questionable control on redaction critical work" and proceeded with a method that does "not assume the two-source theory, nor any other source theory, for that matter" (1982d:1).

3) On the intended purpose of such an interpretive method, Talbert observed:

> The end sought in the earlier approach is basically a history of the tradition, including not only the pre-gospel stages of the church's transmission but also the question of the historical Jesus. The later trend has been to look for a message of the text in its canonical form. The earlier method uses the Gospel as a window through which to see something else (the development of the tradition); the latter as a mirror to reflect its own narrative world (1986a:337).

Talbert described his approach in *Reading Luke* as "a type of redaction criticism heavily influenced by nonbiblical literary criticism" (1982d:2). As such, the interest in Luke is almost exclusively at the level of the *Sitz im Leben Kirche*.[31] That is, he focused on the text as a religious document and was eager to unfold its theological character and message (see 1986f:280).

4) Finally, he commented on the shift to a "post-Conzelmann era" (a phrase used in 1979b:342): "Whereas the dialogue partners of Lucan scholars prior to 1974 were basically Conzelmann and his colleagues, the post-1974 period seeks to dialogue with Greco-Roman literature and with modern literary criticism" (1986a:337). The fact that *Reading Luke* has no references to *The Theology of St. Luke* highlights the degree to which Talbert himself now eschews Conzelmann's redaction-critical agenda.

Some would rightly dispute that this description of the "new way of doing Lucan studies" fits all of the work on Luke-Acts since 1974, but

---

[31]Occasionally, though, Talbert exchanged mirror for window and discussed the meaning of some passages, especially parables, within the context of Jesus' ministry (e.g., 1982d:122-24). As Tyson (341) observed: "One may not quarrel with this procedure if one is trying to learn something about the meaning of the parable in the context of Jesus' life, but the relevance of this information to the literary meaning of Luke is at best questionable."

there can be little doubt that Talbert has here described the procedure he followed in writing *Reading Luke*![32] In this volume he has provided numerous new perspectives on the literary techniques and theological emphases of the Third Evangelist.

A Précis of Talbert's Scholarship. Though there is much that is new in this book which distinguishes it from other commentaries, *Reading Luke* is "vintage Talbert." If one does not appreciate the way he has drawn upon his own previous work in this commentary, then one misses the insight that *Reading Luke* "brings together in one volume the mature insights of a major North American interpreter of Luke-Acts."[33] Below are summarized four ways in which *Reading Luke* may be understood as a précis of Talbert's previous work.

1. *Genre Criticism.* The most obvious indebtedness *Reading Luke* owes to Talbert's previous work is in the area of genre criticism: "This book operates from a perspective indebted to genre criticism. Luke-Acts belongs to the ancient biographical tradition" (1982d:2).

2. *Literary Patterns.* In dealing with the Lukan "large thought units" Talbert made numerous references to the architectural designs of Luke-Acts noted earlier in *Literary Patterns*. In addition to the three explicit references to *Literary Patterns* (1982d:42, 115, 186), he noted a large number of parallelisms and chiasms, many of which were drawn from his previous work, all of which are informed by it.[34]

3. *Purpose of Luke-Acts.* In *Reading Luke* Talbert still assumed that the Gospel of Luke is functioning as a defense against heresy. This view, of course, was first presented in *Luke and the Gnostics* and was sharpened in subsequent publications (1968a; 1970a; 1974d). That Luke was combatting overrealized eschatology was explicitly assumed by Talbert in his discussion of 17:22-37 and 19:11-27 (1982d:166-69; 177-78). An anti-Docetic function is implied in the commentary on Luke 24:36-43 (1982d:228-29). Though much less significant now than twenty years ago, this Lukan apologetic purpose has remained a part of Talbert's system.

---

[32] A point Talbert himself makes in his review of Robert Tannehill's *The Narrative Unity of Luke-Acts* (1988c:136). In this review, Talbert makes the same four points about the differences between the traditional and more recent approaches to Lukan studies, though he no longer marks 1974 as the watershed date.

[33] Robert J. Karris, *TS* 44 (1983) 533.

[34] See his coments on the chiastic structures at 3:21-22; 4:16-20; 6:39-45; 7:37-50; 9:51-19:44; 9:52-10:24; 9:57-62; 14:1-24; 17:11-19:44; 21:8-36; passim. One wonders if chiasm was a more favorite literary technique of Talbert than Luke!

4. Methodology. Talbert's decision to employ a type of "redaction criticism" which assumed no particular source theory was the upshot of a growing dissatisfaction with the "critical consensus." Earlier he had observed: "Employing Mark as a control today is about as compelling as using Colossians and Second Thessalonians to describe Paul's theology. It may very well be legitimate to do so, but so many have problems with the procedure that such an assumption narrows considerably the circles with whom one can converse" (1976c:393-94). This methodological concern finds full expression in *Reading Luke.*[35]

Though there was some concern for certain aspects of Talbert's exegesis,[36] structure,[37] or use of Greco-Roman parallels,[38] the immediate response to *Reading Luke* was almost uniformly positive. Joseph Tyson hailed it as "a pioneering effort."[39] Jerome Kodell called it a "first-rate guide to the Gospel of Luke."[40] Frederick Danker labeled it "a very helpful and sensitive exposition of Luke's literary strategy and techniques."[41] Though not written for peers, *Reading Luke* received generally high marks from the scholarly guild for applying "contemporary insights and approaches and awareness of the world of the Gospel in a way that builds ordinary people's faith."[42]

---

[35]Not only do the previous emphases of genre criticism, literary patterns, and the purpose of Luke-Acts guide Talbert in this commentary, but a "source analysis" demonstrates a close literary relationship between *Reading Luke* and previous writings of Talbert where blocks of varying material have been taken over with few or no editorial modifications. These literary "roots" may be found in 1967d; 1968a; 1970a; 1974d; 1976c; 1980a; 1982c; and 1982e. It is not surprising that Talbert should draw upon the fruits of previous, intensive research in Luke-Acts; however, this "source analysis" does serve to buttress my argument that *Reading Luke*, while an innovative interpretation of Luke, in many ways is the culmination of a twenty-year pilgrimage in Lukan research.

[36]See Tyson, 341; Mikeal C. Parsons, *PersRelSt* 11 (1984) 284; Kurz, 417; Archie L. Nations, *Faith and Mission* 1 (1983) 96; Robert L. Brawley, *CumSem* 21 (1983) 26.

[37]Despite his concern for the architecture of Luke, at several points, Talbert displaced material in order to consider it with texts on a similar theme. Jerome Kodell (*BTB* 14 [1984] 158) noted that this procedure caused Talbert to overlook completely Luke 1:18-25 and led him "to violate his principle of following the author's compositional design." See also Kurz, 417.

[38]Frederick W. Danker, *CBQ* 46 (1984) 377.

[39]Tyson, 342.

[40]Kodell, 159.

[41]Danker, 377.

[42]Kurz, 417.

Reading Acts

As one would expect, Talbert also applied his methodology of close readings to Acts (1984a). One reviewer, Roger Omanson, remarked: "An appropriate sub-title for this most recent commentary would be 'A Literary and Theological Commentary on Acts.'"[43] The methodological assumptions are the same as in *Reading Luke*: 1) Acts is a succession narrative of one sub-genre of ancient biography and "portrays the Twelve and Paul in such a way that they reproduce in their careers the prototypical events of the career of the earthly Jesus" (1984a:3). 2) The focus is on large thought units. There are three major sections: a) The Commission: A Mission to Do (1:1-14); b) The Commission Fulfilled: Stage One (1:15-12:24); and c) The Commission Fulfilled: Stage Two (13:1-28:31). These last two sections are each divided into twelve subsections. In each subsection, Talbert examined the literary patterns, now called the surface structure (borrowing a term from structuralism),[44] and gave some indication as to the theological message of the text. 3) As might be expected there is little emphasis on the anti-heretical purpose of Acts (though see 1984a:86-88). 4) Since Acts has never been hampered by any particular source theory, Talbert did not have to justify his particular method of comparing Acts with Jewish (cf. Acts 6:1-7) or Greco-Roman parallels (e.g. Acts 28:1-10). To date, the volume has received little attention from reviewers.[45] My own evaluation of *Acts* as a companion volume to *Reading Luke* will follow later.

New Perspectives from the SBL Seminar

The second volume generated by the Luke-Acts Seminar appeared in 1983. In the "Preface," Talbert remarked: "This volume of essays is an attempt to bring together some of the work done between 1979 and 1983

---

[43]Roger L. Omanson, *RevExp* 82 (1985) 443.
[44]In addition to parallel structures at Acts 1:3-11; 13:44-52; 15:36-18:22; 18:23-21:26; 13:16-52; and 18:5-18a, Talbert noted chiasms in Acts 1:16b-19; 1:23-26; 4:32-35; 6:8-8:4; 9:1-25; 10:22-33; 15:1-5; 20:19b-27; 20:28-31; 20:31b-35; 23:12-24:27. Interestingly, the chiastic surface structures found in Acts 20:28-31 and 20:31b-35 do not match the chiasms discovered by Talbert and Cheryl Exum almost twenty years earlier (1967c).
[45]See though the review by Richard C. White, *LexThQ* 21 (1986) 29-30.

by those related directly or indirectly to that seminar" (1983f:vii).[46] Many of the contributions, both to the volume and the Seminar, demonstrated shared interest with, and in some cases an indebtedness to Talbert, particularly in the area of Greco-Roman parallels and Luke-Acts.[47] Not intended as a replacement for *Perspectives on Luke-Acts* (1978e), Talbert expressed his hope that "this book, like its predecessor, will serve as a stimulus to further study of the Lucan writings" (1983f: vii). For a decade, the participants in the program segment of the SBL on Luke-Acts, through their publications and presentations, have insured that this hope was not in vain.

Reading Corinthians

As in the earlier periods, Talbert soon applied his refined method to other NT material.[48] The fruit of this labor was the recently published

[46]Interestingly, only two of the twelve essays (Jones and Richard), which represent "new perspectives from the Society of Biblical Literature seminar," appeared on the program of the SBL Luke-Acts Seminar 1979-83 (See Appendix Two).

[47]As Robert Smith (*CurTM* 13 [1986] 55-56) noted about these essays: "all illustrate the conviction that Luke-Acts must be interpreted within the broad Mediterranean milieu and make good use of Greco-Roman as well as OT materials, convictions nurtured and promoted by editor Talbert over the years, and rightly so." In the Seminar, see especially the work of Tyson, Robbins, Praeder, Danker. In the *Luke-Acts* volume see the essays by Brodie, Barr and Wentling, Brawley, and Kurz. Talbert's article in this volume, "Promise and Fulfillment in Lucan Theology," appeared in a modified form in Excursus A in *Reading Luke*. For other evaluations of this volume, see the reviews by Arthur A. Just, Jr., *ConcorThQ* 49 (1985) 217-18 and Jane E. Via, *BTB* 18 (1988) 37-39. Jane Via provided a rather extensive critique of this volume and concluded: "Talbert's volume challenges the exegetical community to do not only exegesis but also theology in order to render their work meaningful to the believing Christian community and helpful in understanding its relationship to other believing communities." While the volume may be vulnerable to such criticism, Via's comments should not be generalized to include Talbert's work as a whole (see especially 1982e, 1983a, 1986b, 1986g, 1986h, 1987b, 1987g, 1987h, and 1989b) where Talbert moved from a descriptive analysis of the context of the NT writing to the contemporary context of the believing community.

[48]Talbert's intention to leave the familiar territory of Luke-Acts is seen also in his collaboration with Jack Dean Kingsbury in a SBL Consultation on Matthew and his editorial leadership of two volumes, one on 1 Peter (1986c), the other a *Festschrift* for Frank Stagg (1985c). For reviews of *Perspectives on 1 Peter*, see Jerome Neyrey, *CBQ* 49 (1987) 690-691; Thomas Lea, *SWJTh* 29 (1987) 57-58; and J. Ramsey Michaels, *PersRelSt* 15(1988) 286-288. On *Perspectives on the New Testament: Essays in Honor of Frank Stagg*, see the review by C. Thomas Rhyne, *CBQ* 49 (1987) 176-177.

Reading Corinthians: A Literary and Theological Commentary on 1 and 2 Corinthians (1987a), an eminently readable, theologically sensitive treatment of the Corinthian correspondence. In his review, Calvin Roetzel claimed that "the work succeeds, because its incisiveness, synoptic grasp of the literature, fresh appraisals, and independent judgments will surely provoke fresh investigation and understanding of the text."[49] The opening lines situate this book in the context of Talbert's ongoing work: "Like its predecessor, *Reading Luke*...his volume...is concerned to understand large thought units and their relationship to Pauline thought as a whole. The focus, moreover, is on a close reading of the text" (1987a:xiii). After more than two decades of challenging Luke-Acts scholarship with new perspectives, Talbert is now applying those insights to other parts of the NT, aiding both the scholar and the general reader "to feel at home in the biblical text."[50]

Contributions to Lukan Scholarship: Experiments in Method

Charles Talbert appeared on the scene of Lukan studies in *die Mitte der Zeit*. By the time he completed his doctoral work and published his first book, the work by Conzelmann would cause W. C. van Unnik in 1966 to speak of Luke-Acts as a "storm-center" in NT scholarship.[51] Responses to Conzelmann's agenda took several tacks. A number of conservative scholars attempted to correct what they considered to be a radically critical approach. I. Howard Marshall is representative. He defended the historical reliability of Luke-Acts, maintaining that Luke was both historian and theologian, but as the the title of his book evinces, his emphasis was on Luke as historian.[52] Other scholars, and by

---

[49]Calvin Roetzel, "A Provocative New Commentary," *Int* 43 (1989), 301. See also the generally positive evaluation in the review by Alan C. Mitchell, *TS* 49 (1988) 157-58; and the brief reviews by Earl Ellis, *SWJTh* 30 (1988) 48, and Graydon Snyder, *CTS Register* 77 (1987) 46-47.

[50]This phrase first appeared in Talbert's review of R. E. Brown's *The Birth of the Messiah* (1978d: 215). Since that time, he has used it repeatedly, and it serves as a convenient summary of Talbert's changing understanding of what a biblical commentary should be (see 1982a: 163; 1982d: 2; 1987a: xiii; 1988e: 178).

[51]W. C. van Unnik, "Luke-Acts, a Storm Center in Contemporary Scholarship," *Studies in Luke-Acts* (eds. Leander E. Keck and J. Louis Martyn; Nashville: Abingdon, 1966) 16.

[52]See I. Howard Marshall, *Luke: Historian and Theologian* (Grand Rapids: Zondervan, 1971). See also H. Flender, *St. Luke: Theologian of Redemptive History*. Trans. Reginald H. & Ilse Fuller (Philadelphia: Fortress, 1967); W. Gasque,

158   *Mikeal C. Parsons*

far the larger number of them, accepted the redaction-critical method
and engaged in the task of sustaining, modifying, and rejecting
Conzelmann's picture of Luke's theology. Surveys of this research
abound and there is no need to rehearse it again here.[53]
    The third major area of response to Conzelmann was in the area of
methodology. Talbert has made his greatest contribution here,
facilitating the shift of Lukan scholarship to a "post-Conzelmann" era.
In a recent essay, "Luke-Acts," Talbert offered his assessment of Lukan
scholarship over the past three decades, organizing his discussion
around four questions (1989a).[54] At one point in the discussion, Talbert
addressed the place of redaction criticism in Lukan studies, particularly
of the gospel, and raised the question: "Is the Method Workable?"
(1989a:306). Since Talbert has been at the forefront of methodological
experimentation, it is fitting to raise his own question about his
approaches to Luke-Acts: "Is the method workable?"

Redaction Criticism and the Purpose of Luke-Acts

    The purpose of Luke-Acts has attracted much attention. Luke's
purpose in writing has been variously defined as 1) evangelism (F. F.
Bruce, J. C. O'Neill); 2) a defense of Paul at his trial (A. J. Mattill); 3) a
Christian apology to the Roman empire (B. S. Easton; E. Haenchen); 4) a
defense against Jewish Christian attacks on Paul's memory (F. C. Baur;
S. G. F. Brandon; to some extent J. Jervell); 5) a response to the delayed
parousia (Conzelmann); and 6) the need to defend the continuity of
salvation history (Maddox).[55] One other alternative is that of Talbert:
Luke-Acts is a defense against Gnosticism.
    What began as an explicit reference to anti-Gnostic heresy in *Luke
and the Gnostics* was gradually effaced in Talbert's later writings. In

___

A History of the Criticism of the Acts of the Apostles (Grand Rapids: Eerdmans,
1975).
    [53]See especially, Francois Bovon, *Luc le theologien: Vingt-cinq ans de
recherches (1950-75)* (Neuchatel: Delachaux & Niestle, 1978); Earl Richard,
"Luke—Writer, Theologian, Historian: Research and Orientation of the 1970's,"
BTB 13 (1983) 3-15; W. Ward Gasque, "A Fruitful Field: Recent Study of the Acts
of the Apostles," *Int* 42 (1988) 117-31. Note Talbert's contribution to this task,
especially in modifying Conzelmann's views of Lukan eschatology and
Heilsgeschichte.
    [54]This article serves as a companion and update to Talbert's earlier article,
"Shifting Sands" (1976c).
    [55]For a discussion of this issue, see Robert Maddox, *The Purpose of Luke-Acts*
(Göttingen: Vandenhoeck & Ruprecht, 1982) 1-30.

Literary Patterns, he spoke of Gnosticism, but more specifically of anti-Docetism. Overrealized eschatology was the occasion mentioned in *What Is a Gospel?* Finally, in *Reading Luke*, Talbert referred explicitly to overrealized eschatology and implicitly to anti-Docetism in several specific passages, but identified neither of these concerns in his introduction.

Talbert has since rejected the redaction-critical method which engendered his understanding of the Lukan occasion; the occasion, however, has not been abandoned. It has simply been submerged, surfacing now and then in his exegesis of certain passages. In fact, his understanding of Luke-Acts as a legitimation document presupposes some type of opposition to (or in) the Lukan community, and when he has attempted to identify it, he usually did so as some form of heresy. Talbert himself observed: "...redaction criticism has been unable to delineate either the Lucan purpose or the Lucan *Sitz im Leben*" (1989a:305).[56] The earlier criticisms raised against *Luke and the Gnostics* still apply. Any argument from silence is questionable, and Talbert has not adequately explained the "silence of Acts" on the heresy issue.

Architecture Analysis

Talbert's next stop along his methodological sojourn was the study of parallelisms and chiasms as discerned by architecture analysis. The study of parallelisms in Luke-Acts has a long history, dating back to the nineteenth century. Noteworthy among Talbert's predecessors are the works by F. C. Baur, E. Zeller, R. Morgenthaler, and M. D. Goulder.[57] Talbert had already anticipated some criticism regarding his proposal to combine architecture analysis with redaction criticism:

> At this point I am aware of being caught in a crossfire. On the one hand, opponents of the two source theory will be unhappy because I assume it here....On the other hand, New Testament scholars under the influence of certain currents of modern literary criticism will claim that such source analysis is unnecessary and should be discarded (1974d:14).

---

[56]Some recent work on Christian origins, however, lends support to Talbert's thesis by pressing the diversity in early Christianity in the first century (see especially the work of Helmut Koester, James Robinson, and Dominic Crossan).

[57]For a summary and critique of scholarship on Luke-Acts parallels, see Susan M. Praeder, "Jesus-Paul, Peter-Paul, and Jesus-Peter Parallelisms in Luke-Acts: A History of Reader Response," *1984 SBL Seminar Papers* (Chico: Scholars, 1984) 23-39.

The most incisive critique of Talbert's methodology in his work on parallelisms was offered by Norman Petersen, and his criticisms fall into the latter camp identified by Talbert above. Petersen claimed: "Talbert's selection and application of a literary model largely uninformed by general literary criticism leads me to doubt that he has succeeded in explaining what Luke did and why he did it."[58] He did not criticize Talbert's choice to combine "complementary models" but maintained that in doing so, "the possibilities of a literary model have been restricted even before they have been explored."[59] Petersen's conclusion is worth quoting:

> In consequence of his premature abandonment of a more comprehensive literary model, Talbert also precludes answers to the question of style and content that might come from a strictly internal analysis of the stylized sections of Luke's composition. Thus he does not and cannot proceed from a literary analysis of stylized content to its functions within Luke's narrative,...as literary critics do in their work generally.[60]

Petersen's comments are on target and indicate a methodological flaw in Talbert's work during this period. Though he has yet to adopt a "comprehensive literary model"—or at least not the type which Petersen probably had in mind—he does partially redress the situation by developing his own interpretive model which is free from problematic source theories.

Genre Criticism

During the 1970s, gospel genre was a burning issue. Genre studies were published which were antecedent to or slightly later than Talbert's work, and a Gospel Genre Group was active in the Society of Biblical Literature at this time. The cumulative effect was a mounting challenge to the posture that the gospels were *sui generis*. In general, the alternatives concerning the genre of the gospels were two. 1) The gospels took their generic conventions from the Jewish milieu and had parallels with the OT, or they were Christian midrashim patterned on the Jewish lectionary cycle.[61] 2) The gospels were influenced by the

---

[58]Norman R. Petersen, *JBL* 96 (1977) 456.
[59]Ibid.
[60]Ibid., 457.
[61]Old Testament parallels were suggested by D. A. Baker, "Form and the Gospels," *Downside Review* 88 (1970) 13-26; and R. E. Brown, Jesus and Elisha," *PersRelSt* 12 (1971) 85-104. The liturgical origins of the gospels were argued more thoroughly by P. Carrington, *The Primitive Christian Calendar: A Study in the*

literary conventions of the Greco-Roman milieu.[62] With regard to Luke
and Acts specifically, several options are available. In addition to the
ancient biography proposed by Talbert, Luke and Acts have been
characterized as having generic features similar to a type of ancient
history[63] or the ancient novel.[64]

Talbert's most recent—and I would add, most compelling—defense
of his thesis that early Christians utilized the ancient biographical genre
is found in a *Semeia* article, "Once Again: Gospel Genre" (1988a). His
discussion of the purpose and significance of genre criticism at the
beginning of that article is worth quoting in full:

> The basic rule for all reading is: a text is to be interpreted in light of its
> context. For example, a word means what it means in its sentence; a
> sentence means what it means in its paragraph; a paragraph means what it
> means in its section; a section means what it means in the document as a
> whole. But what does the document as a whole mean? … It is at this point
> that genre criticism enters the picture. By locating the individual text
> within the context of those documents of a similar literary type and by
> noting both likenesses and differences, one has a handle on at least a
> primary dimension of the meaning of the individual text as a whole. It is,
> therefore, important to ask about the genre of the early Christian gospels if
> one wants to understand them as wholes (1988a:53).

Talbert maintained that the constitutive feature of ancient
biography may best be seen in contrast to ancient history: "Whereas
history focuses on the distinguished and significant acts of great men in

---

Making of the Marcan Gospel (Cambridge: Cambridge University, 1952); M. D.
Goulder, *Midrash and Lection in Matthew* (London: S.P.C.K., 1974); idem, *The
Evangelists' Calendar: A Lectionary Explanation of the Development of Scripture*
(London: S.P.C.K., 1978). This theory is harshly criticized by Leon Morris, "The
Gospels and the Jewish Lectionaries," in *Gospel Perspectives: Studies in Midrash
and Historiography* (eds. R. T. France and D. Wenham; Sheffield: JSOT, 1983) 3.
129-56.

[62]On the gospels as biography, see H. Cancik, "Die Gattung Evangelium: Das
Evangelium des Markus im Rahmen der antiken Historiographie," and "Bios
und Logos: Formengeschichtliche Untersuchungen zu Lukians 'Demonax,'" in
*Markus-Philogie: Historische, Literargeschichtliche, und Stilistische
Untersuchungen zum zweiten Evangelium* (Tübingen: J. C. B. Mohr, 1984). Other
suggestions for Greco-Roman parallels are chronicled by Talbert (1983b: 197-202).
For a survey of the problem, see R. A. Guelich, "The Gospel Genre," in *Das
Evangelium und die Evangelien* (ed. P. Stuhlmacher; Tübingen: J. C. B. Mohr,
1983) 183-219.

[63]F. F. Bruce, "The New Testament and Classical Studies," *NTS* 22 (1976) 229-
242; most recently Aune, *The New Testament in Its Literary Environment*, 77-157.

[64]See especially Richard I. Pervo, *Profit with Delight: The Literary Genre of the
Acts of the Apostles* (Philadelphia: Fortress, 1987).

the political and social spheres, biography is concerned with the essence of the individual" (1988a:55). He went on to argue that the Christian gospels (canonical and non-canonical) share this constitutive feature (even though they demonstrate great diversity in what he calls "accidental features"): "it is difficult to believe that on first acquaintance the canonical gospels, at least, would not have been considered biographical by Mediterranean readers/hearers" (1988a:60-61). This position has grown in popularity over the past decade on both sides of the Atlantic, and Talbert deserves much of the credit for this emerging consensus. And David Moessner was certainly correct to observe that in this most recent essay Talbert has presented "a model of clarity with remarkable depth in surveying a broad and complex body of literature."[65] Still, problems remain with Talbert's specific thesis about the generic pattern of Luke-Acts.

Talbert reiterated his position that the Lukan writings imitated the a+b pattern of didactic biographies which attempted "to indicate where the true tradition is in the present" (1988a:58). In *The New Testament in Its Literary Environment,* David Aune has leveled three telling criticisms against this view: 1) the usual pattern of life + successor + teachings which Talbert claimed was typical of Diogenes' *Lives* is found in only six of the eighty-two lives; 2) contrary to Talbert's view, Diogenes is concerned only with who succeeded whom, not with the legitimacy of their views; and 3) to speak as Talbert does of a succession *narrative* in ancient biography is an "inappropriate description of brief *lists* of students or successors."[66]

Aune himself has most recently argued that Luke-Acts belongs to the genre of Hellenistic general history, though he does accept the identification of the other three canonical gospels as ancient biography. The basic problem with classifying the Lukan writings as biography, according to Aune, is stated as follows:

> The Gospel of Luke and the Acts of the Apostles originally constituted a two-volume work by a single author....By itself, Luke could (like Mark,

---

[65]David Moessner, "And Once Again, What Sort of 'Essence?' A Response to Charles Talbert," *Semeia* 43 (1988) 75. In this response, Moessner rightly calls for Talbert to nuance more carefully, in light of the "long history of God's dealings with Israel" (82), Talbert's central tenet that the gospels present the essence of Jesus' character.

[66]Aune, *The New Testament in Its Literary Environment,* 79. Even those sympathetic with Talbert's work are critical at this last point. See David Barr and Judith Wentling "The Conventions of Classical Biography and the Genre of Luke-Acts: A Preliminary Study" (1983f: 63-88).

Matthew, and John) be classified as a type of ancient biography. But Luke, though it might have circulated separately, was subordinated to a larger literary structure. Luke does not belong to a type of ancient biography for it belongs with Acts, and Acts cannot be forced into a biographical mold.[67]

Most genre critics, like Aune and Talbert, assume that Luke and Acts are to be taken together. In fact, the assumption of the generic unity of Luke and Acts has led to Aune's double edged appraisal. On the one hand, though he disagreed with Talbert's conclusions, Aune commended Talbert's proposal because it "has the merit of attempting to find an analogy in genre to Luke-Acts as a whole."[68] On the other hand, Aune is critical of Richard Pervo, the most notable exception to the assumption of the generic unity of Luke and Acts. Pervo argued that Acts employs the generic conventions of the ancient novel.[69] Aune argued: "Luke-Acts *must* be treated as affiliated with *one* genre, but Pervo treats Acts in isolation."[70]

After reading Aune's description of the generic features of Luke-Acts, however, one could turn Aune's argument on its head and make an apt critique of his own work: Acts does not belong to a type of ancient history for it belongs with Luke, and Luke cannot be forced into an historiographical mode. Though both Talbert and Aune affirmed that genre studies must address the genre of Luke-Acts as a whole, Talbert's genre study favors the gospel and argues for biography, while Aune's study favors Acts and argues for historiography. Again, both scholars evidently assume generic unity on the basis of authorial unity, subsuming one narrative under the other. Pervo is willing to separate the two volumes, but has not yet provided full justification for doing so.[71]

The basic question is this: Is the same real author capable of producing works belonging to two distinct genres of literature? Herodotus, Thucydides, and Xenophon have all been credited with writing both in biographical and historical genres. In fact, Xenophon treated the life of Agesilaus twice, in the biography *Agesilaus*, and historically in *Hellenica* 3-6.

---

[67]Aune, *The New Testament in Its Literary Environment*, 77.
[68]Ibid., 79.
[69]See Pervo, *Profit with Delight*.
[70]Aune, *The New Testament in Its Literary Environment*, 80.
[71]But see his article on the generic unity of the Lukan writings, "Must Luke and Acts Belong to the Same Genre?" *SBL 1989 Seminar Papers* (ed. David J. Lull; Atlanta: Scholars Press, 1989) 309-16.

To move beyond the current debate in genre studies of Luke and Acts, the basic *opinio communis* of the unity of Luke-Acts needs thorough re-evaluation.[72] That Luke could have written in multiple genres seems not only plausible, but perhaps probable. The Third Gospel could share the generic conventions of the ancient biography; Acts might well share more in common with the ancient novel or historiography. Further, genre critics could benefit from a more self-conscious understanding of the theoretical moorings which underpin their assumptions.[73] Despite Talbert's efforts, the genre of the Lukan writings is still, for most scholars, an unresolved issue.

"Non-Biblical Literary Criticism"

Talbert finally "stumbled on the combination found in *Reading Luke*: a synthesis of close reading, use of parallels from Jewish and Greco-Roman worlds, and focus on the theological message."[74] This method, particularly its sensitivity to the way in which Luke-Acts participated in the literary conventions of Greco-Roman antiquity, has a long and distinguished heritage, recalling the work of Cadbury and Dibelius.[75] Talbert's new method was forged, in part, by a disenchantment with redaction criticism. On the first page of *Reading Luke*, he claimed that

---

[72]See the volume by Mikeal C. Parsons and Richard I. Pervo, *Rethinking the Unity of Luke and Acts* (Philadelphia: Augsburg/Fortress, forthcoming). Talbert himself has observed "...is it not ironic that as biblical scholars influenced by non-biblical literary criticism begin to emphasize the organic unity of the biblical texts, much recent literary criticism seems intent on denying the very organic unity of literary texts that biblical scholars seek to affirm?" (1988c:138). Evidently Talbert has not yet seen the force of his own comments with regard to the problem of the unity of Luke and Acts.

[73]A number of literary theorists have dealt helpfully with the issue of genre and present options which range from the authorial intention model of E. D. Hirsch (*Validity in Interpretation* [New Haven: Yale University, 1967]) to the post-modern treatment of genre by Adena Rosmarin (*The Power of Genre* [Minneapolis: University of Minnesota, 1985]); see also the article by Mary Gerhart, "Generic Studies: Their Renewed Importance in Religious and Literary Interpretation," *JAAR* 45 (1977) 309-325, and volume 43 of *Semeia* devoted to the study of genre in which Talbert's essay appeared. Talbert has taken a step forward in this direction when he distinguished between those who "use genre for classifications that have no necessary ties to a particular social matrix that is limited by time and space" and those who "speak of genre in the sense of a literary grouping tied to a particular time, place, and cultural milieu" (1988a: 54).

[74]Private correspondence, dated 2 February 1987.

[75]See H. J. Cadbury, *The Book of Acts in History* (London: Adam & Charles Black, 1955); Martin Dibelius, *Studies in the Acts of the Apostles* (ed. Heinrich Greeven and trans. Betram L. Woolf; New York: Charles Scribner's Sons, 1956).

others share this disillusionment: "This volume reflects the widespread loss of confidence in the two-source theory that has occurred during the past fifteen years" (1982d:1). Fitzmyer has challenged the extent of this "loss of confidence": "It is characteristic of a small group of students of the Synoptic relationships, mostly American, a few British, and still fewer Continental scholars."[76] But judging from recent publications and professional meetings, this disenchantment is becoming increasingly widespread in the scholarly community.

Experimentation in new methods of interpreting Luke-Acts by North American interpreters has thus far developed along two parallel, but distinct paths.[77] Some, like Talbert, have emphasized the location of Luke and Acts in their historical and literary milieu. Others, like Robert Tannehill, have emphasized "using selected aspects of narrative criticism to gain new insights into Luke-Acts."[78]

Using Tannehill and Talbert as representative of these distinct perspectives, one may observe the practical differences between the two approaches by noting that Tannehill made ten references to ten non-canonical ancient sources in the entirety of *The Narrative Unity of Luke-Acts*, while Talbert referred twenty-nine times to fifteen ancient non-biblical sources in the first eleven pages alone of *Reading Luke!* Though both eschew the two-source theory and traditional historical criticism, the concerns and interests of these two approaches are obviously different. Tannehill is heavily indebted to modern literary theory, but he does not make use of the comparative materials from the larger literary

---

[76]J. A. Fitzmyer, *The Gospel according to Luke* (AB 28A; Garden City, NY: Doubleday, 1985) 2:x. Fitzmyer goes on to comment (ibid.): "Fortunately, there is much good in Talbert's commentary, which saves it from the fate that it might otherwise encounter."

[77]One ought also mention the recent work by biblical scholars in sociological exegesis (e.g., John Elliott, Bruce Malina, and Jerome Neyrey) and social history (e.g., Wayne Meeks, Abraham Malherbe, and David Balch) which is now being employed in Lukan studies. See, for example, the Luke-Acts project, tentatively entitled, *The Social World of Luke-Acts: Models for Interpretation*, ed. Jerome Neyrey (Peabody, MS: Hendrickson, 1991).

[78]See Robert C. Tannehill, *The Narrative Unity of Luke-Acts: A Literary Interpretation* (Philadelphia: Fortress, 1986) 1:1. In his review of Tannehill (1988c:137), Talbert argued that Tannehill's "approach is closer to the old 'New Criticism' which focused on the text as an organic unity whose meaning was discerned by tracing the interconnections of its parts than it is to the newer 'Narrative Criticism' which focuses on narrator, implied reader, narrative time, etc."

environment of Luke's writings.[79] Talbert has a telling criticism of this type of narrative-critical work:

> Perhaps the question which all those who practice narrative criticism must answer is: What is the extra pay-off from the use of such a method? What can you tell us that we do not already know from other methods? If it is a narrative criticism divorced from a careful use of comparative materials from Greco-Roman antiquity, the answer must be: "Not much" (1988c:138).

Talbert, on the other hand, has fully utilized the Mediterranean sources outside the Bible, but seems uninformed by recent literary criticism. Stephen Moore correctly made the following observation about Talbert's work: "...I find his claim that he investigates Luke 'with a type of redaction criticism heavily influenced by nonbiblical literary criticism' a puzzling one. There are no references to works of nonbiblical literary criticism in this commentary, and no signs that he has any familiarity with the area."[80]

What is needed is a poetics of biblical narrative based on a broad corpus of Greco-Roman, Jewish, and Christian writings of antiquity and informed by the most recent trends in literary criticism.[81] Such a program places such heavy demands on the interpreter that the future of biblical studies may well rest on our ability to work together in collaborative efforts, pooling our resources and expertise.

Is Talbert's method workable? The answer to this question is a qualified "yes." One may and should examine Luke's literary context for

---

[79]And Talbert (1988c:137) is right in suggesting that since Tannehill's "work with the Pronouncement Story Group of SBL guarantees his knowledge of such [comparative] materials, one must chalk their neglect up to his methodology."

[80]Stephen D. Moore, "Narrative Commentaries on the Bible: Context, Roots, and Prospects," *Foundations and Facets Forum* 3,3 (1987) 37. Moore (37-38) goes on to argue that Talbert's method fits better under the rubric of composition criticism than literary criticism. If we are to call what Talbert does "literary criticism," we should take note of the careful nuance provided by Dennis Smith (*JAAR* 53 [1985] 137): "Literary analysis as Talbert practices it however is historically conditioned; that is, he seeks for models for the literary form of Luke from the literature of Luke's day."

[81]I am aware that such a statement makes a great many theoretical assumptions about texts and the locus of meaning of those texts. I am unable to provide a full justification of that statement here, but I hope to do so in a forthcoming commentary on Acts in *The Narrative New Testament Series* (eds. R. Alan Culpepper and Werner Kelber; Sonoma, CA: Polebridge, forthcoming). Meir Sternberg (*The Poetics of Biblical Narrative: Ideological Literature and the Drama of Reading* [Bloomington, IN: Indiana University, 1985]) and Robert W. Funk (*The Poetics of Biblical Narrative* [Sonoma, CA: Polebridge, 1988]) have taken steps in this direction.

parallels which enlighten the literary conventions employed in the narrative. This procedure has and will continue to be applied to biblical texts in fruitful ways. To engage fully in Talbert's method in interpreting Luke-Acts, however, may require accepting Talbert's presuppositions regarding the purpose, architecture, and genre of Luke-Acts—all of which are, as yet, unsettled issues. In that sense, Talbert's method is an idiosyncratic one and may explain why the full model has not been appropriated by other scholars in significant measure.

In fact, one could argue that Talbert himself has not yet explored the full implications of his model, particularly with regard to Acts. Though nothing inherent in the model itself would preclude its application to Acts, the fact remains that such a comprehensive application of the method as is found in *Reading Luke* is missing on Acts. While helpful insights are scattered throughout the book, one is not made "to feel at home in the biblical text itself," as one is in *Reading Luke*. The stated aim of the "Knox Preaching Guides" in which this volume is published, is to "offer realistic, professional assistance for the vital task of proclaiming the word of God" (1984a). The generic form, content, and function of this series may contribute, in part, to the book's shortcomings. In *form*, most volumes in this series rarely exceed 150 pages—they are "designed for quick reference." Talbert's slim volume is no exception, with 105 pages of exposition. In terms of *content*, significant portions of these volumes give sermon ideas or outlines—at least, it is evident that such were the editorial instructions to the contributors. *Acts* follows this pattern, and at the end of each unit, several paragraphs are devoted to sermon ideas which emerge from the text. A conservative guess would categorize approximately seventeen of the 105 pages of Acts as devoted to homiletical issues.

Though the Library of Congress has catalogued these books as biblical exegesis rather than homiletics, the *function* of the series at least is intended to "offer invaluable resources...for renewing and reviving possibilities of biblical preaching today." Such aims are admirable, and certainly Talbert's work fulfills this aim better than some, but the intended purpose of a "preaching guide" is at points in direct conflict with Talbert's stated aim in his Introduction: "The object in reading the two volumes is to enter into the narrative world of the text and listen to what Luke-Acts wants to say about religious reality. It is the Lukan theological point of view that is sought" (1984a:3). Because of the type of literature in which this volume appears, the "Lukan theological point of view" is often shortchanged. Those looking for a companion volume worthy of *Reading Luke* will not likely find it here.

The Usefulness of a Method: Two Test Cases

By Talbert's own standards, the value of a new method is in its ability to assist in dealing with "the problem of an author's thought taken as a whole" and to offer something "useful or new on the passage under consideration" (1989a:309). Based on these criteria, the changes in Talbert's methodology usually, though not always, produced changes in perspective on the text at hand. By observing the way he has applied different methods to the same passage, we may gauge the degree to which Talbert's method does or does not inform his interpretation.

Talbert's treatment of martyrdom in Luke-Acts is a good test case for the ways in which his method informs or shapes his interpretation. In *Luke and the Gnostics*, Talbert argued that Luke parallels the martyr deaths of Jesus and Stephen, not only to accent the unity between Jesus and the church, but also "to defend against the Gnostic denial of the legitimacy of suffering-martyrdom for the Christian" (1966b:82; cf. 76-81).

In *Literary Patterns*, Talbert viewed the parallels between the deaths of Jesus and Stephen as part of the larger "correspondences between the career of Jesus in the Third Gospel and the life of the apostolic church in Acts..." (1974d:99). Since the biography of the ancient philosopher tried to link the philosopher with his successors, Talbert concluded that by connecting the founder, Jesus, with his followers, the disciples, Luke had employed these correspondences to "contribute to the overall Lucan appropriation of the Hellenistic image of the philosopher..." (1974d:99). Finally, in *Reading Luke*, Talbert argued: "Any appreciation for the Lukan understanding of Jesus' martyrdom must come from a knowledge of pagan, Jewish, and early Christian attitudes toward martyrdom" (1982d:221; see also 1983a). He then marshalled examples from these various sources to argue that Jesus' death legitimated his profession (1982d:221-224). He also drew parallels with the death of Stephen, slightly different from those noticed before: "This legitimation is evidenced in the conversion of the criminal on the cross: Jesus' martyrdom had such evangelistic benefits (cf. Acts 8:1, 4; 11:19ff. for the evangelistic benefits of Stephen's martyrdom)" (1982d:224).[82]

These passages demonstrate that for Talbert, a change in method does entail a change in interpretation. Such changes in perspective are expected. What is surprising are the places where the method yields little that is new. Below is printed one example where the method has changed, but little is altered in the material argument. Column 1 is taken from a 1967 redaction-critical analysis of Luke 4:31-9:50. Column 2 is from *Reading Luke* which disavows any source theory:

In Luke 7:1-10 we find a Q tradition (cf. Matthew 8:5-13) to which the Evangelist has added vv. 3-6a. Thus, we have a story of a pious centurion who sends others to secure assistance for him. The point of the tradition as it stands here is the centurion's faith as contrasted with Israel's lack of faith (v. 9) (1967d:491-92).

In Luke 7:1-10 is tradition also found in Matt 8:5-13. In Luke's version, vss. 3-6a are distinctive. Thereby it becomes a story of a pious centurion who sends others to secure assistance for him. The point of the tradition as it stands in Luke is the centurion's faith as contrasted with Israel's lack of faith (vs. 9) (1982d:53).

The removal of the reference to "Q" in *Reading Luke* has the cosmetic effect of ignoring problematic source theories. Pragmatically though, Talbert drew conclusions regarding the meaning of Luke 7:1-10 based on Luke's redaction of traditional material, rather than on his conformity to or deviance from literary conventions of contemporary Greco-Roman parallels. Such "lapses" are infrequent, but occur often enough to question how much previous conclusions based on intensive redaction-critical analysis have shaped Talbert's interpretation of certain passages, and how much "new" his new interpretive method really discovers.

Conclusion

Recently, Talbert predicted: "A new methodology seems likely to emerge which...will be able to come to terms with the unity of Lucan thought" (1989a:311). Ironically, the real difficulty with Talbert's method

---

[82]Some of these earlier emphases on martyrdom are present in *Reading Luke*, but by no means do they constitute the major focus of his comments (see 1982d:223; 225).

of interpretation has been the failure to incorporate Acts in a convincing way into his interpretive model. This problem has plagued his methodological explorations throughout his career. The "silence of Acts" was the weakest link in the argument that the purpose of Luke-Acts was to serve as an apologetic against Gnosticism. One of the severest criticisms lodged against Talbert's genre studies was the way Acts so poorly fit the biographical genre. Finally, the most recent method of close reading and observing parallels is certainly as applicable to the text of Acts as to Luke, but the point remains that Talbert has yet to do so in a thorough-going way.[83]

Over a decade ago, Talbert closed his insightful survey of Lukan studies with these words: "At present, widespread agreement is difficult to find, except on the point that Conzelmann's synthesis is inadequate. Until the scholarly community can agree on a proper procedure for studying Luke-Acts, there is little likelihood that another synthesis will fare any better" (1976c:395). More recently, Talbert has been somewhat more optimistic: "It is still too early to see the final shape of a methodology that will supersede redaction criticism. It is not unlikely, however, that it will combine elements of modern literary criticism, genre criticism, and the type of comparative study now being done in Acts" (1989a:310). That Talbert has significantly shaped this new method is clear; that his own particular method is unlikely to emerge as the one which replaces redaction criticism is equally obvious. Nonetheless, the assessment of *Literary Patterns* by Norman Petersen still rings true for Talbert's scholarly endeavors as a whole:

> We are therefore left with the need for a more comprehensive literary model than the one proposed by Talbert....Although Talbert has prematurely abandoned the search for such a model, he can nonetheless take comfort in knowing that his efforts to rectify the eclipse of biblical narrative have been as suggestive in their failures as they have been in their successes. At this point in critical time, that is no little achievement.[84]

In closing, we should remember that Talbert's many accomplishments have not been limited to the academic guild. His vocation as a scholar and his confessional commitments are two sides of

---

[83]Failure to deal with the "unity of Lukan thought" may reflect not so much Talbert's personal shortcoming as much as it underscores a problem shared by the larger scholarly community, the futility of implementing that to which we have all paid lip service, the unity of Luke-Acts. See Parsons and Pervo, *Rethinking the Unity of Luke and Acts*.

[84]Petersen, 457-58.

the same coin. In "Biblical Criticism's Role," Talbert reflected on the various roles of the scholar who relates to a confessional community: "Some scholars do pioneer research and writing and shape the disciplines of ancient Near Eastern and early Christian studies. Other scholars take what has been discovered by the pioneers and popularize it for the more general reader, especially within the church. Both serve the church through the exercise of their gifts of teaching" (1987g:70-71).[85] For nearly twenty-five years, Charles Talbert has managed to facilitate the meeting of Athens and Jerusalem (see 1981g). As a theologian of the church, he has offered a healthy corrective for those in his own confessional community whose dogmatism has held a stranglehold on their scriptures. As a world-renowned NT scholar, he has provided a creative impulse in the academic community of the Society of Biblical Literature. He has provided new perspectives on the texts of Luke and Acts and the methods used to understand their religious message. His own methodological pilgrimage has both mirrored and shaped the quest of these larger communities, providing new insights in both success and failure. As one of a growing number of younger scholars who have profited both from the generous benefaction of Talbert the scholar and from the genuine piety of Talbert the churchman, may I return to Charles Talbert a blessing he often bestows upon his colleagues: "May his tribe be legion!"[86]

---

[85]One could make the argument that Talbert has fulfilled both these roles. In his first twenty years or so Talbert spent his energies attempting to shape the discipline of NT (particularly Lukan) studies, and recently he has given more time writing for the life of the church.

[86]A "Talbertian" blessing found in several recent reviews (cf. 1982c:22; 1983c:23).

APPENDIX ONE:
PROGRAM OF THE SBL LUKE-ACTS GROUP
1974-78

1974   Consultation on the Acts of the Apostles
Charles H. Talbert, Wake Forest University, Convener

A Critique of Richard F. Zehnle's Peter's Pentecost Discourse
Karl Paul Donfried, Smith College

A Spectrum of Opinion on the Value of Acts as a Source for the
Study   of Paul: Tradition and Redaction in the Pauline Portions of Acts
A. J. Matill, Jr., Winebrenner Theological Seminary

The Title Kurios *in Luke-Acts*
Donald L. Jones, University of South Carolina

1975   SBL/Luke-Acts Group
Charles H. Talbert, Wake Forest University, Chair

Luke's Method in the Annunciation Narratives of Chapter One
Raymond E. Brown, Union Theological Seminary, New York

A Critical Review of C. H. Talbert, Literary Patterns, Theological
Themes and the Genre of Luke-Acts
Gerhard Krodel, Lutheran Theological Seminary at
Philadelphia

A Critique of J. Jervell, Luke and the People of God
Mary Moscato, College of St. Teresa

The Prologues of Luke-Acts and the "We" Passages in their Relation to the Tendency of the Author
Schuyler Brown, General Theological Seminary

Anti-Jewish/Pro-Roman Sentiments in Luke-Acts
Karl Paul Donfried, Smith College

The Significance of the Stephen Episode in Acts
T. C. Smith, Furman University

1976   SBL/Luke-Acts Group
Charles H. Talbert, Wake Forest University, Chair

Salvation to and from Zion: The Lukan Birth Narrative in Tradition and Redaction
Lloyd Gaston, Vancouver School of Theology

The Lukan Sitz im Leben: *Methodology and Prospects*
Robert J. Karris, Catholic Theological Union

Panel Discussion: *Semitisms in Luke-Acts*
Fred L. Horton, Wake Forest University
Jerome D. Quinn, St. Paul Seminary

By Land and by Sea: A Study in Acts 13-28
Vernon K. Robbins, University of Illinois at Urbana

The Picture of Paul in Acts and the Pastorals
S. G. Wilson, Carelton University

The Accounts of Paul's Conversion in Acts
P. Boyd Mather, Dubuque Theological Seminary

1977   SBL/Luke-Acts Group
Charles H. Talbert, Wake Forest University, Chair

Establishing a Text for Luke-Acts
Frank Stagg, Southern Baptist Theological Seminary

Some Aspects of Prayer in Luke-Acts
Allison Trites, Acadia Divinity College

Weeping for Jerusalem: Luke 10:41-44 as vaticinium post e ventum
David L. Tiede, Luther Theological Seminary

Karl P. Donfried, Smith College, presiding

Acts 3:19-26 as a Test of the Role of Eschatology in Lukan Christology
William S. Kurz, Marquette University

The Defense Speeches of Paul in Acts
Frederick Veltman, Pacific Union College

Some Dead Ends in Lukan Research
Charles H. Talbert, Wake Forest University

1978   SBL/Luke-Acts Group
Charles H. Talbert, Wake Forest University, Chair
Karl P. Donfried, Smith College, presiding

Prefaces in Greco-Roman Biography and Luke-Acts
Vernon K. Robbins, University of Illinois, Urbana-Champaign

An Interpretation of Acts 7:35-37: From the Perspective of Major Themes in Luke-Acts
E. Jane Via, University of San Diego

The Circumferential Speeches of Luke-Acts: Patterns and Purpose
Donald R. Miesner, Concordia College

Panel Discussion: *New Directions for Lukan Research*
P. Boyd Mather, The Schools of Theology in Dubuque
Horst R. Moehring, Brown University
Stephen G. Wilson, Carleton University

1979   SBL/Luke-Acts Seminar
Charles H. Talbert, Wake Forest University, Chair

Windows and Mirrors: Literary Criticism and Luke's Sitz im Leben
Robert J. Karris, Catholic Theological Union

Luke, Josephus and Rome: A Comparative Approach to the Lukan
Sitz im Leben
Benjamin J. Hubbard, University of Waterloo, St. Jerome's
College

The Problem of Food in Acts
Joseph B. Tyson, Southern Methodist University

On Finding the Lukan Community: A Cautious Cautionary Essay
Luke T. Johnson, Yale Divinity School

1980   SBL/Luke-Acts Seminar
Charles H. Talbert, Wake Forest University, Chair

Luke-Acts and the Relationship between the Church and Judaism
David M. Scholer, Gordon-Conwell Theological Seminary

Law in Luke-Acts
Stephen G. Wilson, Carleton University

The Divine Purpose: The Jews and the Gentile Mission (Acts 15)
Earl Richard, Somerville, Massachusetts

Luke-Acts and Historiography in the Greek Bible
William S. Kurz, Marquette University

1981   SBL/Luke-Acts Seminar
Charles H. Talbert, Wake Forest University, Presiding

Laudation Stories in the Gospel of Luke and Plutarch's Alexander
Vernon K. Robbins, University of Illinois at Urbana-
Champaign

Luke-Acts and the Ancient Novel
Susan Praeder, Boston College

The Endangered Benefactor in Luke-Acts
Frederick W. Danker, Christ Seminary-Seminex

1982   SBL/Luke-Acts Seminar
Charles H. Talbert, Wake Forest University, Presiding
Theme: *Christology and Soteriology in Luke-Acts*

The Title Pais in *Luke-Acts*
Donald L. Jones, University of South Carolina

The Salvation of the Jews in Luke-Acts
Jack T. Sanders, University of Oregon

Does Luke Make a Soteriological Statement in Acts 20:28?
Waldemar Schmeichel, Kalamazoo College

*Jesus and the "Wilderness Generation": The Death of the Prophet
Like Moses According to Luke*
David P. Moessner, Basel, Switzerland

1983   SBL/Luke-Acts Seminar
Joseph B. Tyson, Southern Methodist University, Presiding

Paul and the Pattern of the Prophet Like Moses in Acts 3:45
David P. Moessner, Louisiana State University

The Lukan Writer's Stories about the Call of Paul
Norman A. Beck, Texas Lutheran College

The Paulusbild *in the Trial of Paul in Acts*
William R. Long, Reed College

Paul in Acts as martus *and* hupertos
Boyd Mather, The Schools of Theology in Dubuque

Miracle Worker and Missionary: Paul in the Acts of the Apostles
Susan Praeder, Boston College

Paul in Luke-Acts: The Savior Who Is Present
Glenn R. Jacobson, Lewisburg, Pennsylvania

TALBERT'S NEW PERSPECTIVES ON LUKE-ACTS: THE ABC'S OF ANCIENT LIVES

J. Bradley Chance

Introduction

In the preceding essay, Mikeal Parsons has offered an excellent survey of the rich contributions which Charles Talbert has made to the study of Luke-Acts. In addition, he raised helpful questions which might guide the guild as it continues in its study of these documents. Two of the most intriguing are the suggestion that Luke and Acts represent different genres (See Parsons, 163-64 above) and the fruitfulness of blending modern literary critical theory with Talbert's approach to literary studies, which focuses on the reading of Luke-Acts in the context of the literature of antiquity (See Parsons, 165-66 above). Each of these issues lies close to the center of what has concerned Talbert throughout his career: how to read a text.

The clarity and breadth of Parsons' essay allow me the luxury of presenting an examination of Talbert's contributions which is narrower in its focus and more modest in its scope. Certainly a most significant aspect of Talbert's agenda for reading Luke-Acts has been his study of genre. Genre offers the one key of literacy which allows the interpreter to approach a text holistically and to unlock "at least a primary dimension of the meaning of the individual text as a whole" (1988a:53; cf. 1989:310).

Talbert argues that Luke-Acts follows a pattern of ancient lives of philosophers in which part (a) describes the "life" of the founder of a school (= Luke) and part (b) offers information concerning the successors of this founder (= Acts). Talbert has focused much attention on the existence of such a pattern in a number of the lives of Diogenes Laertius'

Lives of Eminent Philosophers. He summarizes well his thesis in his most recent discussion of gospel genre:

> Another social function of didactic biographies in antiquity seems to be to indicate where the true tradition is in the present.... This is found first of all in "lives" of founders of philosophical schools that contained within themselves not only a life of the founder but also a list or a brief narrative of his successors and selected other disciples, an (a+b) form. In Diogenes Laertius certain "lives" of philosophers reflect this pattern. There is (a) the life of the founder, followed by (b) a brief list or narrative of his successors and selected other disciples, followed by (c) an extensive statement of the teaching of the philosopher....Examination of Laertius' references to the sources for these "lives" shows that the material in (c) comes from a different origin than that in (a+b). This permits the inference that Laertius took over individual biographies that were written in terms of the (a+b) pattern and added the (c) component himself (1988a:58).

Such an inference is supported by evidence, found outside of Laertius and to which I shall refer below, pointing to the existence of *individual* lives which followed such a pattern. Talbert concludes, "Taken together, this evidence establishes the existence of individual 'lives' of founders of philosophical schools that contained within themselves not only the biography of the founder, but also a narrative, however brief, about his successors and selected other disciples" (1988a:59). Two things must be noted in order to offer a fair assessment of Talbert's case. First, Talbert is interested in comparing Luke-Acts with "lives" of founders of philosophical schools, not simply "philosophers" in general. Hence, the observation offered by Aune, and echoed by Parsons in the preceding essay, that in Laertius "only six of eighty-two lives have this [a+b+c] pattern"[1] is *not* the devastating criticism it appears to be at first glance. The founders upon whom Talbert focuses are Aristippus, Plato, Aristotle, Antisthenes, Zeno, Pythagoras, and Epicurus (1974d:125). He also refers in *Literary Patterns* to Socrates (1974d:131).

Second, Talbert is more interested in the sources which lay behind Laertius than in Laertius himself. He fully recognizes that Laertius is a *collection* of lives, whereas Luke-Acts is an *individual* life (Jesus, plus successors). "It is a fact," Talbert notes, "that biographies of philosophers in antiquity developed in two directions: one, that of individual biographies, the other, that of collections of Lives. Luke-Acts obviously belongs to one, Laertius to the other. In both cases, however,

---

[1]David E. Aune, *The New Testament in Its Literary Environment*, Library of Early Christianity (ed. Wayne A. Meeks; Philadelphia: Westminster Press, 1987) 79, and Parsons, 162, above.

the biography could, and often did, contain both the life of the founder and a succession list or narrative" (1974d:130). Hence, the (a+b) pattern was *not* dependent upon the "collections" sub-genre.[2] Talbert believes that *behind* Laertius there existed sources of "individual" lives which followed the (a+b) pattern. It is *this*, the individual life, following the (a+b) pattern, *independent* of any collection's sub-genre, to which Luke-Acts is comparable.

In the next section of this essay, I shall examine the sources referred to by Laertius to determine to what extent we can find evidence for individual lives which—"apart from a collection of...Lives," to quote Talbert (1974d:131)—contained the (a+b) pattern of biography. Getting behind Laertius to his sources is tedious business. He cites more than 200 ancients, covering a host of genres, only a fraction of which he probably actually used.[3] Our purpose, however, is not to uncover the actual sources used by Laertius, but to attempt to uncover the existence of an (a+b) pattern in the biographical sources which preceded Laertius, whether or not he actually looked at such materials. Even if Laertius did "lift" from a source actually before him references to other biographical materials,[4] such information can still offer clues concerning the content and structure of these ante-Laertian lives. Hence, in the following discussion, when I make reference to one of Laertius' biographical sources, I am not implying that such a life was used by Laertius, but only referring to a life which preceded him, independent of any judgment of sources actually consulted by him.

I shall also focus my attention, as does Talbert, on selected "founders." Talbert notes seven, as mentioned above, in addition to the reference he makes to Socrates. I shall add Pyrrho to this list since Laertius does view him as the founder of the Skeptical school, though he does acknowledge debate on this matter,[5] and, like most of the other founders examined by Talbert, Pyrrho's life too follows the (a+b+c) pattern.[6]

---

[2]"A single Life of a philosopher with a succession list or narrative could exist apart from a collection of such Lives" (1974d: 131).

[3]See the introduction to Diogenes Laertius, *Lives of Eminent Philosophers*, LCL, 1.xv-xxx.

[4]A common practice among writers of antiquity. So Kurt von Fritz, *Pythagorean Politics in Southern Italy: An Analysis of the Sources* (New York: Columbia University Press, 1940) 22.

[5]See Laertius, 9.70-73.

[6]We could, perhaps, look at other "founders," e.g., the founders of the ten ethical schools to whom Laertius refers in 1.19 who, in addition to Plato,

184   *J. Bradley Chance*

The (A+B) Pattern in Individual Ante-Laertian Lives

Socrates. (2.18-47). This life follows the (a) [2.18-46] + (b) [2.47] pattern. It must first be noted that Laertius cites no specific source for the list of successors, save for a reference to "the traditional list" (*ton de pheromenon*). One could infer from this that knowledge of successors could have existed in the sphere of general knowledge, and need not be derived from a particular written source tied to the preceding life. Second, 2.47 shows signs of composition by Laertius himself, for he uses this brief paragraph to outline the order of the following presentations. Third, though Laertius cites no specific sources for this succession list, he does cite four biographical sources within the "life" section, none of which is an "individual" life.[7] Hence, even if we should grant that the succession list of 2.47 was drawn from one or more of the biographical sources cited by Laertius, we would have to conclude that such a list came from a life of Socrates found within a *collection* of lives. Evidence for an independent "Life of Socrates" consisting of an (a+b) pattern is not present.

Aristippus (2.65-104). This life follows the (a) [2.65-85a] + (b) [2.85b-86a] + (c) [2.86b-104] pattern. The (c) component is not only a summary of doctrine, but a summary centering around specific followers of Aristippus, namely Hegesias (2.93-96), Anniceris (2.96,97), and Theodorus (2.97-99). Here we find some rather detailed discussion of followers of the founder *within* the life of the founder itself, and not within their own separate "lives" as Laertius generally dealt with

---

Aristippus, Aristotle, Zeno, and Epicurus, include Lacydes (4.59-61), Phaedo (2.105), Euclides of Megara (2.106-112), Menedemus of Eretria (2.125b-144), and Clitomachus of Carthage. He devotes a life to all but the last and follows the (a+b) pattern for all but Menedemus. In addition other (a+b) lives include Theophrastus (5.36-57), Metrocles (6.94-95), Timon (9.109-116), and perhaps Stilpo (2.113-120) which offers no list of successors but a list of pupils he drew away from other schools (2.113-14a). Deference to space and the concern to be illustrative with respect to patterns, not exhaustive with respect to all data, justify the narrower focus.

[7]Hermippus of Smyrna (2.38), Satyrus (2.26), Antisthenes of Rhodes (2.39), and Alexander Polyhistor (2.19). In the case of the first two, Laertius does not cite the specific works to which he was referring, but while we know that Hermippus and Satyrus did compose collections of "Lives" (see 5.2 and 6.80, respectively), we have no indication from Laertius that either composed an individual "Life of Socrates." With respect to Antisthenes and Alexander Polyhistor, Laertius specifically states that the reference to them came from their respective *Successions of Philosophers.*

successors. At first glance, this is fertile ground for comparison with Luke-Acts, where *detailed* discussion of Jesus' successors is part of the larger "life" of Jesus. If, however, we follow Talbert's own hypothesis that the (c) component of the (a+b+c) pattern derives from sources other than those employed by Laertius for the (a+b) components and that *Laertius* is responsible for adding the (c) component, then we must conclude that Laertius, and not his sources, is responsible for this detailed discussion of Aristippus' followers *within* the "Life of Aristippus." If so, then the fertile ground for comparison becomes shallow and rocky.

One comment should be made, however, before rushing to this conclusion. Laertius notes two biographical sources used within the (c) segment, both in reference to Theodorus.[8] Laertius' discussion of Theodorus is of a different quality than that of Hegesias and Anniceris, being more gossipy and anecdotal. We can deduce from the character of this section and the explicit reference to *biographical* sources that Laertius drew from "lives" (as opposed to handbooks or synopses of philosophical doctrines) for his discussion of Theodorus. The question then is whether this material on Theodorus came to Laertius incorporated *within* a life of Aristippus, or as a separate life of Theodorus. There is simply no evidence for the former, so we would be begging the question not to conclude that it was Laertius himself who appended this material on Theodorus to his "Life of Aristippus." Laertius' "Life of Aristippus" offers no evidence that *detailed* discussion of Aristippus' followers was included within an ante-Laertian "Life of Aristippus."

Is there evidence, however, that Laertius employed an individual, discrete life of Aristippus whence came, at least, the *list* of successors? As in the case of Socrates, Laertius mentions no specific source for his list of successors (see 2.85b-86a). If one *assumes* that such a list of successors would make best sense only if appended to a preceding life, one can perhaps infer that the (b) component was probably preceded by some sort of (a) component in Laertius' sources. However, the two biographical sources cited by Laertius for his "Life of Aristippus" are both *collections* of "lives."[9] Hence, we have no evidence, based on what

---

[8]Antisthenes (*Successions of Philosophers*, see 2.98) and Amphicrates (*Upon Illustrious Men*, see 2.101).

[9]Sotion, *Successions*, see 2.75, 85 and Diocles of Magnesis, *Lives*, see 2.82. He also refers to Phanias of Eresus in 2.65. No specific text is cited here, but we know he wrote a work entitled *On the Socratics*, see 6.8.

Laertius tells us, that he drew upon any *individual* life of Aristippus. If Laertius found the (a+b) pattern in his sources, such sources were collections of lives, not an individual life.

Plato (3.1-109). This life follows the (a) [3.1-45] + (b) [3.46-47a] + (c) [3.47b-109] pattern. Of the many lives noted by Laertius, only that of Aristoxenus, was an individual life of Plato.[10] Based on what Laertius tells us (see 3.8), we can draw no conclusions concerning its structure. Unlike the lists of successors examined thus far, Laertius does cite some specific sources for his list of Plato's successors, of which only Dicaearchus (*Lives*) and Sabinus (*Materials for Criticism*, citing Mnesistratus of Thasos) are of real relevance.[11] The reference to Sabinus indicates that materials other than "lives" offered names of successors, which should caution us against always assuming that references to a successor of a certain philosopher must be preceded by a "life" of the philosopher. Dicaearchus is the only source cited by Laertius in both the "life" (3.4, 38) and the "list of successors" (3.46) of Plato. Note, however, that this is not an individual life of Plato—it is part of a collection of lives, as evidenced not only by the title, but the fact that Dicaearchus also wrote on Pythagoras (see 8.40). Laertius' "Life of Plato" offers no evidence that Laertius made use of an *individual* life of Plato which followed the (a+b) pattern.

Aristotle (5.1-35). This loosely follows the (a) [5.1-35a] + (b) [5.35b] pattern, if we allow a brief reference to Aristotle's having many disciples, with special note of Theophrastus, to constitute the (b) component. Further, one finds *within* the life a summary of teachings, perhaps allowing for an (a+c+b) pattern.[12] Laertius cites three biographical sources in "Aristotle," two of which are from collections of lives, one of which, Hermippus' *On Aristotle*, offers an individual biography.[13] Ingemar Düring has proposed a cautious reconstruction of

---

[10]Hermippus (3.2, no specific source cited, but presumably *Lives*, cf. 5.2), Anaxilaïdes (*On Philosophers*, see 3.2), Alexander Polyhistor (*Successions of Philosophers*, see 3.4, 5), Dicaearchus (*Lives*, Bk 1, see 3.4, 38), Timotheus the Athenian (*Lives*, see 3.5), Satyrus (presumably *Lives*, cf. 6.80, see 3.9), Idomeneus (presumably *On the Socratics*, cf. 2.20, see 3.36), and Aristoxenus (3.8, no specific source cited but presumably *Life of Plato*, cf. 5.35).

[11]Laertius cites other sources for successors, but offers no clue as to the character of such sources: Chamaeleon (3.46, no specific source given), Polemo (3.47, no specific source given).

[12]Talbert notes this in 1974d: 127.

[13]Hermippus' *On Aristotle* (5.1) and *Lives* (5.2) and Timotheus the Athenian's *Lives* (5.1).

Hermippus' life of Aristotle.[14] He concludes that this biography did contain a notification that Aristotle was the disciple of Plato, and he also offered an anecdote concerning the succession of Theodorus. If one will grant a single anecdote concerning succession sufficient to view Hermippus' life as (a+b) and grant the accuracy of Düring's reconstruction (which I am not competent to challenge), then we do find here a concrete example of an individual life which, as part of the life of the founder, offered notification of the founder's successor.

Antisthenes (6.1-19). We should perhaps diagram this life as (a | | b), for the brief reference to successors is found not at the end, but prior to the list of Antisthenes' writings and record of his death. Laertius credits Antisthenes for laying the foundation for Cynicism-Stoicism (6.14-15), noting specifically Diogenes', Crates', and Zeno's indebtedness to him. He cites no sources for this information of the (b) component. Laertius cites three biographical sources within the (a) component of his "Life of Antisthenes," all of which are collections of lives, not individual biographies.[15] The existence of an (a+b) (or [a | | b]) biographical pattern in an individual life finds no confirmation in the sources cited by Laertius.

Zeno (7.1-160a). This life follows the (a) [7.1-35] + (b) [7.36-38a] + (c) [7.38b-160a] pattern. Laertius cites three biographical sources for this life, one, probably two, of which were individual lives.[16] In addition, he makes two references to Hippobotus (7.25, 38), possibly referring either to his *On Philosophical Sects* (cf. 1.19) or *On the Sages* (cf. 1.42). The title of the former work implies more of a didactic than biographical character. Laertius notes no sources for his list of successors, save for Hippobotus (7.38), who was the source for a portion of Laertius' list. If Laertius is referring to Hippobotus' didactic work, evidence is offered once again (cf. above our discussion of Sabinus under Plato) that sources other than "lives" provided a discussion of a teacher's successors. If Laertius is referring to Hippobotus' *On the Sages*, then this reference to successors was found in a collection of lives, not an individual life. If we

---

[14]Ingemar Düring, *Aristotle in the Ancient Biographical Tradition*, Studia Graeca et Latina Gothoburgensia 5 (Göteborg: Göteborgs Universitets Årsskrift, 1957) 464-67.

[15]Hermippus (6.2, no specific source given but presumably *Lives*, cf. 5.2), Sosicrates of Rhodes (*Successions of Philosophers*, see 6.13), and Diocles of Magnesia (6.12, 13, no specific source given but presumably *Lives*, cf. 2.54).

[16]Apollonius of Tyre (*On Zeno*, cf. 7.2, see 7.1, 2, 6, 24, 28), Antigonus of Carystus (no specific source given, but Laertius did know that Antigonus had composed a *Life of Zeno*, cf. 3.66, see 7.12), and Timotheus of Athens (*Lives*, see 7.1).

grant that the successors not specifically drawn from Hippobotus came possibly from Laertius' other biographical sources, then the *individual* lives of Zeno by Antigonus and Apollonius *may* have included within them a list of successors. This, however, is the most we can say on the basis of what Laertius tells us.

Talbert calls to our attention the evidence from Herculaneum papyrus 1018 (1974d:133; 1988a:58). This lengthy papyrus does offer a discussion of Zeno and a number of his followers, and even disciples of certain followers.[17] This work on Zeno is probably a fragment from Philodemus' *Successions*, a work which Laertius does cite, but only with respect to his "Life of Epicurus" (10.3). Even if Laertius did not use this work in his "Life of Zeno," it does offer evidence of a "life" which includes within itself some extensive discussion of the "founder's" followers. Note, however, that Philodemus' work was a "collection" of lives, not an individual life.

Pythagoras (8.1-50). Talbert outlines this life according to the (a) [8.1-45a] + (b) [8.45b-46a] + (c) [8.48-50] pattern. The bulk of the (c) component consists of a brief allusion to Pythagoras' work in mathematics and physics and a brief letter from Pythagoras to Anaximenes. The letter actually tells us nothing of Pythagoras' teachings. The bulk of the teachings material is actually found within the "life" section (8.25-35), which is drawn from "the Pythagorean memoirs" which Laertius lifted from Alexander's *Successions of Philosophers* (8.25). The fact that such a detailed summary of teachings was found by Laertius in Alexander's collection of "lives" indicates that at least in this instance Talbert's generalization that the (c) component of the life, detailing the "teachings of the school," was drawn from sources other than those used by Laertius for the "life and successors" components is not accurate. Laertius, apparently, did not always add the "summary of teachings" section himself based on other, non-biographical, sources.

In addition to Alexander, Laertius cites a number of other biographical sources. One of these sources, Hermippus, was an *individual* life; another, Aristoxenus, *might* have been. The remaining were collections of lives.[18] Significantly, Laertius' brief list of the end of

---

[17]See Augustus Traversa, *Index Stoicorum Herculanensis* (Genova: Istituto di Filologia Classica, 1952).

[18]Hermippus of Smyrna (*On Pythagoras*, see 8.1, 10, 40, 41), Satyrus (8.40, 44[?], lifted from Heraclides' *Epitome of Satyrus*, who wrote a collection of *Lives*, cf. 8.53), Sosicrates (*Successions*, see 8.8), Aristoxenus (8.1, 20, cf. 46 [?], *On Pythagoras and His School* [?], cf. 1.118, or *Rules of Pedagogy* (*paideutikon nomon*) [?], cf.

the Pythagorean line *implies* that Aristoxenus is the source.[19] Granting that some literary source of Aristoxenus did contain the list of Pythagoreans, and granting the possibility that the source was Aristoxenus' *On Pythagoras and His School*, then we may have evidence here of an *individual* life of Pythagoras which contained the (b) component of the (a+b) pattern. The title of the work, *Pythagoras and His School*, if indeed this was the work to which Laertius intends to refer, certainly points to the appropriateness of such a list. It needs to be noted, however, that the only source by Aristoxenus which Laertius actually cites *within* his "Life of Pythagoras" is *Rules of Pedagogy* (8.16), a work on Pythagoreanism, but not a "life." Hence, this non-biographical source may have been Laertius' source for this list, offering, once again, evidence that a list of successors need not be preceded by a "life."

Finally, it should be noted that even if *Pythagoras and His School* was not the source to which Laertius was referring in his "Life of Pythagoras," this work, as reconstructed by J. Mewaldt "contained a biography of Pythagoras and a history of the Pythagoreans in chronological order."[20] Talbert infers from this description of the work that it too followed the (a+b) biographical form (1988a:58). Hence, while we may not have any direct evidence that Laertius referred to this specific source of Aristoxenus in his "Life of Pythagoras," there did appear to exist a life by Aristoxenus which included within itself a discussion of Pythagoras' followers.

Pyrrho (9.61-108). The life follows the (a) [9.61-69a] + (b) [9.69b-73] + (c) [9.74-108] pattern. Laertius cites three biographical sources, one of

---

8.16), Antiphon (*On Men of Outstanding Merit*, see 8.3), Aristippus (*On the Physicists*, see 8.21), "Aristotle" (spurious) (*On the Pythagoreans*, see 8.34, 36), and Sotion (8.7, lifted from Heraclides' *Epitome of Sotion*).

[19]"For the last of the Pythagoreans, whom Aristoxenus in his time saw, were Xenophilus from the Thracian Chalcidice, Phanton of Phlius, and Echecrates, Diocles and Polymnastus, also of Phlius, who were pupils of Philolaus and Eurytus of Tarentum" (Laertius, 8.46 [LCL]). Fritz states that "there can be scarcely any doubt that this fact was mentioned by Aristoxenos [sic] himself." But Fritz offers no speculation regarding in which of the four works on Pythagoreanism by Aristoxenus such mention would have been made. See *Pythagorean Politics in Southern Italy*, 21.

[20]*De Aristoxeni Pythagoricis sententiis et vita Pythagorica* (Disset., Berlin, 1904) cited from Fritz, ibid., 22 n. 3.

which was Antigonus' *On Pyrrho*.[21] Laertius lists no sources for the successors of Pyrrho. Interestingly, Hicks argues that Laertius' primary source for the "life" [(a)] portion of his biography was Antigonus' individual life *On Pyrrho*. However, Hicks believes Laertius' use of Antigonus concludes with 9.67, *before* the discussion of successors. Furthermore, he believes the list to be in some way connected with the summary of Skeptical doctrine found in 9.74-108 *and* the concluding list of Skeptical successors which is found at the end of the "Life of Timon" (9.115-116).[22] If this is the case, then Laertius used a source which could be diagramed, using Talbert's method, as (b+c+b´), with Laertius' discussion of Timon's life inserted between the (c) and (b´) components. This is all most tentative, but it might suggest, once again, the possibility that a list of pupils of a certain school did not have to be preceded by a life of the founder of said school. If we follow Hicks, then we would have to conclude that *none* of Laertius' biographical sources, including even the collections he cited, provided him with an (a+b) pattern.

   Epicurus (10.1-154). This life follows the (a) [10.1-22a] + (b) [10.22b-26] + (c) [10.29-154] pattern. A reference to Epicurus' prolific writing activity plus a select bibliography are found between (b) and (c) (10.27-28). Laertius cites eight biographical sources within the "life" section of Epicurus, two of which are individual lives,[23] one of which is polemical,[24] and one which apparently focuses on a portion of Epicurus' life in a desultory fashion.[25] In addition, he cites four collections of lives.[26] No sources are listed for the successors, so we cannot determine whether the individual lives, the collections of lives, or other sources provided Laertius with this information.

   It is interesting to note that we find more in the (b) segment than a mere list; we actually find "mini-lives" of three of Epicurus' followers. In the case of Metrodorus (10.22b-24a) we find a record of his parents, hometown, death, and a list of his writings. Laertius' statement

---

[21]Antigonus of Carystus (*On Pyrrho*, see 9.62), Alexander Polyhistor (*Successions*, see 9.61), and Diocles of Magnesis (9.61, 65, no specific source cited but presumably *Lives*, cf. 2.54).

[22]Laertius, *Lives*, LCL 2.480 n. c.

[23]Apollodorus the Epicurean, *Life of Epicurus*, see 10.2, 13; Ariston, *Life of Epicurus*, see 10.14.

[24]Theodorus, *Against Epicurus*, see 10.5.

[25]Herodotus, *On the Training of Epicurus as a Cadet*, see 10.5.

[26]Sotion (*Successions*, from Heraclides' *Epitome*, 10.1); Hermippus (no source cited but presumably *Lives*, cf. 5.2 or *On the Sages*, cf. 8.88, see 10.2, 15); Philodemus (*On Philosophers* [= *Successions*], 10.3); Diocles of Magnesia (*Epitome of Philosophers*, 10.11, 12).

concerning Polyaenus (10.24b) offers a record of his father, place of citizenship, and a statement concerning his good character. Concerning Hermarchus (10.24b-25) we have a record of his father, place of citizenship, list of writings, and his death. There is also some brief discussion of other followers. This material, as brief as it is, does offer evidence that *within* the biography of a founder we can find material concerning successors which goes beyond a mere list.

Unfortunately, we cannot conclude that the *individual* lives cited by Laertius, or even the collections, structured their presentations of Epicurus in this manner. For all we know, Laertius himself, knowing that he intended to conclude his work with the "Life of Epicurus," summarized material relating to Epicurus' successors which he found as *separate lives* in his sources and placed it within his "Life of Epicurus." This is sheer guesswork on my part, but no more of a guess than saying that Laertius' sources included this rather detailed material on Epicurus' successors *within* the life of Epicurus.

Conclusions. "Examination of Laertius' references to the sources for these 'lives' shows that the material in (c) comes from a different origin than that in (a+b). This permits the inference that Laertius took over individual biographies that were written in terms of the (a+b) pattern and added the (c) component himself" (1988a:58). So Talbert summarizes what may be gleaned from Laertius concerning the existence of individual lives composed according to the (a+b) pattern. With the one exception noted above under Pythagoras, it is fair to infer that Laertius himself added the (c) component to his lives, drawn, with the exception of Theodorus (cf. above under Aristippus), from non-biographical sources. That we may further infer that the (a+b) pattern was consistently found by Laertius in individual lives to which he added this (c) component is not, however, so clear.

In the first place, numerous statements by Laertius allow for the possibility that on a number of occasions his "list of or narratives about successors" came from sources other than those referred to in the "life" of the founder. He makes reference in his presentation of Socrates' successors to a "traditional list." Sabinus' *Materials for Criticism* offered a list of successors of Plato. Hippobotus' *On Philosophical Sects* possibly listed successors of Zeno. Aristoxenus was likely the source for Laertius' list of the last generation of Pythagoreans, but the work to which Laertius may have been referring was not Aristoxenus' "life," but his work entitled *Rules of Pedagogy*. Finally, according to Hicks' reconstruction, the list of Pyrrho's successors *introduced* a summary of

skeptical doctrine; it did not *conclude* Antigonus' *On Pyrrho*. All of this
serves to caution against the inference that a list of successors at the end
of a life in Laertius means that Laertius was following sources which
offered an (a+b) pattern. Such an (a+b) pattern in Laertius does not
necessarily translate into (a+b) in his sources.

Second, should we *grant* that Laertius generally drew the list of
successors from his *biographical* sources even in those numerous
instances when he offers no source for his list, it was shown above that
the majority of ante-Laertian lives were collections.[27] This would seem
to allow the inference that *if* Laertius found the (a+b) pattern in his
sources, it just as likely would have been found in a life contained within
a "collection" of lives, not necessarily from a discrete, individual life.
This does not harm the thesis of an (a+b) pattern, but it does raise the
question whether such a pattern within antiquity was *most* (though not
exclusively) conducive to the "collections" sub-genre of lives and not
individual lives. If the "collections" sub-genre was the most suitable
home for the (a+b) pattern, its appropriateness for comparison with
Luke-Acts, which is not a collection, may not be so immediately
apparent.

Third, solid evidence for the (a+b) pattern can be found in only four
instances, twice in individual lives (Aristotle [Hermippus] and
Pythagoras [Aristoxenus' *On Pythagoras and His School*]), and twice in
a life found within a collection (Plato [Dicaearchus] and Zeno
[Philodemus]). We also could add as relevant *The Life of Pachomius*. This
is a fourth century CE Christian life of which about eighty percent is
devoted to Pachomius and twenty percent to the followers of Pachomius
and their history.[28] The late date of this cannot be ignored, but neither
can it be exaggerated for we cannot assume its structure to be *sui
generis*. *Pachomius* does point to the existence of an (a+b) pattern and

---

[27]Collections of lives were cited by Laertius in each of his lives. Individual lives
are cited in Plato (one [though Laertius offers absolutely no hints on its structure],
plus seven collections, see n. 12), Aristotle (one, plus two collections, see n. 15),
Zeno (two, plus one collection, see n. 18), Pythagoras (one, possibly two, plus six
collections, see n. 20), Pyrrho (one [but if Hicks is right [see above under Pyrrho] it
did *not* contain a succession list], plus two collections, see n. 23), and Epicurus
(four, two of which were negative, plus four collections, see nn. 25-28).

[28]See Apostolos A. Athanassakis, tr., *The Life of Pachomius*, Texts and
Translations 7, Early Christian Literature Series 2 (ed. Birger A. Pearson, Missoula:
Scholars Press, 1975) 1-117 focuses on Pachomius; 117-150 on his followers and
their history.

does show evidence that the (b) component could offer more than a mere list or brief collection of narratives.

Fourth, even if one can isolate only four clear instances of the pattern in ante-Laertian lives, the fact that Laertius chose to use the pattern with some frequency in his collection does allow the *possible* inference that such a pattern was more common and prevalent than the unambiguous evidence indicates. Even if, for example, it was Laertius, and not his sources, who was wholly responsible for appending the "mini-lives" of Epicurus' followers to his "Life of Epicurus," can we assume that Laertius was doing something without some sort of precedent? This question cannot be answered dogmatically either positively or negatively. We are at an impasse.

Even granting a negative response to the preceding question, the following concluding comment is still in order: The (a+b) pattern was not a dominant pattern in ancient biographical literature. Of the plethora of lives, noted by Talbert himself for example (see 1988a:54-59), only a handful offer such a pattern. And only a number out of this handful offers much more than a mere list of successors. Such a lack of numbers proves nothing on a purely theoretical basis, but does allow one to ask whether the pattern was prevalent enough that the author of Luke-Acts could have expected his readers to pick up on this pattern and interpret the function of his two-volume work accordingly.

More importantly, granting the existence, however limited, of the pattern, we need to ask whether such a pattern, most especially the (b) component of it, actually offers a suitable comparison with Luke-Acts. Those uncomfortable with Talbert's generic conclusions can note that the brief list of or narrative about successors at the end of a life is not sufficiently similar to the whole of Acts to warrant viewing Acts, even preceded as it is with such a detailed discussion of Jesus, as a continuation of the "biography of Jesus."[29] Talbert himself anticipated such a criticism in *Literary Patterns*. There he recognizes that Luke's (b) component is much longer and more detailed than the (b) component of other comparable "lives." But *length*, he would contend, does not determine a *pattern*.

---

[29]The comment by David L. Barr and Judith L. Wentling, "The Conventions of Classical Biography and The Genre of Luke-Acts: A Preliminary Study" (1983f: 73), is illustrative: "There is…a serious problem of scale. In all the surviving examples of this organizational pattern the material about the disciples is very brief—often no more than a list of successors with perhaps an anecdote or two."

...in Laertius' *Lives* the (b) component is not as fully developed as in Acts.... There can be no doubt that the Lucan Acts is more fully developed, containing as it does a mass of material equal to the amount in the Third Gospel.... We must recognize that the mere expansion of content in the (b) component of Acts need not necessarily involve a denial of its participation in the biographical genre (1974d:131- 32).

Discussion of patterns alone leaves the genre question wide open. There was such a pattern, though not very prevalent, in antiquity. But, despite Talbert's argument cited just above, the brevity of the (b) component in most such texts suggests to many that Acts is not well suited as the (b) component of a "life of Jesus." It is apparent that function must be considered in addressing the genre question. It is to this that I now turn.

The Function of the A+B Biographical Genre and Luke-Acts

Talbert's thesis of the (a+b) biographical pattern, both as it applies to Luke-Acts and to philosophical biographies, is indissolubly linked to his understanding of the function of such a generic pattern. A most important function of Luke-Acts, according to the early investigations of Talbert, is to fight heresy. Methodologically, Talbert is to be commended for linking his examination of genre to his earlier studies of Luke's anti-heretical concerns. It offers to the guild an excellent model of how one's scholarship is to evolve, building on and complementing previous conclusions. The way in which Talbert's "anti-heresy" thesis evolved into his "(a+b) genre" thesis is easy to trace, due to the clarity with which Talbert has consistently presented his arguments.

Talbert's public entry into the study of Luke-Acts began with the publication of his doctoral thesis *Luke and the Gnostics* (1966b). The thrust of the book was to argue that Luke was concerned to combat Gnostic heresy. Two significant articles emerging from the early period of Talbert's investigation of Luke-Acts, "An Anti-Gnostic Tendency in Lucan Christology" (1968a) and "The Redaction Critical Quest for Luke the Theologian" (1970a), furthered the investigation of this theme, focusing on Luke's arguments against Docetism and overly-realized eschatology. In "Redaction Critical Quest" Talbert lays forth in some detail his thesis of the legitimate succession of the gospel from Jesus to the Twelve to Paul to the Elders, a thesis of succession which would eventually feed directly into Talbert's study of the genre of Luke-Acts. The succession motif was employed by Luke to indicate where the true

Christian tradition could be found, implying that a false tradition needed to be combatted. This false tradition was a Gnostic heresy. It was, in short, Talbert's conviction that Luke's occasion was to combat heresy that laid the foundation for his later work in generic studies. The succession motif, soon to be so important in determining the genre of Luke-Acts, served the anti-heresy motif.

Talbert's works dealing with genre criticism (*Literary Patterns* [1974d] and *What is a Gospel?* [1977a]) build heavily on his thesis that Luke-Acts is an anti-heresy document. In *Literary Patterns,* Talbert gives careful attention to the many parallels between Luke and Acts and between the first and second parts of Acts, interpreting the meaning of these parallels in the context of the succession motif. Parallels between Luke and Acts are explained within the larger context of the popular Mediterranean image of the philosopher and his successors. The primary function of succession lists in philosophical literature was to point one to the locus of the true tradition of a given philosophy. As Talbert states, "The philosophical succession lists function to point to those who had 'lived' a doctrine as the locus of the true teaching. This was the importance of a living succession. It was a school's comment on where the true tradition was to be found" (1974d:92).

The parallels between Jesus and the apostolic church serve to point to the latter as the locus of the true tradition.

> The parallels between Paul and Jerusalem serve the same succession mentality. In terms of the philosophic image, the "living voice" is found in the Pauline tradition because he embodies the same life and speech which are found in Jerusalem (i.e., the eyewitnesses). The tradition of Jesus which found embodiment in the eyewitnesses of Jerusalem has also found embodiment in Paul. This means that when the Ephesian elders look to Paul as their pattern and imitate him, they are a "living voice." To indicate correspondences between Paul and Jerusalem, therefore, seems both to legitimate Paul and the line of successors from Paul (1974d:99).

When Talbert elaborates on the need of such a succession, i.e., the need of locating a "living voice," such need is found in Luke's polemic against Gnostic heresy, specifically the docetic heresy of Cerinthusian Gnosticism (1974d:119). It is on the basis of this specific occasion that Talbert proceeds to discuss the genre of Luke-Acts. Luke-Acts is a succession biography, patterned most similarly after a certain type of Hellenistic philosophical biography, which Talbert summarizes in the (a+b) formula.

The purpose of the succession biography in the philosophic tradition is described by Talbert as being the same as that of the succession pattern in Luke-Acts, namely to identify the locus of the true philosophical tradition of the founder, presumably as opposed to a false tradition. While I could find no instances where Talbert explicitly uses the term "anti-heresy" with respect to the function of philosophical biographies, he comes close to saying as much in *Literary Patterns.*

> Faced with the existence of continual clashes not only among the various philosophical schools but also within any given school, the different philosophical communities developed lives of their founders to which were appended lists or narratives of the legitimate line of succession as a means of meeting the need to say where their true tradition was to be found. Such biographies said precisely where the "living voice" was located (1974d:135).

Given that this statement follows closely on the heels of the statement that "the Lucan community was one that was troubled by a clash of views over the legitimate understanding of Jesus and the true nature of the Christian life" (1974d:135), and given that Talbert has made clear that in the context of Luke-Acts such clashes were the result of conflicts with heresy, it would not seem unfair to conclude that Talbert views the function of philosophical succession biographies to be precisely the same as the anti-heresy succession biography called Luke-Acts. In short, both with respect to the (a+b) philosophical biography and Luke-Acts, the occasion for the genre is to combat heretical (or false) versions of the true tradition and to locate the legitimate line of that tradition. Succession genre and anti-heresy polemic go hand-in-hand.

Talbert's next major work, *Reading Luke* (1982d), was clearly based upon his generic studies and centers, once again, on the theme of Luke-Acts as a document which emphasizes "legitimation." In his introduction the legitimation motif is dominant. Talbert reiterates his thesis that the (a+b) biographical pattern is adopted by Luke "to say [that] the true tradition is that which comes from Jesus through the Twelve to Paul and from him...to the Ephesian elders (Acts 20). This Lukan motif would inevitably function as legitimation in the same twofold way the philosophical biographies did" (1982d:3). But while legitimation is still very much at the core of the genre of the Lukan document, the heresy issue has virtually disappeared as the occasion which prompted Luke to write such a legitimation document. To be specific, in *Reading Luke* Talbert devotes only nine of 246 pages to anti-heresy issues.[30]

This pattern leads to some problematic consequences. Talbert's investigation into Luke-Acts emerged with the thesis that Luke was very much concerned to battle heresy by providing the reader with the true, legitimate understanding of the Christian faith. From the hypothesis of this occasion emerged Talbert's generic and literary studies. The literary patterns and the genre employed by Luke to identify for his readers the legitimate line of tradition complemented and supplemented Talbert's thesis that Luke was fighting heresy. In *Reading Luke*, the concern for legitimation is still there; the concern to combat heresy appears now to be only tangential. The anti-heresy occasion of Luke-Acts provided us with a historical and sociological rationale which gave explanation to the genre of Luke-Acts as a legitimizing succession biography. But when the anti-heresy occasion becomes so thoroughly minimized, can an understanding of genre which grew so consistently out of such a proposed occasion remain unaffected?

Talbert's particular understanding of the genre of Luke-Acts is so indissolubly tied to his understanding of the occasion, that to question the occasion, or even to minimize it as Talbert seems to have done, allows one to question the conclusions concerning genre which so thoroughly reflect such an occasion. When I read the Hellenistic (a+b) biographies, either as they are found in the whole of Laertius, or as individual lives separated from Laertius, I simply do not see anything intrinsic in the (b) component to point to a "living voice," *as opposed to some "false" (heretical) voice.* Talbert's statement concerning the function of Hellenistic (a+b) lives, which offered "the legitimate line of succession as a means of meeting the need to say where their true tradition was to be found" (1974d:135), is not, I think, intrinsic to these lives, but heavily shaped by Talbert's conclusion that Luke-Acts, which he views as an (a+b) life, was anti-heretical in its intent. David Aune, who is echoed by Parsons in his contribution to this volume, is not overly harsh to say that such succession lists were "concerned only with who...succeeded whom, not with the legitimacy of their views."[31]

---

[30]See 1982d: 166-69; 177-78; 228-29. Cf. Parsons, 154 above.

[31]See Aune, *The New Testament in Its Literary Environment*, 79; Parsons, 162 above. Cf., e.g., Laertius' opinion concerning Dionysius, one of Zeno's followers, whom he describes as one who turned from the Stoic ideal of indifference to pleasure, because his ophthalmia was too severe to bear (7.37). It would not seem

Talbert has shown that there did exist, though without prevalence, a type of biography to which was appended information concerning who studied with and followed after the founder-philosopher. Evidence indicates that in limited instances information other than a name and brief description was offered about such followers. That such lives offered such information to counteract false "Academics," "Pythagoreans," "Stoics," or whatever is not apparent, at least to me. Still, "Luke-Acts" has a certain attractive structural affinity with a "founder-follower" form of biography. But if such an (a+b) biographical pattern is to prove informative for the reading of Luke-Acts, some occasion other than "heresy in the church" and function other than "fighting heresy" needs to be found.

Talbert himself hints at such a different occasion in his most recent discussion of genre [1988a], which offers a restatement of an earlier essay (1979d = 1981c). In this earlier essay Talbert discussed all the Gospels, arguing that attention to "a particular understanding of the divine presence [in Jesus] and to a distinctive view of discipleship" (1981c:20) motivated the formation of the canonical gospels. Such a particular understanding of Jesus and discipleship seeks to "avoid the reductionism of seeing the presence of God in Jesus in only one way and attempts to set forth a comprehensive and balanced understanding of both the divine presence and the discipleship it evokes" (1981c:22). Thoroughly complementary to his concern is the canonical gospels' offering of "a model for dealing with error/heresy," which Talbert defines as "Christians' absolutizing a part of the truth at the expense of the whole" (1981c:25).[32] In each of the essays, Talbert's application of his discussion to Luke-Acts relates the Lukan texts to a specific *Sitz im Leben*: the promulgation of an overly realized eschatology ("heresy") which needed to be addressed (1981c:21; 1988a:66). Heresy has not totally disappeared, but one can ask whether this proposed *Sitz im Leben* truly can explain Luke-Acts as a whole. In fairness to Talbert, one cannot overlook the fact that even this brief discussion of a specific anti-heretical concern is subsumed under the larger concern which he argues was evident in all the canonical gospels: an appropriate understanding of Jesus and what it meant to be a disciple.

---

that Laertius would wish the reader to see Dionysius as a representative of the "living voice" of Zeno.

[32]In Talbert's more recent essay, he substitutes "subversion of the gospel" for "heresy," but comparison of the shape of the discussion reveals that he is moving along a similar track (1988a: 62-64).

While offering no panacea to explain all the interpretive issues and problems relating to the Gospels, this "larger agenda" (Christology and discipleship) is not an unfair assessment of what was important to the Evangelists, including Luke. It is here, in this "larger agenda," as opposed to the narrower agenda of fighting heresy, that the (a+b) biographical pattern might still prove useful. The concern of the gospels to offer holistic explications of Christology and discipleship finds specific treatment in Luke-Acts, with Luke, focusing on Jesus, offering Luke's assessment of the proper understanding of "the divine presence in Jesus" and Acts, focusing on his followers, offering Luke's detailed portrait of what it means to be a disciple. This is not to say at all that Christology is absent from Acts or discipleship from Luke, but it might prove helpful to explore the possibility that Luke consciously shaped his two-volume narrative in some conscious awareness that two critical issues were facing the Christians of his generation: who was (is) Jesus and what does it mean to follow him?

Assuming for now the generic unity of Luke-Acts, which will itself begin to come under some serious critique,[33] the Third Evangelist might have found useful for his discussion of Christology and discipleship a biographical pattern which loosely followed an analogous structure: the life of a leader/founder followed by some discussion of his followers. Given that genre study is not a prescriptive science, the possibility may be worth exploring that what influenced the expansion of the (b) component for Luke was his concern, shared broadly by many of his Christian contemporaries, to offer a clear statement about what it meant to be a follower of Jesus. Such a clear statement demanded more than a list of followers. It would demand even more than a mere expansion of such a list. For such expansion, Luke would have had no real model—he was free to expand using any number of literary conventions which might suit his purpose; historical narrative and romantic drama being the most immediately obvious.

Such a suggestion addresses the valid objection raised by Parsons that Acts' silence with respect to heretical concerns makes "anti-heresy" an unlikely occasion for the documents (See Parsons, 159). It also does not link Luke's broad use of a basic biographical pattern to any assumptions about how such an (a+b) pattern functioned in philosophical lives, namely to point to "legitimate" followers of a teacher. The function of (b) in philosophical lives seemed to be merely to

---

[33]See the Parsons essay in this volume, n. 72.

let the reader know who studied with the founder. But Luke wanted to
do more than let the reader know who followed Jesus, not because any
genre he found helpful specifically had such a concern, but because the
Christian community of which he was part had such a concern. This
suggestion modestly proposes simply that Luke might have found an
(a+b) pattern helpful to talk about Jesus and his followers, for it helped
to express the indissoluble connection between the Master and his
disciples.

Conclusion

Talbert has isolated a type of individual biography which can
legitimately be said to offer a "life" of a founder of a movement
succeeded by some discussion of the founder's followers. Such an
individual life was not as prevalent as Talbert's "inference" from the
existence of such a pattern in Laertius might imply, and even less
prevalent was something beyond a simple list of successors.
Furthermore, Talbert's interpretation of the function of such a pattern
seems too heavily influenced by his own conclusions concerning the anti-
heretical function of Luke-Acts. These are weaknesses in his thesis. Yet,
if one is to assume the generic unity of Luke-Acts *and* conclude that the
gospel's affinities with ancient lives, including the other three canonical
"lives of Jesus," cannot allow Luke to be placed in another generic
category (such as history or romance),[34] Talbert's thesis is still
promising, particularly if it can be shown to be useful apart from his
proposed "anti-heretical" function.

Whether or not one can follow Talbert's reading of Luke-Acts, he has
made significant contributions to the study of these documents. He has
sensitized the guild to the need to read these texts holistically in the
context of the *literature* of antiquity, not merely in the context of the
ideas of antiquity (history of religions) or through the examination of the

---

[34]History, of some sort or another, seems to many a more suitable genre. See,
e.g., Robert Maddox, *The Purpose of Luke-Acts* (ed. John Riches, Edinburgh: T. &
T. Clark, 1982) 15-18 (theological history); David P. Moessner, "And Once Again,
What Sort of 'Essence?': A Response to Charles Talbert," *Semeia* 43 (1988) 75-84,
and his essay in this volume. Moessner's view is similar to that of Barr and
Wentling, "The Conventions of Classical Biography and The Genre of Luke-Acts"
(1983f: 63-88), i.e., Hebrew historiography which "is almost wholly person-
oriented" (1983f: 75); David Aune, *The New Testament in Its Literary
Environment*, 77-141, esp. 138-41 (general history). Richard I. Pervo has proposed
romance for Acts in *Profit with Delight: The Literary Genre of the Acts of the
Apostles* (Philadelphia: Fortress, 1987).

alteration of inherited traditions (redaction criticism, cf. esp. 1989a). This is a significant advance. Talbert's particular thesis for reading Luke-Acts has not created a consensus among his fellow interpreters. With respect to genre, the "jury is still out" (1989a:310). But it is the good work of Charles Talbert that has, to a very great extent, shaped the issues for the jury's deliberations.

RE-READING TALBERT'S LUKE:
THE *BIOS* OF 'BALANCE' OR THE 'BIAS' OF HISTORY?

David P. Moessner

Introduction

More than any other scholar of the modern post-War period, Charles H. Talbert has shed light upon the Lukan writings by placing them within the larger world of Greco-Roman antiquity. In so "opening up the Scriptures" of Luke-Acts, he has forced us as readers to ask: How would this or that notion in Luke-Acts be perceived by persons living in the Mediterranean basin of the first century CE? The texts he has marshalled and the comparisons drawn in his own responses have not only illuminated smaller sections or ideas in Luke or Acts; they have also opened up the entire field of Lukan studies by demanding that interpreters come to terms with the overall phenomenon—Luke-Acts— *as one work* and ask precisely how this unity would be construed generically within Greco-Roman literary history. It is indeed in his genre studies of Luke-Acts and the Gospels as a whole that Talbert has distinguished himself as one of the most important modern scholars in Gospel studies and as one who will continue to occupy a leading place as an interpreter of Luke-Acts in the twentieth century.

In his essay in this volume, Mikeal Parsons has provided a very fair and insightful appraisal of Talbert's work. As I understand my task, I am not to respond to his review so much as I am to engage some aspect of Talbert's contribution, though I shall take issue with Parsons on one basic point.

Talbert's clearest, most forceful arguments for the gospels, and Luke-Acts in particular, sharing the features of the Greco-Roman *bios/vita* more constitutively than any other genre is in a 1988 *Semeia* article in which he states:

> ...biography is concerned with the essence of the individual.... Biography is interested in what sort of person the individual is, his involvement in the historical process being important only insofar as it reveals his essence. Whereas history attempts to give a detailed account in terms of causes and effects of events, biography presents a highly selective, often anecdotal account of an individual's life with everything chosen to illuminate his essential being (1988a:55-56).

Based on both the discussions of ancient writers and upon his own inductive analysis of many texts, Talbert draws the distinction between what is "essential" to biography, viz. to set forth the "essence" (*fusis*) or "character" (*ethos*) of the individual, and what is "accidental," such aspects as the extent of the life covered, the style of narration, the use of myth, primary social function, lack of sequential or organic development, and so forth. In my response to Talbert in that same *Semeia* issue, I argue that, on the contrary, according to Talbert's own instructive formulation, Luke-Acts looks far more like history than his essential biography.[1] I do not intend here to repeat all that I have said there. Rather, I want first to highlight certain fundamental disagreements between Talbert and myself in assessing his categories before looking briefly at Talbert's genetic theory of gospel composition. Although certain of the following points *may* apply to other canonical gospels as well, in keeping with the theme of this book I shall focus my arguments with respect to Luke-Acts.

I. Points of Disagreement

1. In echoing a phrase from G. N. Stanton that "it is difficult to believe that on first acquaintance the canonical gospels, at least, would not have been considered biographical by Mediterranean readers/hearers" (1988a:53, 60-61),[2] Talbert strikes a chord to which most readers could chime in. Certainly a book that focuses on one individual for a significant part of his or her career *looks like* a biography and is surely biographical in its content. On this score, yes, to

[1] D. P. Moessner, "And Once Again, What Sort of 'Essence?': A Response to Charles Talbert," *Semeia* 43 (1988) 75-84.
[2] Cited from G. N. Stanton, *Jesus of Nazareth in New Testament Preaching* (SNTSMS 27; Cambridge: Cambridge Univ., 1974) 135. Stanton himself, it should be pointed out, does not agree with this "first acquaintance" *conclusion* for gospel genre (117-36, 186-91).

readers on first acquaintance, the gospels look like *lives* of a distinguished person. But the reason for pause—why in fact scholars like K. L. Schmidt[3] and R. Bultmann could not accept the *bios* theory—is that upon greater familiarity, one is struck with the way in which the singular life of Jesus of Nazareth is subsumed to an even greater process, the Kingly Rule of God. And all of Jesus' sayings and actions appear to be subordinated to a concluding event of rejection and vindication which reveals most sublimely the "essence" and "character" of this overriding process for the entire career of this great individual in the greater history-consummating plan of God. Talbert himself says clearly: "Whereas history focuses on the distinguished and significant acts of great men in the political and social spheres, biography is concerned with the essence of the individual" (1988a:55). He goes on to illustrate this distinction by using Dio Cassius' appropriation of *biographical* material about Augustus into his *Roman History* (45-56) in order to change the "aim" of this material "from concern with Augustus' individual essence to his place in a social and political process." Talbert further argued that: "Biography is interested in what sort of person the individual is, his involvement in the historical process being important only insofar as it reveals his essence" (1988a:55-56).

It is difficult to believe that upon further reading one could conclude that the canonical gospels are so concerned with Jesus' individual

---

[3]Talbert rightly concludes that a *bios* for K. L. Schmidt is impossible, given Schmidt's categorization of the canonical gospels as *Kleinliteratur* (folk literature) and not primarily the products of individual *literary* personalities (1988a:60). But *contra* Talbert, redaction criticism did not overturn Schmidt's fundamental insight that the "Kultlegende" background for the formation of the gospels includes self-conscious editors (i.e. the evangelists) linking individual units into a biographically-oriented order and overall format. After all, Schmidt found the closest parallels to the canonical gospels to be the Dr. Faust collections, medieval legends of the *chasid*, and certain ecclesiastical "lives of the saints" ("Die Stellung der Evangelien in der allgemeinen Literaturgeschichte," *Eucharisterion: Hermann Gunkel zum 60. Geburtstage* [ed. H. Schmidt; Göttingen: Vandenhoeck & Ruprecht, 1923] 2.68-75, 79-124). The main reason Schmidt, *contra* Talbert, rejected the literary Greco-Roman *bios* hypothesis is that all the smaller forms of the canonical gospels show a process of growth and formation from worshipping communities who, *along with* the evangelists, are convinced that God through the death and resurrection of Israel's Messiah has appeared on earth to establish the eschatological people of old and new covenants ("Jesus Christus," *RGG*[2] [1929] cols. 114-16). That is to say, both process and final form are explicable only as all the Jesus material is subsumed to cultic and kerygmatic contexts which place Jesus into a larger historical and meta-historical process. Focus on Jesus' *individual* essence is simply not endemic to the canonical gospels.

essence that his relation to the Jewish people in the setting of first-century Galilee and Judea, his role in the larger history of this people Israel, and his ultimate significance in the larger process of the events of God's salvation for the whole world are at best external framework, an outer husk which serves the greater purpose of allowing telling glimpses into the enduring character traits (*ēthē*) of Jesus. It is difficult to believe, upon careful scrutiny, that the development of opposition crescendoing through the four canonical gospels, the growing division of the people of Israel, tension with their leaders and misunderstanding of the disciples, all of which lead to the climax of the story in which eschatological salvation is to be offered to the whole world—in short, what most literary critics would call the *plot* of these gospels—that all of this material is immaterial to the presentation except as it might reveal "what sort of person" Jesus was. And that "insignificant gestures or passing utterance" (Plutarch, *Alexander* 1; *Demosthenes* 11:7) might have sufficed just as well in exposing "the essence" of Jesus of Nazareth is likewise suspect (1988a:56).[4] For as Talbert insists, the critical quality which determines the *bios* character of the gospels is what they share with other "lives," that "what is revealed in the narratives about Apollonius, or Pythagoras, or Moses, or Jesus is the same—their distinctive nature" (1988a:61).

2. That the events and words of the featured individual are clearly secondary to the ongoing, unchanging character traits, and that both deeds and sayings are in fact *via media* to the enduring essence of the individual is emphasized in Talbert's use of Plutarch's discussion. As is well known, during the Hellenistic period interest in the roles of individuals within their historical setting increased significantly from the classical period in which writers like Herodotus and Thucydides were far more concerned to trace *trans*-personal forces and causes of the events they were describing.[5] Yet this growing biographical interest

---

[4]Cf., e.g., A. Dihle, "Die Evangelien und die biographische Tradition der Antike," *ZTK* 80 (1983) 38: "Eben deshalb aber ist es für den Leser einer Alexander-biographie wichtiger zu wissen, wie er sich räusperte und spuckte, als seine weltbewegenden Taten erzählt und erläutert zu erhalten."

[5]See, e.g., A. Momigliano, *The Development of Greek Biography* (Cambridge: Harvard Univ., 1971) esp. 65-104; A. Dihle, ibid., 37-40; idem, *Die Entstehung der historischen Biographie* (Heidelberg: C. Winter, Universitätsverlag, 1987) esp. 7-22, 64-80; D. E. Aune, *The New Testament in Its Literary Environment* (Philadelphia: Westminster, 1987) 29-31; D. L. Barr and J. L. Wentling, "The Conventions of Classical Biography and the Genre of Luke-Acts: A Preliminary Study," in 1983f:67-71.

within Greek history writing[6] did not lead to a self-contained biographical sub-genre in which the famous individual himself becomes an epitome of an entire period or culture in a way in which the individual essence of the person might become primary in representative fashion. Rather, the events themselves and the way the individual illuminates the significance of those events remain uppermost.[7] It is in this larger context of a growing overlap of biographical and historical interests that Plutarch makes his observations.

> Do not expect a thorough account of even one, let alone of the many significant events in the lives of Alexander and Caesar that I am writing in this book, since I am not writing histories (*historiai*) but lives (*bioi*).... Accordingly, just as painters get the likenesses in their portraits from the face and the expression of the eyes, wherein the character (*ethos*) shows itself, but make very little account of the other parts of the body, so I must be permitted to devote myself rather to the signs of the soul in men, and by means of these to portray the life of each, leaving to others the description of their great contests.
> (*Alexander* 1:2, 3-LCL).

Ironically, a biographer will research the commonplace events and sayings of an individual to glean significant glimpses into the individual's distinctive character, whereas an historian is interested in the distinctive private life and details in order to gain insight into the significant events associated with that person's time period (e.g., Plutarch, *Pompey* 8:6). Indeed, given the extensive overlap of biography and history in the period in which the canonical gospels were written, it is no wonder that they, and Luke-Acts in particular, exhibit marked interest in both the significant events in which Jesus participates and through these "what sort of person" Jesus was. Again, I am arguing that the canonical gospels are thoroughly *biographical*.[8] But when it comes

---

[6]Dihle ("Evangelien," 37) points to Theopompus' *Philippika* (mid-fourth century BCE) as representative.

[7]E.g., Dihle (ibid., 38): "Genau an diesem Punkt aber, nämlich der Erklärung denkwürdiger, in die Gegenwart fortwirkender Taten durch Informationen über Charakter und Lebensumstände der Akteure, liegt nach griechischer Auffassung der Unterschied zwischen Biographie und Geschichtsschreibung"; cf. Momigliano (*Greek Biography*, 64): "Before Aristotle, I would say that there were experiments of a biographical and autobiographical kind which normally were kept outside political historiography as transmitted to the fourth century in the models of Herodotus and Thucydides."

[8]Talbert himself points to Dio Cassius' use of "Augustus" biographical material in Books 45—56 in which, for instance, we learn of his parents (45.1.1), of visions, divinations, prophecies, and signs attending Augustus' birth (45.1.2-2.7), his patrician education in oratory, military service, and politics (45.2.8), and at the end

to the crucial benchmark in genre between biography and historiography, Talbert comes down decidedly on the side of the "eyes," to use Plutarch's image, rather than on the full body of the portrait. By doing so, Talbert commits a wide and diverse body of writing to this Plutarchan definition and relegates the "history-like narrative" that many biographies utilize to a non-essential, "accidental" status.[9]

It is just here that Talbert's definition will not work for Luke-Acts:

(i) Luke states in his proemium (Luke 1:1-4) that he is writing in a particular order or sequence (*kathexēs*, 1:3) in order to lend "certainty" or "assurance" to the narrative (*diēgēsis*, 1:1) of events (*pragmata*, 1:1) that he is relating.[10] In light of the fact that "many" others already before him have set their hand to the same task using the same eyewitness traditions/material (*paredosan hēmin*, 1:3), one should probably conclude that he is not fully satisfied with their accounts and that, in fact, his new or different *sequence* will distinguish his account and give it greater credibility. In any case, Luke is saying to Theophilus and to all his readers: "If you want to understand the significance which

---

of his public career, of his death and omens attending his burial and rumors of his ascending to heaven (56.46)—in short, the same formal categories as in the Gospel of Luke, and like Luke-Acts, subsumed to the larger story or history (i.e. of the rise and reign of Rome). In other words, the kind of material found in Luke could be, generically speaking, equally "at home" in either historiography or biography.

[9]Talbert's use of the Plutarchan distinction to encompass a vast array of works which focus on one person will not work, e.g., for Tacitus' *Agricola*, where the historical framework and conditions are crucial in describing Agricola's *life* in a way in which Agricola becomes a mirror or representative of a period in Roman history. Chaps. 39—42, for instance, portray a considerable amount of information about life in the last years of Domitian's reign, not only to illuminate what Agricola was like, but also what Rome was like and Agricola's role in that period. Cf., e.g., Dihle (*Entstehung*, 31): "Diese Erwägung erweist Tacitus' 'Agricola' als historische Biographie im mittelalterlich-neuzeitlichen Sinn, als Werk also, in dem eine geschichtliche Epoche im Spiegel eines individuellen Lebens dargestellt wird, ein individuelles Leben aber eine Epoche repräsentiert."

[10]Cf., e.g, Aune (*Literary Environment*, 116): "By substituting the term 'narrative' for Mark's 'gospel,' Luke indicated his intention to write history." Cf. (ibid., 121): "The 'events completed among us' indicates a historical rather than biographical focus." Although *pragmata* can (obviously) be used with many different referents in any genre of writing, including the 'events'/'affairs' of an individual in a *bios*, it is telling that it is a stock term for *historians* precisely in their *preface* or in digressions where they discuss the purpose and scope of their work (e.g., Polybius, *The Histories*, 1.3.9; Diodorus Siculus, *Library of History*, 1.4; Dio Cassius, *Roman History*, 1.2; Dionysius of Halicarnassus, *Roman Antiquities*, 1.3; cf. Lucian, *Historia [How to Write History]* 47; 55). Moreover, they avoid using the term *bios/vita* in those contexts (see below, n. 12).

I am assigning to the material that follows, you must read with the sequence of the text,[11] lest you miss precisely the connections I am trying to make and, in particular, the greater clarity or certainty of those events." Now this kind of comment, coming as it does at the beginning of a work, runs counter, as we have seen, to Plutarch's comments in his introduction to *Alexander* and *Caesar*. Though Plutarch utilizes Alexander's deeds and follows overall a rough chronological order in his history-like narrative, no significance at all is attached to one *event* per se as compared to another, much less to any sequence of events. Luke, on the other hand, is taking to heart what Lucian says should be the aim of every good *historian* in writing up the material one has at hand:

> Let the narrative (*diēgēsis*) be arrayed with the virtues proper to narrative, progressing smoothly....let its clarity appear brightly, achieved both by style, as I have said, and by the inter-weaving of the events (*pragmata*)....When he has finished the first event, he will introduce the second, attached to it and linked with it like a chain, so as to avoid breaks and a multiplicity of narratives lying juxtaposed to one another; rather always the first and second events must not only be adjacent, but must also have common material and overlap (*Historia*, 55—trans. mine).

However successfully Luke has carried out his own objective and met Lucian's expectations, it is clear that if the choices for Luke's intent be either biography or history, the answer must fall squarely on the latter. Luke is indicating (rather) that the sequence (and significance) of the events is part and parcel of the larger story of "fulfillment" (1:1b) that he is relating, and in no way ancillary or convenient scaffolding for a more essential elucidation of Jesus' essence.[12]

(ii) Like Matthew, Luke is interested in a biographical expansion of the Markan outline which gives his Part One (Gospel) the fuller profile of a "life" (according, for example, to Theon's proprieties

---

[11]I.e. a "synchronic," not chronological reading.

[12]T. Callan ("The Preface of Luke-Acts and Historiography," *NTS* 31 [1985] 578) has shown that *if* a biography has a preface where the purpose and scope of the work is discussed, then invariably the term *bios* or *vita* is used to categorize its genre (with 8 examples from 4 authors, 581 n. 10). Even when Luke in Acts 1:1 summarizes the first half of his work, which has focused almost entirely on the career of one person, he does not refer to volume one as the "life" of Jesus but rather as "all the things/events (*panta*, cf. Luke 1:3-*panta*, i.e. the *pragmata* of Luke 1:1) of which Jesus began to do and to teach until the time he was taken up." Volume two is thus going to relate more things/events that continue the events of fulfillment (Luke 1:1) that Jesus began and which his witnesses are to continue within the overarching story of the Kingdom of God through Israel (Acts 1:3, 6-8); see nn. 29, 30 below.

[*Progymnasmata* 8]). Yet this fuller sketch is, generically speaking, equally "at home" in biography or in historiography, depending upon the larger context and literary aims into which the source material is placed.[13] That Luke dovetails his birth narratives of Jesus *and* John, his description of Jesus' childhood and relation to parents, and the genealogy of Jesus, all into the greater story of the fulfillment of Israel's salvation for the whole world illustrates again the subordination of biographical details into a larger story—a sequence in which the events themselves are revelatory, pregnant with meaning not only for the identity or essence of Jesus but for the story of Israel and the history of the whole human race as well. Announced by heaven as both son of David and Son of the God of Israel in the longed for fulfillment of the oath to Abraham, Luke indicates that the historic line of David and the eschatological reign of God are merging together in unprecedented fashion. Portents and signs divulge that this "Son" and "Lord" will bring about the hoped for glory of the people Israel, even as he is a light of revelation of the one God to all nations. But he will be a "sign" of this God's world-saving act as one contradicted and rejected and the cause of the people of Israel to be torn into division (Luke 1:26-38, 39-56, 67-79; 2:8-14, 25-38). In other words, Luke is announcing from the beginning that his story of fulfillment of salvation has a distinctive plot in which the events of rejection and of falling and rising are constitutive of the character or essence of Jesus.

"What sort of person" Jesus is cannot be revealed apart from this larger story and interface with the responses of an historical people. The truth is that Luke, like an historian, according to Talbert (1988a:56), is interested in *cause* and *effect* in events. Thus, he emphasizes the judgment that awaits Israel *because of* their repeated rejections of the one sent to them for their liberation (e.g., Luke 10:13-16; 11:47-52; 13:34-35; 17:22-35; 19:41-44; 21:20-24).[14] Indeed, it is hard to conceive of an

---

[13]See n. 8 above. Cf., e.g., Aune (*Literary Environment*, 65): "By adding background material, genealogies and birth narratives...and resurrection appearances... Matthew and Luke have moved closer toward the *biographical and historiographical* expectation of pagan readers" (emphasis mine). Cf. Dihle ("Evangelien," 36): "Die Biographie Jesu als Aufgabe für den Schrifsteller in der christlichen Literatur des 1. und 2. Jahrhunderts zunehmende Bedeutung gewann." But for Dihle neither Mark nor Matthew or Luke exhibit the overall concerns of the *bios*: "Dieser biographische Rahmen widerum gehörte aber von vornherein in einen mit der Tradition des Volkes Israel vorgegebenen heilsgeschichtlichen Zusammenhang" (p. 46).

[14]The fact that Israel's rejection is part of a larger plan or necessity of God's salvation does not excuse Israel's rejection on the level of human responsibility:

essence for Jesus apart from this involvement in the social and political process of Israel, to use Talbert's definition of the focus of history (1988a:55-56). Nor, judging from the denouement of Part One, in which Jesus commands the disciples to take the eschatological salvation to Israel and the nations (see below), can it be the case that Luke is simply choosing a history-like or connected interaction of Jesus with Israel as one of several, in principle equally good, modes for presenting an essential nature that is more fundamental than any particular interaction in time and space with Israel. No, for Luke, *there is no character Jesus nor exalted Christ apart from his role in Israel's life and character:* "Today this Scripture is fulfilled in your hearing" (Luke 4:21).

(iii) A. Dihle has shown how integral to Plutarch's definition (and thus Talbert's) of a *bios* genre is the notion of human nature as a static, unchanging composite of virtues and vices based on the individual's own choices in developing various character traits *ēthē* which together build a person's "character" or "essence."[15] The aim of biography, then, whether explicitly didactic or not, is to let the various actions, sayings, and general behavior patterns divulge the unchanging character that transcends all temporal and historical contingencies. Whether an Agesilaus or a Pompey, a Demosthenes or a Cicero, an Alexander or a Caesar, meaningful comparisons of persons from totally different backgrounds, times, and circumstances can be made, since fundamental character traits are trans-personal and trans-historical and are in principle achievable (whether good or bad) by any person of any status or station. The Plutarchan (and Talbert's) definition of the aim of all biography, then, is a description of "what sort of person" an individual is *with respect to these traits.*

How striking by contrast is Luke's interest in Jesus' character: The Third Evangelist is intent to show that Jesus appears in the public arena in a specific time and under particular political conditions: "In the fifteenth year of the reign of Tiberias Caesar...in the high priesthood of Annas and Caiaphas, the word of God came to John..." (Luke 3:1-2). That this *synchronism* is not narrative decoration becomes evident when Luke ties the heavenly annunciation of Jesus as "Son" through the historical baptizing movement of John to the genealogy of Jesus that

---

e.g., Acts 3:18-19—"What God proclaimed in advance through the mouth of all the prophets—that the Messiah must suffer—God thus fulfilled. Repent *therefore* and turn in order that your sins might be removed."

[15]Dihle ("Evangelien," 40-42); idem, *Studien zur griechischen Biographie* (Göttingen: Vandenhoeck & Ruprecht, 1956) 57-103.

ascends all the way to Adam "son of God" (3:21-22, 23-38).[16] The "mightier one" announced by John who is "coming" upon the historical scene is the Son of God whose own baptizing with Holy Spirit and fire will spark the eschatological division and judgment of "all flesh" even as foretold long ago by Israel's prophets (3:15-17, 4-9). Moreover, this Son of God is himself the "Savior" (2:11, 30), the "Anointed One, the Lord" born in the days of Caesar Augustus when Quirinius was governor of Syria (2:1-2, 10-14).[17] By tying Messiah Jesus' public ministry to Israel through these historical synchronisms at the beginning of his two volumes,[18] Luke is demonstrating that "the sort of person" Jesus is can be grasped only through his connection to a unique and unrepeatable set of world and political circumstances and events.[19]

(2) Luke again demonstrates his historical interest in the character of Jesus in his statements about Jesus' *development* (Luke 2:40, 52; cf. 1:80). Such growth in "wisdom, stature, and favor before God and humankind" anticipates and prepares Jesus for his sending as the beloved Son of this God (3:22; 4:1-14) and as one eminently qualified to bring salvation to all flesh (3:6) through a mission of "release" to all nations (24:47 and Acts). Again, Talbert's delineation of biography having "virtually no interest in tracing development" since the "essence of a person was not examined in its chronological development but only as a fixed constituent in a 'life'" (1988a:56) does not conform with Luke's portrayal. Rather, as the Deuteronomic historians subsumed the many biographical details of David including his "continuing to grow in stature and in favor with the Lord and humankind" (1 Sam 2:26; cf. 2:21b!) to David's significance in the historical events of the reign of God over Israel through the monarchy, so Luke has done with the Jesus material. Luke shows not the slightest interest in divulging some character trait of Jesus as Son of God that somehow supersedes his historical mission as a more eternal, transcendental quality. "If you are

---

[16]For the Lukan genealogy, see W. S. Kurz "Luke 3:23-38 and Greco-Roman and Biblical Genealogies," in 1983f:169-87.

[17]See, e.g., W. C. van Unnik, "The Purpose of Luke's Historical Writing," *Sparsa Collecta* (NovTSup 29; Leiden: Brill, 1973) 1.6-15, esp. 9.

[18]I am indebted to Prof. J. H. Charlesworth who in private correspondence pointed out Luke's way of emphasizing his historiographical intent by placing the synchronisms at the *beginning* of his two volumes.

[19]See, e.g., Dihle ("Evangelien," 45) on Luke-Acts: "Die sorgfältigen Datierungen und andere Details...rücken das berichtete Geschehen in einen geschichtlichen Zusammenhang, der die ganze Heidenwelt einschliesst."

the Son of God, command this stone to become bread....A human shall not live by bread alone" (4:4)!

(3) It seems that whenever the question of "what sort of person" Jesus is breaks open as a public issue, Luke has Jesus "correct" the expectations of his disciples and the crowds with a presentation of Jesus' understanding of his own *mission to Israel*. For instance, in the opening scene of his public activity (4:16-30) Jesus perceives that the "fame" that has already preceded him (4:14-15) has framed certain expectations of his identity that do not square at all with the Isaianic promises of the anointed prophet-Servant's role that he has come to fulfill (4:18-19). "Is this not Joseph's son?" is answered by the "beloved Son" (3:22, 23; 4:18) who, like rejected prophets before him, must go "outside" Israel with God's salvation (4:23-27).[20] Or again after a significant amount of the Galilean activity is recounted, the one who served to introduce Jesus to the public as "the Christ" (3:15-17) is now questioning Jesus' identity precisely because of that activity (7:18a, 18b-23). As in Nazareth, Jesus indicates who he is, his "essence," by pointing solely to the nature of his calling *with Israel* and again in the language and demonstration (7:21!) of the Isaianic expectations of the final salvation (7:22; *emoi*, v. 23).[21] Moreover, Luke once again has Jesus define himself in light of Israel's history of the reception of its prophets sent by Wisdom/God, this time by contrast (and continuity) with the mission of John (7:24-35, esp. vv. 27-28). Numerous other examples could be cited (e.g., 9:18-36; 10:21-24; 15:1-2, 3-32; 22:66-71, etc.) which illustrate that the "character" that emerges from the Gospel of Luke is totally absorbed in his sending to Israel.

It is not by accident that the author organizes much of his plot in the journeying of Jesus to Jerusalem and its Temple, and places Jesus under a divine compulsion to complete the "exodus" of God's salvation to Israel (and the nations) there (9:31; 24:47).[22] Nor is it "accidental" that the author in the finale has Jesus lift the veil of mystery that has enshrouded his own identity among the people from the very beginning by having Jesus point to the whole of Israel's Scriptures as the clue to

---

[20]Note how Luke's *narrator's* description of the Holy Spirit "upon him" (*ep' auton*) in 3:22a is reaffirmed by Jesus in 4:18 using the words of Isa 61:1. Both "voices" thus attest to the "voice from heaven" (3:22b) that Jesus is the "beloved Son/Servant" in whom God delights (Isa 42:1).

[21]Notice how Luke's narrator conjoins "Lord" with John's "coming one" in 7:19 as in 3:4, 16; see also 7:27-28. Cf. *prosdokaō* in 3:15 and 7:19, 20.

[22]See II.(iii) below.

"what sort of person" he is: The story of Israel has come to its crowning point in its suffering Christ (24:25-27, 44-47; cf. 22:37 and 24:19-21; see II below).

It is certainly true that in all of this Lukan sketch of Jesus we do learn a great deal about the sort of person he was: e.g., his compassion for the ill or grieving (e.g., 5:13; 7:13; 13:12); his predilection for "tax collectors and sinners" (5:27-35; 7:34-35, 36-50; 15:1-2; 19:1-10) and the "poor" (e.g., 6:20; 7:22); and his apparent enjoyment of the company of women and treatment of them as disciples (e.g., 8:1-3; 10:38-42; cf. 24:6-11). But in every instance this quality is not linked to a particular moral essence or structure of virtues but rather to the presence or "reign of God" that gives shape and drive to Jesus' mission to Israel. Even when his "character" vis-a-vis the Law is assailed, Jesus' response is "characterized" by his understanding of his *presence among Israel* (e.g., 5:33-39; 6:1-5, 6-11; 7:29-35; 11:37-52).

3. Is then Luke-Acts or even Part One by itself historiography? Yes, but certainly not of the usual variety. As van Unnik pointed out, Polybius' definition holds true for the entire Greco-Roman period: "An historian may include anything he deems necessary, but it has to serve his main theme: the history of the state(s)."[23] Luke or Luke-Acts certainly does not sound or feel like the usual political history; although the fulfillments of the hopes and promises of much of Israel's past form the central plot of both volumes (e.g., Luke 1:32-33, 54-55, 68-79; 24:44; Acts 1:6-8; 3:24-26; 26:6-8; 28:20, 26-28), all interest is focused upon the movement begun by one Jew from Nazareth with very little given about the workings of the Jewish Sanhedrin, Jewish relations with Rome, events leading to the Jewish War, etc. Nor does the center of Jesus' preaching, the Kingdom of God, sound like the usual state rhetoric representing the origins and aspirations of a national consciousness.

Nevertheless, Luke-Acts fits into the broad generic classification of "general history" (e.g., A. Dihle; D. Aune) in two ways: (i) Luke never loses his focus upon the people or *laos* of Israel as a whole, even in Part Two (Acts) where corporate Israel is increasingly deaf and even hostile to the "sect" of Christians (Acts 28:20-22). Luke sounds the hopes of pious Israelites for the fulfillment of ancient promises (Luke 1-2) through the vivid frame of an angelophany at the central shrine where the *laos* are gathered (1:5-23) and the precocious young Jesus teaching the

---

[23]W. C. van Unnik, "Luke's Second Book and the Rules of Hellenistic Historiography," *Les Actes des Apôtres. Traditions, rédaction, théologie* (ed. J. Kremer; Gembloux: Leuven Univ. Press, 1979) 39.

teachers of this people in the Temple at the Passover (2:41-52). He then depicts the interactions of Jesus with the *laos* who follow and eventually journey with him to another Passover in Jerusalem where, gathered in the Temple-precincts (19:46—21:38), they will join with their leaders in crying out for the death of this prophet-teacher (23:13-25), who was "to have redeemed Israel" (24:19-21). Because of the people's rejection of their "king" (cf. 23:3), God will "rain" destruction upon them (e.g., 11:47-51; 13:34-35; 19:41-44; 21:20-24). Here then is a description of an approximately thirty-year period purporting to relate a significant national figure to the origins, character, and ultimate fate of that entire people. In Part Two, irrespective of how final Paul's closing judgment upon Israel may or may not be (28:25-28), Luke continues with another approximately thirty-year period in which the messianic salvation of Israel is taken first to the *laos* of Israel before it is extended through Israel to the nations of the earth. As the chief figure of this second part exclaims to fellow Jews in the closing scene: "It is because of the hope of Israel that I am bound with this chain" (28:20).

(ii) At the same time that a history of a people is being described, Luke depicts a division within this people through which a sect of Israel begins to take on its own identity[24] and to propagate its own legitimation to outsiders or non-Israelites. The great concentration of Paul's defense speeches before Roman procurators and his deliverance from the wrath of *Dikē* (Justice) (28:4) through the sea voyage scenes at the end all make it clear that the "Christian" movement (11:26; 26:28!) is something that "has not taken place in a corner" (26:26). Luke, then, writes something new, a history of the beginnings of a trans-national, trans-political "religious" movement.[25] In this sense, we can speak of a new kind of "writing" or sub-genre within ancient historiography.[26]

Yet by the use of obvious *historiographical* literary forms and conventions such as speeches, travel accounts (*periēgēsis*) dramatic

---

[24]Notice how in Acts 15:14; 18:10 *laos* clearly denotes non-Israelites or Gentiles as incorporated into the *laos* of God. In 18:10 it may be that *laos* designates largely Gentile converts, though incorporated into the first Jewish believers in Corinth as the eschatological or fulfilled *people* of God.

[25]See van Unnik ("Second Book," 39). This, of course, does not mean Christianity is apolitical or necessarily does not have a profound impact on "politics," e.g., Acts 17:5-9.

[26]Cf. Aune, *Literary Environment*, 139: "Luke, rather than Eusebius, should be credited with creating the 'new' genre of church history." If the ca. 60-year period and length of text were determinative, then Luke-Acts would be closer to the historical monograph; on this, see, E. Plümacher ("Die Apostelgeschichte als historische Monographie," *Les Actes des Apôtres*, 457-66).

episodes, sea voyages (*periplous*), letters, summaries, synchronisms, digressions, and parallelisms,[27] Luke is deliberately presenting this movement to a larger audience in a clearly understandable form in order to show the world-wide significance of a group which claims its origins in an ancient people and professes its relevance for all of human history.[28] As in general histories, it is no wonder that Luke is intent to show the impact of fulfilled Israelite ideology/Scripture on leading intellectual and commercial centers with successes among leading social groups and stretching to the center of the Empire—all directed by an overarching, supra-historical "will" of the God of Israel, the one God of the universe.

But how does the canonical separation of Luke-Acts affect this evaluation? Should each volume be considered on its own, perhaps each belonging to a separate genre as, for instance, Mikeal Parsons is arguing? Parsons speaks of "authorial unity" as a false criterion and of an author's potential to write in more than one generic vein (Parsons: 163). But the fact is that neither Talbert nor others like Aune *assume* generic unity because of *de facto* authorial unity; nor do they subsume one book to the other, but rather to a larger whole. As they and I have tried to show, Luke himself states his intention to write a specific work and refers to volume (*logos*) one as he subordinates the subsequent volume (Acts) to a larger program/format of the whole work and not to the gospel by itself. Part One contains "all[29] the deeds and teaching which Jesus began" (Acts 1:1-2)[30] within a scheme which the apostles will

---

[27]See esp. E. Plümacher, *Lukas als hellenistischer Schriftsteller* (SUNT 9; Göttingen: Vandenhoeck & Ruprecht, 1972) 32-137; Aune, ibid., 120-31.

[28]Cf., e.g., Plümacher (ibid., 79) on the speeches in Acts: "Wollte Lk dieses apostolische Wort als geschichtswirkendes Movens charakterisieren, so konnte nichts nützlicher sein, als bei einer bestimmten hellenistischen historiographischen Tradition Anleihen zu machen, die mit ihren Reden etwas Ähnliches auszudrücken gesucht hatte."

[29]"All," though standard rhetorical hyperbole, may well be another indication of Luke's goal to write history. See, e.g., Plutarch (*Alexander*, 1.1-3); Cornelius Nepos (*Pelopidas*, 16.1.1); Lucian (*Historia*, 55); and Diodorus Siculus (*Library of History*, 16.1) who refer to history being a "fuller" or "complete" account. *Panta* (Acts 1:1a) refers back to the *panta* (neut.) of Luke 1:3, i.e. to the "fulfilled" *pragmata* of Luke 1:1b. Luke it seems was intent in giving a fuller account than his predecessors (Luke 1:1) who he *may* have felt did not give an extensive enough account and thus did not render sufficient clarity or import to the events for a wider readership. His fuller account certainly entails the continuation of the fulfilled *pragmata* in his *second* volume (see n. 12 above).

[30]Luke operates with three critical "beginnings": (i) the Scriptures, including all the prophets who announce or interpret in advance the events of Luke-Acts—

continue as authenticated witnesses of the significance of these deeds and words *within the Kingly Rule of God* (1:3). The apostles' question in 1:6, whatever their understanding, lets the reader know in Jesus' response how volume two will continue the history of salvation for the whole world effected by the Kingly Reign of God through Israel's Messiah, even as Luke will end the two volumes with Paul in Rome "preaching to all the Kingdom of God" and "the things concerning the Lord Jesus Messiah" (28:31).

Since Parsons, like Talbert and others, ties reader expectation through genre to at least some level of *authorial intent*, one cannot, because of *de facto* canonical separation suddenly switch the terms of the argument to make a canonical reading the basis of generic disunity. How did Luke intend his readers to relate both parts to each other? What expectations did he set for the reader when he tied the two together?— These are the primary questions when addressing genre *within the parameters of authorial intent*. However, at the *different level* of a canonical reading, clearly the Gospel of Luke "looks" more biographical as a part of a four-fold sketch of one central figure. Yet again, as we have seen, Luke is distinctive among the four in the extent to which this one figure is subordinated to the great events of the Kingdom of God, on the one hand, and is tied to the reigns and conditions of Roman and Jewish governments and to a genealogy spanning universal history, on the other. By itself, the Third Gospel is closer to, e.g., Tacitus' *Agricola*, sc. to biographical history or historical biography.[31]

4. Luke's use of an "omniscient mode of narration"[32] for most of his two volumes needs to be pursued further, particularly in light of the

---

e.g., *archomai* (Luke 24:27; Acts 8:35; cf. *archaios* in Luke 9:8, 19); (ii) Jesus' public ministry, which is the decisive "beginning" of fulfillment and which "begins" with the baptism of John and Jesus' teaching in Galilee—e.g., *archomai* (Luke 23:5; Acts 1:22; 10:37) and with witnesses to this "beginning"—e.g., *archē* (Luke 1:2; cf. Acts 1:22); (iii) the coming of the Holy Spirit at Pentecost which "begins" the world mission in fulfillment of Jesus' final injunctions before his "taking up" which end the "beginning" of "all that Jesus *began* to do and to teach" (Acts 1:1)— e.g., *archē* (Acts 11:15); *archaion* (Acts 15:7); *archomai* (Luke 24:47). This concern for linking different eras and time periods is constitutive of *historiography*, not of biography. See also nn. 29, 12 above.
[31]See n. 9 above; Parsons, along with R. I. Pervo, will be developing these generic questions further in their volume, *Rethinking the Unity of Luke and Acts* (Minneapolis: Fortress/Augsburg, forthcoming).
[32]R. Alter, *The Art of Biblical Narrative* (N.Y.: Basic Books, 1981) 155-77; M. Sternberg, *The Poetics of Biblical Narrative* (Bloomington, IN: Indiana Univ., 1985) 84-128.

distinctive use of this mode in the great biblical histories spanning Genesis to 2 Kings, and Lucian's injunction that an historian should be

> ...like Homer's Zeus, looking now at the land of the horse-rearing Thracians, now at the Mysians' country—in the same way let him look now at the Roman side in his own way and tell us how he saw it from on high...let him hurry everywhere...to avoid missing any critical situation (*Historia* 49—LCL).

We can, however, observe briefly: (i) Though our author introduces himself as a "me," "us," "I," and "we," he, unlike his Greco-Roman counterparts, remains anonymous. Rather, this anonymity parallels *Hebrew historiography*, especially Joshua—2 Kings; (ii) In Part One, after the initial "me" (1:3) and "us" (1:1, 2) in the preface, our unidentified author "Luke" slips behind the narrator in 1:5—24:53 to a consistent third person mode. He quickly establishes his viewpoint "from on high" as he freely moves his readers from one locale to another (e.g., from the Temple to Judea to Galilee, etc.), reveals angelic pronouncements (e.g., 1:11-23, 26-38), "quotes" private thoughts and desires (e.g., 1:25; 2:19), and cites prophetic interpretations of "interior" and supraterrestrial events (e.g., 1:41-45, 46-55, 67-79) etc. In Acts 1:3(2) after again inserting himself as an "I," our author retreats behind an omniscient mode and remains a "third person" narrator until a surprising re-surfacing in 16:10-17 in the first of the famous "we" passages.[33] After such extended lengths of omniscient third person narration this emergence is not only startling but also gives the distinct impression that the "I" of our author is now part of the "we" as an actual participant in the narrated events (see below).

(iii) In Part One, our narrator conjoins his omniscient mode with the divine omniscient perspective of the Lord God of Israel and fuses this perspective with that of the main character, Jesus of Nazareth. For example, "the word of God" to John (Luke 3:2) is pronounced by the *narrator* (3:4-6) as a fulfillment of the prophet Isaiah's oracle (Isa 40:3-5), sc. the narrator is declaring directly what the essence of the "word of God" to John was, i.e. is "speaking" for God (cf. already 1:6; 2:25, 40, 52, etc.). Then the narrator as omniscient witness fuses the direct "voice" of God from "heaven" in 3:22 with Jesus' point of view in 4:1-13 where Jesus now speaks "directly" for the Lord God (4:8, 12) within the

---

[33]Cf. Acts 20:3-15; 21:1-18; 27:1—28:16; on this whole issue, see J. Wehnert (*Die Wir-Passagen der Apostelgeschichte. Ein lukanisches Stilmittel aus jüdischer Tradition* [Göttingen: Vandenhoeck & Ruprecht, 1989]).

narrator's omniscient frame (4:1, 13). In Part Two the narrator wastes no time. After he links the "I" of authorship to Part One (Acts 1:1), and reasserts this omniscient perspective, he has Jesus (cf. 1:1) interrupt the third person narration of verses 3-4a by abruptly *taking the words out of the narrator's mouth!*—"... the promise of the Father which 'you heard from *me.*'" Through this amazing "intervention" Luke asserts the fundamental *narrative unity* of the two volumes by fusing their divine omniscient point of view, linking "the promise which 'you heard from *me*'" (1:4b) to the words of Jesus in "the promise of *my* Father" in Luke 24:49c. In full accord with this transition the narrator continues on in third person, relating the omniscient speech of the "two men in white" who give "heaven's" perspective (Acts 1:11) on Jesus' words to the apostles in 1:7-8. In short, it would appear that the only parallels to such lengthy uninterrupted stretches of *divine* omniscient narration are the biblical histories.[34]

(iv) Not only does Jesus speak directly for God in Part One (e.g., Luke 5:23-24; 6:20; 10:16, 22-24, etc.), but also in the many speeches in Part Two, the apostles-witnesses proclaim the mind or will of God directly to the people (e.g., Acts 2:16-36; 3:13-26; 4:10-12; 5:29-32, etc.). Unlike Greek or Roman historiography in which roughly half of narrated speech is *indirect*, Luke consistently relates *direct* speech similar to the preferred direct speech of Hebrew historiography.[35] (v) In Luke's relatively few *digressions* in Part Two (e.g., 1:18-19; 17:21; 23:8), he avoids a "first person" comment or speculation, unlike his Greco-Roman counterparts[36] but consistent with the omniscient mode of Hebrew historiography.

To sum up, in terms of sheer uninterrupted length it would appear that Luke's anonymous, divine omniscient mode most closely parallels Hebrew historiography. Here it is curious that Lucian's remarks about an omniscient vantage point (49)[37] come in the middle of his discussion

---

[34]See, e.g., Sternberg, *Poetics,* 72-83.
[35]See, e.g., W. C. van Unnik, "The Book of Acts: The Confirmation of the Gospel," *NovT* 4 (1960) 53: "The speeches in Acts are in the *oratio recta* and not *obliqua,* as often in pagan historiography; they are not a record of the message only, but a direct message itself"; Plümacher, *Schriftsteller,* 32-38; Aune, *Literary Environment,* 91-93, 107-08; M. Dibelius, "Die Reden der Apostelgeschichte und die antike Geschichtsschreibung," *Aufsätze zur Apostelgeschichte* (ed. H. Greeven; FRLANT 42; Göttingen: Vandenhoeck & Ruprecht, 1951) 120-25.
[36]On digressions in Greco-Roman historiography, see, e.g., Aune (*Literary Environment,* 93-95).
[37]See n. 34 above.

about the *credibility* of the historian's account (47—51): the necessity of "investigating the events/facts" (*pragmata*, 47; cf. Luke 1:1b—*pragmata*) in "a painstaking way" (cf. Luke 1:3a), if at all possible himself to be an "eyewitness observer" (*paronta kai ephoronta*, 47), and failing that to "listen to those with the most impartial account" (47; cf. Luke 1:2-3a—*autoptai... akribos*), and once "a body of notes" or "material" has been gathered (cf. Luke 1:2a—*paredosan*; 1:3a—*pasin*) "to arrange them into an order" (*taxin*, 48; cf. Luke 1:3b—*kathexēs*), adding the "beauty" or "expression," "figure," "rhythm" of a completed narrative (48; cf. Luke 1:1, 3a—*diēgēsis... ka'moi*)—all for the purpose of presenting the most "credible" account possible (47—*pithanoteros*; cf. Luke 1:4—*asphaleia*!). Luke's use of an eyewitness "we" in Part Two in the midst of an extensive omniscient narrative mode, which through a particular ordering of the events lends greater credibility to his narrative, divulges the distinctive practice and pursuit of historiography—*not* biography.

II. Talbert's Genetic Theory of Gospel Composition

Talbert argues that the canonical four gospels (and Acts) are *balanced* composites in *bios* form of four different conceptions of divine presence in Jesus, each of which derives from a distinct type of Jesus tradition/material (display of power [miracles]; moral guidance for living [sayings of the wise]; secrets of one's ultimate origin/destiny leading to repentance [apocalyptic revelations]; forgiveness of sins and faith [passion narrative]). He suggests that "...the canonical gospels appear to be attempts to avoid the reductionism of seeing the presence of God in Jesus in only one way and attempts to set forth a comprehensive and balanced understanding of both the divine presence and the discipleship it evokes" (1988a:66-67).

Talbert speaks of the new "wholes" (e.g., 1988a:68; 1979d:361), "inclusive reinterpretation" (e.g., 1979d:361, 362), their "controlling context" (e.g., 1988a:64, 67), and "the order and connection" of the narratives (e.g., 1988a:69) as safeguards against misunderstanding the nature of "the God who was manifest in Jesus" (1988a:68). Yet he never develops nor discusses narrative poetics in any way that makes it clear just how a new connected whole organizes the different types of divine presence into any *coherent* divine presence.[38] One gets the impression,

---

[38]For instance in his *Reading Luke* (1982d), one searches in vain for the role that, e.g., summaries, flashbacks, synchronisms, repetitions, etc. might play in

rather, that the gospels force the reader to confront the different types of presence all within the framework of the *bios* of one figure in a way that ensures that no one presence will unduly assert itself over the others.[39] So, for example, in Luke-Acts, "...Luke designed a picture of Jesus that would show him not only in terms of power, morality, and knowledge—all of which emphasize authority over the world—but also in terms of suffering and death. He enters into his glory only *after* experiencing his suffering (Luke 24:26)" (1979d:357-58; 1988a:66).[40]

Yet, it is as we look more closely at Talbert's notion of divine presence in Luke-Acts that we confront a basic contradiction in his "composite plus passion narrative" model (1979d:356; 1988a:65, 68). On the one hand, Luke gives his passion narrative no soteriological significance, and throughout the two volumes, asserts Talbert, "only Luke fails to speak of the connection between Jesus' death and the forgiveness of sins" (1988a:66; also cf. 1979d:357). His passion narrative amounts to a "grand rejection story...the human NO to God's messenger" (1988a:66; 1979d:357). Yet on the other hand, in following "the order and connection" of the narrative of Luke-Acts, "it comes clear" that

> it was not until after Jesus' death-resurrection-ascension-exaltation-gift of the Spirit that the disciples were effectively attached to him and the kingdom. From the order and connection of Luke's biographical narrative, one sees first that the kingdom is not so much a moral as a christological reality...and second that the experience of the kingdom...is mediated not so much by the language of Jesus as by what happened to him—death, resurrection, ascension, exaltation, receipt of the promise from the Father—and as a consequence of what happened to him (1988a:69).

---

tying various parts of the narrative together. On these and the notion of plot and story utilized below, see, e.g., N. Petersen, *Literary Criticism for New Testament Critics* (Philadelphia: Fortress, 1978) esp. 33-48.

[39]E.g., Talbert (1988a:68): "...a certain type of biographical narrative (composite plus passion narrative) was admirably suited to express the wholeness and balance of the good news about Jesus"; and (1979d:358): "The canonical gospels are not so much kerygma as reflections of the controversies about the legitimacy of the various forms of proclamation in the ancient church. They come into their present shape not so much as the result of a gradual attraction of Jesus tradition around the core magnet of a passion narrative but rather as the result of a conscious and deliberate composition related to a clear-cut theological stance about the nature of God and the nature of discipleship" (cf.also 1988a:67).

[40]In his *What Is A Gospel?* (1977a:119-20), Talbert speaks of Luke's stages of salvation history as a "controlling context, in order to indicate the legitimate hermeneutical use of the earthly Jesus" and finds precedent in Paul in, e.g., 1 Corinthians 15.

222   *David P. Moessner*

Is it conceivable that with Talbert one can read Luke-Acts in sequence (cf. Luke 1:3) and conclude that the "consequence of what happened" to Jesus in his rejection and death at the hands of his own people Israel has no soteriological significance in establishing the effective christological reality of the Kingdom of God where the presence of God is experienced as the forgiveness of sins? Has Luke actually relegated the total development of opposition and rejection that culminates on the cross only to a negative foil for the suddenly new and now saving events of resurrection, ascension, etc.? Could we not with Talbert's interpretation conclude that Jesus' suffering has no integral bearing on the kingdom at all, that it is a function of human sin and its No to God, so that now, after the resurrection, exaltation, and the gift of the Spirit one looks only to the *real saving* effective divine presence of God in Jesus through *those* events for the triumphant, even realized life of the forgiveness of sins, the experience of power, revelations of ultimate destiny, and so forth? Does not Talbert's interpretation of suffering and cross actually work directly against the kind of situation of over-realized eschatology that Talbert claims Luke is correcting in his two volumes?[41] As Parsons has pointed out (161, above), Talbert unfortunately has neither operated from an overall literary model nor moved very far from his redaction-critical method in which small tradition units are compared from one gospel to the next; so, for example, if Luke does not contain the parallel to Mark 10:45, nor the phrase, "for the forgiveness of sins" in Matt 26:28, then, somehow these "omissions" become telling for the whole "order and connection" of Luke's story.[42]

---

[41]If, as Talbert agrees, the resurrection, ascension, exaltation, gift of the Spirit have eschatological import, then his argument—that Luke in fighting an over-realized eschatology places emphasis on Jesus remaining in the world and enduring suffering *before* these eschatological, soteriologically effective events in order to show his readers that they must also bear the same conditions (i.e. Jesus' passion) "does not take one immediately out of the world" (1988a:66)—is void of all parenetic not to mention soteriological power. The same *conditions no longer apply.* According to Peter's first speech, quoting Joel, those who receive the Spirit are already living in the last/final days (Acts 2:17). Would Luke's audience after reading about the sufferings and death of the apostles-witnesses in Acts come to Talbert's conclusion: "...Luke, just as the other canonical Evangelists, does not tell his story of Jesus merely as a passion narrative. Rejection, suffering, and death are not the essence of the Christian's life, even though a Christian still experiences them" (1988a:66)?

[42]E.g., Talbert (1979d:356-57). Talbert in the same connection finds it soteriologically significant that Mark has the rending of the Temple curtain (he mentions nothing of Luke's account of this [23:45]) and the centurion's confession (again silent on Luke's account [23:47]). Talbert also apparently finds no special

Within the limits here we obviously cannot launch into a fuller treatment of all that Luke understands by the death of Jesus. Nevertheless, consider the following ways that Luke has organized his plot around the events of death *and* resurrection at the end of Part One:

(i) Simeon's double oracles (Luke 2:29-32, 34-35) reveal that Jesus' reign as son of David, Son of God, in which the Lord God, Savior of Israel has "put down the mighty from their thrones" (Mary) in "remembering his holy covenant, the oath which he swore to Abraham" (Zechariah) is effected only as Jesus is himself a "controverted sign" who spurs the "falling and rising of many" in Israel as God's "saving act" to all nations.[43] What the pious of Israel are expecting as the "divine presence" of their liberator (e.g., 2:38) is going to look different indeed (e.g., 2:35—Mary).[44]

(ii) At the beginning of the Galilean ministry, Jesus' rejection at Nazareth serves as a template for the whole mission of "release"/"forgiveness" that Jesus came to fulfill. The eschatological mission of the anointed prophet and Servant of Isaiah is being fulfilled in the very rejection of Jesus by his own countryfolk (4:21-30). Like the prophets of old, sent with redemptive gestures but rejected out of hand by their own folk, Jesus' eschatological mission to Israel (and eventually to those "outside the land" [the Acts]) is depicted in solidarity with Israel's past *history* of its stubborn rejection of the prophets (4:24-27).[45] Again this is not the kind of "divine presence" that sits well with pious, worshipping folk. And that Luke links Israel's rejection of Jesus already during his public ministry to a *mediation of salvation/release* is made clear by Jesus' preaching good news of release to the poor of Israel, the "sinners" and "tax collectors," the ill and handicapped and women who

---

soteriological significance to Jesus' words of forgiveness from the cross to the one malefactor (Luke 23:40-43), though with Mark's centurion Talbert states, "That God gives his presence to those who rejected his Son is the equivalent to saying that God forgives sinners" (!) (1979d:357). See also his "Martyrdom in Luke-Acts and the Lukan Social Ethic" (1983a: 99-100) where Luke 22:19-20 and Acts 20:28 are somehow devoid of atonement or soteriological significance, even though "both speak about the death of Jesus as the seal of the new covenant" (109 n. 2).

[43]See further, D. P. Moessner, "The Ironic Fulfillment of Israel's Glory," *Luke-Acts and the Jewish People: Eight Critical Perspectives* (ed. J. B. Tyson; Minneapolis: Augsburg Publishing House, 1988) 35-50; D. L. Tiede, "'Glory to Thy People Israel': Luke-Acts and the Jews," *Luke-Acts and the Jewish People,* 21-34.

[44] Quite differently apparently from Talbert, who in his *Reading Luke* (1982d) does not treat the Simeon oracles.

[45]See further, D. P. Moessner, "The 'Leaven of the Pharisees' and "'This Generation': Israel's Rejection of Jesus according to Luke," *JSNT* 34 (1988) 21-46.

hear "today" the "forgiveness of your sins"; while at the same time this divine bearing of salvation causes growing opposition by the leaders of the populace and the towns and villages as a whole to refuse Jesus' "good news" of repentance ("release"/"forgiveness" [aphiemi/aphesis: 5:20-24; 7:47-49]; "today" [sēmeron: 13:32-33; 19:5, 9; etc.]; refusal to "repent" [metanoēo, Galilee—10:13-15; Journey—11:29-32; 13:1-5; 15:1-2, 7, 10; 16:29-31; cf. 11:47-52; 12:54-59; 13:34-35; 19:41-44]).

(iii) Nearly 40% of Luke's Gospel is devoted to a long journey to Jerusalem (9:51-19:44) and is characterized as a fulfillment of Jesus' "exodus"/"departure"/"death," which he discusses with the scorned and persecuted prophets of the Exodus-Horeb theophanies and covenant, Moses and Elijah (9:28-36, esp. 9:31). From 9:51 all movement in both words and deeds of Jesus is fixed upon Jerusalem, where Jesus will receive the prophets' "reward" (13:33).[46] Though the "poor" continue to receive eschatological release, the crowds as a whole continue to increase in their opposition to heeding the voice from the mountain as is punctuated by Jesus' pronouncements of judgment upon an obdurate people (e.g., 11:29-32, 50-51; 12:57-59; 13:24-30, 35; 14:24; 17:26-30; 19:27, 41-44). The journey, then, not only leads to Jesus' rejection in Jerusalem, it is itself a journey of rejection.

But is this rejection devoid of saving significance in the larger movement of Luke-Acts? (a) Jesus first announces a denouement in Jerusalem once the disciples utter the fact of his messianic status. But this christological reality involves a "necessity" (dei) of Jesus as Son of Humankind "to suffer many things," "be rejected and killed" by the Sanhedrin in Jerusalem, and "on the third day to be raised up" (9:22). (b) Moreover, Jesus announces that his journey there necessitates the continual bearing of a cross with him by all who would "save" (sozo) their life. The journey therefore is corporate in nature, entailing the "following" of Israel of their crucified Messiah. And by calling upon the verdict of the final court of God (9:26), Jesus clearly signifies this "saving" and "forfeiting" life as an eschatological reality. (c) Furthermore, Jesus connects this journey of saving and forfeiting (cf. falling and rising) to the reality of the Kingdom of God (9:27). By Luke linking "these words" (9:27-28) with the revelation on the mountain of the glory of Jesus and of Moses and Elijah, Jesus' journey becomes an eschatological fulfillment of Moses and Elijah, rejected prophets who by

---

[46]For a fuller treatment, see D. P. Moessner, Lord of the Banquet. The Literary and Theological Significance of the Lukan Travel Narrative (Minneapolis: Fortress, 1989) esp. Part III, 81-257.

their death (Moses)[47] and "taking up" (Elijah)[48] anticipate the death and taking up (9:31, 51) of the Christ, who "alone" (9:36) is the "Chosen One" of the final Reign of God (9:35). It is no wonder again that this kind of "divine presence" remains mystifying (9:33, 40-41, 44-45) and unthinkable (9:45, 46-48, 49-50). (d) The journey is laced with "passion predictions" by Jesus and bound up in his own messianic consciousness with the whole history of Israel's rejection of God's messengers, on the one side, but also with God's overarching plan or necessity to effect salvation *precisely through this rejection*, on the other (11:47-54;[49] 12:49-53; 13:31-33; 14:27; 17:25; 18:31-34; cf. 19:14). In 18:31-34 as the journey nears its end (cf. 18:35), Jesus summons the twelve, those representative of the whole nation, to emphasize that his rejection *and* raising up in Jerusalem is a completion of *all* the things written by the prophets. As in 4:16-30, Israel's Scriptures are in some way a telling template for Jesus' rejection and resurrection. It would appear then that the entire journey of rejection, death, and being raised up has soteriological significance, in some sense a recapitulation, but more importantly, a consummation of *Israel's* history of salvation.

(iv) At table with the *twelve* (22:14-38) before Jesus' "suffering many things" (9:22; 17:25) reaches its conclusion (22:15), Jesus interprets his rejection as a voluntary *giving* and *shedding* of his body and blood "on behalf of"/"for the sake or benefit of" the twelve. To be sure, this rejection does not go unjudged (22:15b); but already forgiveness is promised to the disciples who, though they be "ashamed of Jesus and his words" (9:26a; 22:34!) when the Son of Humankind comes (9:26b; 22:22, 54-62), "turn" from their own participation in his rejection (22:32). Not only is forgiveness thus linked to repentance, as it will be again in the preaching in Acts, but it is tied to the pivotal voluntary, vicarious giving over to death on Jesus' part as a culmination of this rejection. Moreover, Jesus gives peculiar stress to the fact that his rejection by his own people is a necessary crowning and bringing to its intended goal the fate of the righteous suffering Servant of Isaiah who by his own folk "was reckoned as one unrighteous/without the Law" (Isa 53:12—Luke 22:37). It is totally beside the point that the Servant's voluntary giving up of his

---

[47]Deut 1:37; 3:26; 4:21-22; 31:2, 14; 34:1-6.

[48]Cf. *analambanō* (and cognates) in Luke 9:51; Acts 1:2, 11, 22 and 4 Kgdms 2:9, 10, 11.

[49]Luke's comment in Luke 11:53-54 connects Jesus' comments—about his own generation being held accountable for the death of all the prophets—to Jesus' own death.

life for the sins of the many is not quoted by Jesus. Jesus has already signified his coming death in those terms and the analogous situation of Jesus to the Servant of Isaiah is obvious enough. By placing the quote at the end of Jesus' public ministry and having Jesus point to that passage as its summation, Luke places Jesus' *death* at the center of the entire "saving act of God" (cf. 2:29-35).

(v) Luke ends Part One with two scenes (24:13-35, 36-49) which summarize "all that Jesus began to do and to teach" (Acts 1:1), even as they launch the events and preaching (speeches) of the one continuing history of Israel's salvation in Part Two. (a) The two disciples of the Emmaus journey recount what will become the essence of the preaching in Acts—Jesus a mighty prophet, crucified by Israel's leaders but now alive (24:19-23). Yet, though they were hoping he would redeem/liberate Israel (24:21a), they do not "see" the living Jesus journeying in their midst (cf. 24:24b). Jesus points to *"all* the things spoken by the prophets" and singles out two particular necessities (*dei*)[50] of Scriptural fulfillment: "the Messiah must suffer (many) things (pl.) and/so as to enter into his glory" (24:25-26). The entire rejection culminating in Jesus' death is coupled to the resurrection/entering glory. As at table with the twelve, Jesus' *rejection/death* becomes programmatic for the life that will accrue to Israel (and to the nations). Far from being a negative foil that is overcome in the resurrection, Messiah's suffering many things and death stands at the center of the positive *whole* of the Scriptures. If read with "open eyes" (24:31, 32b), the Scriptures divulge a divine necessity which forms a subject and object of faith/belief (24:25). Yet these Scriptures "are not opened" for the Emmaus disciples until their "eyes are opened" "through/in the breaking of the bread" (24:31a, 32b). Already "on the road" their sluggish "hearts" were being "fired" by Jesus' "opening up" to them the central thrust of all the Scriptures (24:25, 32b). But it was not until they heard and saw Jesus *"break* and *give* the bread" that they *"remembered* him," (see 24:8—*mnēmoneuō*) just as Jesus had told the apostles at table when he signified his broken body "for you"—"to remember me" (*ana-mnesis*, 22:19b). Messiah's death "for you" is the key that unlocks and "opens up" the significance of the entire plot of Jesus' rejection, suffering, and exaltation to glory.[51] (b) In 24:36-49 the divine necessity (*dei*) of Messiah Jesus' suffering *and*

---

[50]See further, C. H. Cosgrove, "The Divine *Dei* in Luke-Acts," *NovT* 26 (1984) 168-90; J. T. Squires, "The Plan of God in Luke-Acts," unpublished Ph.D. Dissertation, (Yale University 1988) esp. 228-77.

[51]Notice the strong link in language with Luke 22:37!

resurrection is linked explicitly by Jesus in another "opening" of the Scriptures to the "forgiveness/release of sins" and the "preaching of repentance" to Israel and the nations. That which by God's necessity must be fulfilled from the Scriptures for the soteriological-christological reality for the whole world involves *both* the suffering/death and resurrection of Messiah.[52]

Conclusion

To sum up: 1. The entire movement of the Gospel of Luke is directed to Jesus' death and resurrection in such a way that Jesus' rejection, suffering, and death are especially highlighted as soteriologically significant in the overall plan of God. It is difficult to conceive how one reading with the "order and connection" of the narrative can possibly disconnect Jesus' death from the forgiveness of sins. 2. Talbert's genetic theory of the gospels as "composite plus passion narrative" in guarding against subversion and reductionism in divine presence is not borne up by Luke's Gospel nor by Acts. Luke subsumes all of the Jesus traditions to the peculiar divine presence of a rejected, suffering, dying and exalted Messiah of Israel which effects a fulfillment of salvation for and to Israel and through Israel to the nations. Whatever problems and perversions of the gospel Luke may be addressing, he does *not* do so by coordinating and balancing different notions of divine presence. Instead, in both volumes Luke relates the whole career of Jesus to his cross and resurrection both backward and forward in the history of Israel and through that history to the whole world. 3. Jesus' place and the divine presence represented by him in the history of Israel are not "accidental" to a greater narrative concern of Luke-Acts to expose a deeper "essence"

---

[52]One may wonder why more Scriptures are not explicitly cited in Luke-Acts in describing Jesus Messiah as fulfilling a suffering and exalted figure. The main reason seems to be Luke's emphasis on the larger historical pattern of the rejection of Israel's prophets being repeated in eschatological fashion in the events of Jesus and of the early church. This larger pattern encompasses the whole of the Scriptures, especially "Moses and the prophets" (i.e. the Pentateuch and the former [the histories] and the latter prophets). See esp. Stephen's articulation of this pattern in "his" commentary on the whole movement of events in Luke-Acts in Acts 7. And on this pattern, see further, D. P. Moessner, "'The Christ Must Suffer': New Light on the Jesus—Peter, Stephen, Paul Parallels in Luke-Acts," *NovT* 28 (1986) 220-56; idem, *Lord of the Banquet*, 294-315, 322-25; on the Psalms as integral to the *whole* of Scriptural witness (Luke 24:44), see my "'The Christ Must Suffer,' The Church Must Suffer: Rethinking the Theology of the Cross in Luke-Acts," in *Society of Biblical Literature 1990 Seminar Papers*; ed. D. J. Lull (Atlanta: Scholars Press, 1990) 165-95, esp. 183-91.

as in biography. In short, there is no "life," no "character" Jesus, apart from his role in Israel's life and character.[53] This means, then, that Luke exhibits the concerns associated with the historian and not those of the biographer. Luke's choice of a connected *narrative* for "fulfilled events" may also suggest a special theological concern to tie the Messiah of Israel to the narratives of Israel.

---

[53]It is remarkable that nowhere in Talbert's discussion of the gospels as *balanced* views of divine presence in Jesus (1988a) does he mention *Israel*.

READING CHANCE, MOESSNER, AND PARSONS

Charles H. Talbert

Introduction

That three busy scholars would spend some time in dialogue with my past work is a gracious act on their part. Mikeal Parsons appears to have read virtually everything I have written. For that he needs a purple heart as well as my appreciation. He has correctly perceived that my published work has, in large measure, been a quest for a workable method by which to read the NT. He has recognized rightly that this quest has been an evolution from the start and has yet to find an end. For his attention to detail and his faithful pursuit of an accurate description, I want to express my thanks. Since, however, I have been asked for a response, I assume that more is desired than expressions of appreciation. In the ensuing conversation, let us focus on four areas in the following order: (1) the occasion or purpose of Luke-Acts; (2) the genre of Luke-Acts; (3) the need for a comprehensive method; and (4) the difference that a method makes.

The Occasion or Purpose of Luke-Acts

It is asserted that my method seems to require an anti-heresy occasion/purpose of Luke-Acts, an occasion that has been presupposed in my work from first to last (Parsons and Chance). Traditional redaction criticism took its cue from the study of the Pauline letters. Just as a Pauline letter can be properly understood only if one can specify the particular problem(s) in the church that evoked its writing, so, it is assumed, grasping a gospel's meaning is contingent upon one's being able to determine the specific problem(s) in the community from which it comes and to which it is written as a response. The gospels, like the Pauline letters, are occasional literature best interpreted as arguments addressed to specific pressing problems in the immediate community at the time of writing. When I wrote *Luke and the Gnostics* (1966b) and *Literary Patterns* (1974d), this was my assumption, too. If one can find what looks like a defense against Docetism or over-realized eschatology in the narrative, then it may be inferred that the Lukan community was currently troubled with such problems, problems which in the late sixties and early seventies were normally associated with Gnosticism.

By the time of the writing of *Reading Luke* (1982d), I saw that there were many other tendencies besides these two and that demanded, on redaction-critical assumptions, a broader based occasion. It did not mean that Luke was devoid of defenses against Docetism and over-realized eschatology, but it did mean that his concerns were far broader. By that time, however, I had begun to question the redaction-critical assumption that the canonical gospels were occasional literature analogous to Paul's letters. Foundation documents like the canonical gospels (and Acts) seemed more analogous to systematic theology, albeit in narrative form. That is, they attempt to set forth the Christian position not only in light of problems present and pressing, but also real but past, and real but potential. Such narrative theology tells the story of the community's founder (and in Acts, of the early church) in a way that expresses the values of the group in a balanced way, not just in response to one or more immediate issues that clamor for attention in the community's present. Anti-docetic tendencies while present, like any other tendencies, do not necessitate an inference about a present controversy in the Lukan community. Although it was never explicitly stated, it was with this assumption that *Reading Luke* (1982d) was written. Its references to legitimation techniques used by Luke-Acts and to defenses against over-realized eschatology and Docetism, therefore, do not necessarily presuppose a present and pressing problem in the Lukan community. Luke-Acts offers a balanced presentation of the Christian position in narrative form. I now say explicitly that my method does not mandate an anti-heresy purpose or occasion for Luke-Acts or any other document.

The Genre of Luke-Acts

It is on the question of genre that my colleagues focus especially. That is as it should be. Parsons writes from the point of view of one who is the co-author of a volume arguing against the literary unity of Luke and Acts. Moessner's assumption is that Luke-Acts is a continuation of biblical history. What that means is that the genre of Luke-Acts is history, history like that of Genesis through 2 Kings. Of the three, only Chance seems uncommitted to anything other than what the evidence of the primary sources dictates.

Parsons does not argue the genre issue from the primary sources. Instead he relies on David Aune's "three telling criticisms." (1) The a+b pattern of biography is present in only six of Diogenes Laertius' lives. (2) Diogenes is concerned only with who studied with whom and who succeeded whom, not with the legitimacy of their views. (3) Diogenes Laertius offers brief *lists* of students, not narratives of successors. Aune's own words need to be heard as he allegedly describes my position:

> The only examples of this genre are Diogenes Laertius' *Live of Philosophers*, a lengthy compendium of the lives and teachings of eighty-two ancient philosophers from Thales to Epicurus, written ca. A.D. 250 at the earliest. Talbert regards the similarities between Diogenes' *Lives* and Luke-Acts as remarkable, for both contain the life of the founder of a religious community, a list or narrative of successors, and a summary of the community's teaching (79).

Since Parsons rests his case on Aune instead of the primary sources, let us examine Aune's arguments one by one.

(1) Aune says in the material just cited that the only example of the genre of an a+b biography is Diogenes Laertius and that source is late. In *Literary Patterns* (1974d), I referred to a pre-Christian biography of Aristotle (130-31) and to first century BCE Herculaneum Papyri 1018, 1021, and possibly 1044 (133), in addition to Laertius. In *What Is A Gospel?* (1977a) I spoke of a pre-Christian Life of Aristotle and various collections of Successions of which Diogenes Laertius is the best preserved. In "Discipleship in Luke-Acts," (1985f) I mentioned *The Life of Pachomius* and Hilary of Arles' *Sermon on the Life of St. Honoratus*. At no time did I ever say the sole example of the a+b genre was Laertius or imply its only examples were late.

(2) Aune asserts that although I claim Laertius' biographies "usually" exhibit an a+b pattern, in fact only six lives out of eighty-two do so. In *Literary Patterns* (1974d), I noted that the a+b pattern is characteristic of

five lives of founders of philosophical schools in Laertius (127) and listed them as Aristippus, Plato, Zeno, Pythagoras, and Epicurus (137, n.16). My comment was: "The similarities between the lives of founders of philosophical schools presented by Laertius and Luke-Acts are remarkable" (129). In "Discipleship in Luke-Acts" (1985f), it was specified that only certain lives in Laertius reflect the a+b pattern (63) and six were specified: Socrates, Aristippus, Plato, Zeno, Pythagoras, and Epicurus (74, n.8). From first to last I have contended that only five or six founders of philosophical schools mentioned by Laertius reflect the pattern, not Laertius as a whole.

(3) Aune contends that the a+b pattern of biography has only *lists* of a founder's successors, not a narrative as Luke-Acts does. In *Literary Patterns*, I specified that the biographies of Zeno and Epicurus in Laertius had brief narratives of successors (1974d:137, n.16) and that the pre-Christian biography of Aristotle ended with an anecdote about his choice of a successor (130-31). In "Discipleship in Luke-Acts" (1985f), I pointed out that *The Life of Pachomius* had a long succession narrative. It is true, of course, that the succession principle can be conveyed both by lists and by narratives. Both are found in such biographies in antiquity.

(4) Aune argues that Diogenes is concerned only with who succeeded whom, not with the legitimacy of their views. Chance questions whether or not the b-component of a founder's biography intended to legitimate successors, referring to one of Zeno's followers, Dionysius, who deviated from the founder. *The Life of Pachomius*, 119, says, however, that Pachomius' successor Orsisius zealously emulated the life of the founder. Hilary of Arles' *Sermon on the Life of St. Honoratus*, 8, says Honoratus' successor's task was to do what the founder had done. These two Christian appropriations of the a+b biographical form used for founders explicitly say that the succession narrative was to demonstrate continuity between founder and successor. The succession list found in *Pirke Aboth* certainly has as its aim to assert continuity between the rabbis of the time of writing and the oral law of Moses. The succession narrative of Laertius' "Life of Epicurus" shows continuity, not identity, between founder and successors. Given this context, the example of deviation from Zeno by Dionysius should be understood as a discrediting of the one who deviated. In so doing, the deviation demonstrated the true succession. The a+b biography is concerned to demonstrate continuity between the founder and the true successors and discontinuity between the founder and false followers.

Having looked at Aune's "three telling criticisms" and more, what are we to conclude? I suggest: (a) Aune has not read carefully or reported accurately but opposes a strawman of his construction; (b) his negative assertions do not apply to my thesis and, therefore, constitute no refutation of my thesis about the genre of Luke-Acts; (c) it is better for a scholar to read primary sources than to rely on secondary literature for his case.

There is yet another problem which Parsons has with the hypothesis of the genre of Luke-Acts. He contends that Luke and Acts do not belong to the same genre. He says, "The basic question is this: Is the same author capable of producing works belonging to two distinct genres of literature?" This is not the basic question at all. Of course, the same author can produce works in more than one genre. The basic question is: did the Third Evangelist do it? Is there evidence to support the disunity of Luke and Acts? Henry Cadbury did not think so; nor do I, on the basis of current evidence. One should remember that the architecture analysis of *Literary Patterns* (1974d) was a method borrowed from Classicist Cedric Whitman of Harvard, who used such detection of large patterns to argue, with success, for the unity of Homer's work against its detractors. The large patterns that control the whole of Luke-Acts argue, for me at least, for a unified conception that controls the whole. It is Luke-Acts, not Luke and Acts, about which one must speak in the area of genre, at least until better evidence is forthcoming.

Chance has read Talbert and some of the ancient texts, Diogenes Laertius and *The Life of Pachomius*, and has checked the references to the Herculaneum papyri and the pre-Christian life of Aristotle. After some fine-tuning, which is appropriate, he concludes that there was such a thing as an a+b biography of a founder and that in the case of Laertius' "Life of Epicurus" and *The Life of Pachomius*, the b-component was more than a list of successors. His chief concerns are four: (a) scale discrepancy; (b) paucity of examples; (c) questionable connection with an anti-heresy occasion; and (d) the function of the b-component. The last two questions have already been answered: (c) The genre is not indissolubly tied to an anti-heresy occasion; (d) The function of the b-component is to insure continuity with the founder, either by showing deviance and discrediting the deviant or by showing continuity and legitimating a follower. Let us now turn to the two unanswered issues.

(a) Chance repeats David Barr's complaint about scale. The b-component of such biographies is not as long as the Lukan Acts. The discrepancy in scale, it is alleged, cancels any possibility that Luke-Acts

234 *Charles H. Talbert*

and Laertius' "Life of Epicurus" or *The Life of Pachomius* could belong to the same genre. Scale, however, is not a criterion of genre. Consider the matter of scale in relation to Paul's letters. Since Greco-Roman letters differ in scale as totalities and in their parts from the scale of Paul's writings and their parts, does this mean Paul's writings cannot be letters? Of course not.

(b) Chance also expresses a concern over the relatively few examples of a+b biographies of founders that we have. If a literary form were that scarce, could it have influenced Luke? Is he assuming that what we have extant is what there was? "References in ancient literature to biographies not now extant as well as fragments of numerous 'lives' found among the Oxyrhynchus and Herculaneum papyri show the paucity of the extant remains of the Mediterranean biographical tradition" (1988a, 54). Is he assuming that what was once extant but now is not extant contained no more examples of the a+b biography? Is he assuming that what we have extant showing that Christians appropriated the a+b form on more than one occasion (*The Life of Pachomius* and *The Life of St. Honoratus*) has no bearing on the possibility that Luke could have done the same thing? Is he assuming that Luke could not have appropriated what other Christians did in fact employ?

What should one conclude? I suggest: (a) that Chance's positive reaction to the hypothesis that Luke-Acts belongs by genre to the a+b biographies of founders in antiquity is due to his reading the primary sources instead of relying on Aune; and (b) that his four reservations are not really major problems, given what has been said above.

Moessner's reservations are about the biographical genre's being applicable for Luke-Acts. He thinks the Lukan writings better belong to biblical history that talks about the history of Israel and about what sort of action God is effecting through the human actors in the story.[1] The story is theological, not christological in Luke, theological, not ecclesiological in Acts. The overriding question in Luke is not "What sort of person is this?" but rather, "Who is this person in light of God's dealings with Israel?" We do learn some about the "sort of person" Jesus was (e.g., compassion for the ill and grieving, predilection for tax collectors and sinners, enjoyment of the company of women and treatment of them as disciples), but in every instance this quality is not

---

[1]Moessner's focus on Tacitus' *Agricola* as close to Luke's concern is gratifying since it is a biography.

linked to a particular moral essence or structures of virtues but rather to the presence or reign of God in Jesus. It seems to me that Moessner's concern is to distance Jesus from the Greek world and to insure that it is biblical categories that one uses in speaking of him. I agree. The contents of the Lukan gospel are Jewish in character. Jesus is described not in terms of Greek virtues but in terms of Jewish eschatology. He is the one in whom the Kingdom of God is breaking in and who, therefore, acts like this, and in doing so fulfills the divine will spoken by the Jewish Scriptures, heavenly beings, and living prophets. What I fail to see is where this Jewish eschatological description of Jesus is not "who he is" or "what sort of person he is," that is, biographical. Remember, biography wanted to depict what was particular about the individual. To be the final messenger to Israel, for example, can be what is distinctive about him, what is his essence.

There is no doubt that Luke-Acts begins with a reference to the divine plan ("the things fulfilled among us") and that the subsequent narrative is the working out of this theme of the preface. Is the theocentric theme of the divine plan the background against which the christological/biographical foreground in the gospel and the ecclesiological foreground in the Acts is painted, or is it itself the foreground? Polybius, for example, believed a divine providence ruled the world and expounded this belief in his *Histories*. Nevertheless, this was only the backdrop against which he pursued his dual purpose: (a) providing useful training and experience for the practical politician (3.6.6ff.), and (b) teaching the reader how to bear the vicissitudes of Fortune by describing what had befallen others (1.35.36; 2.35.5ff.). Josephus' *Antiquities* share the cultural belief, although as a Jew he would have viewed the divine necessity as deriving from the personal will of God who is a living person and not a neutral necessity (e.g., 10.8.2-3*142). Nevertheless, this was but the background against which he pursued his aim: to legitimate the Jews by an appeal to their antiquity. The narrative, Genesis through 2 Kings, operates with the theme of the word of God which is fulfilled in the history of the people. This, however, is the backdrop against which an etiological purpose can be worked out: where did the signs of Jewishness like sabbath, circumcision, the law, the priesthood, the sacrifices, the land, the kingship, the Temple, etc., originate (cf. 1 Macc 1:41-50)?

It is my thesis that the Third Evangelist likewise uses the divine plan as a backdrop for the christological and ecclesiological focus of his two volumes. Because the focus is on the founder of the church, a biographical genre is what is appropriate. Because the founder is normative for his followers, a succession narrative, greatly expanded, that shows both deviance and continuity in Jesus' followers is an appropriate second volume for the biography. The culture offered such a model in the a+b biographies of founders; Luke used it and molded it as his circumstances dictated. It is in such terms that I think Moessner must be answered, because neither prologue nor mode of narration is genre specific.

The Need for a Comprehensive Method

Parsons, like Norman Petersen, faults me for lacking a comprehensive literary model, one that is informed by the most recent trends in literary criticism, and cites Stephen Moore's complaint that I seem uninformed by recent literary criticism. The methodological *a priori* of Parsons is the type of literary criticism he learned from his mentor, Alan Culpepper. It is an *a priori* that he shares with Petersen and Moore. For these scholars, literary criticism means "their kind of literary criticism," one that focuses on such things as omniscient narrators and implied readers. Their essential criticism is that I am not doing what they are doing.[2]

Do I have a comprehensive literary model? If their kind, I do not; of another kind, perhaps. In two places Parsons summarizes my method as it had evolved up to *Reading Luke*. In the first (See Parsons, 151-53), he specifies four components. (a) One focuses on large thought units and their relation to Lukan thought as a whole. (b) Source theories are suspended in favor of a close reading of the final form of the text with either rhetorical criticism or modern narrative criticism, followed by the use of a synopsis to compare Luke with the other gospels. (c) The purpose of such reading is not to reconstruct a history of the tradition but to enter into the gospel's own narrative world. (d) The dialogue of the interpreter is with Greco-Roman literature and modern literary criticism rather than secondary sources. In the second place (See Parsons, 164), he speaks of three components: (a) interest in a close reading; (b) constant reference to Greco-Roman parallels; and (c) focus

---

[2]Two recent studies of gospel narrative that seem to be doing what I think I am doing are: Sharyn E. Dowd, *Prayer, Power, and the Problem of Suffering: Mark 11:22-25 in the Context of Markan Theology* (SBLDS, 105; Atlanta: Scholars, 1988), and Susan R. Garrett, *The Demise of the Devil: Magic and the Demonic in Luke's Writings* (Minneapolis: Fortress, 1989).

on the theological message of the text. Parsons recognizes that the method, described by the second set of three points, has been applied not only to a gospel but also to the Corinthian correspondence (and although he missed it, to 1 Peter [1986c, 141-51]). This shows that the method is detachable from the alleged results derived from its use.

It is *my* method in the sense that I used it in *Reading Luke* (1982d) and *Reading Corinthians* (1987a). It is not *my* method in the sense that it is an eclectic assortment of components garnered from elsewhere. The close reading is indebted above all to James Muilenburg's rhetorical criticism (=New Criticism). My focus on the Mediterranean milieu of New Testament writings began under the influence of Lou Silberman and Kendrick Grobel in graduate school, was encouraged by the fruitfulness of such research in the dissertations produced at Harvard and Yale during my first two decades of teaching, and was enabled by two post-doctoral years spent reading Greco-Roman literature. The concern with the religious content of New Testament writings was nurtured by my *Doktorvater* Leander Keck, confirmed by Jacob Neusner[3] and Clifford Geertz,[4] and has been sustained by the fact that I am a churchman. It is an eclectic method.

Why should these components be chosen and not others? Does such an eclectic method have any philosophical underpinnings? Yes, American pragmatism is its philosophical basis. What works? What way of reading makes the best sense of a text? That combination of approaches that yields the best result is "the" correct method. This is the philosophical basis of an eclectic approach to method.

How does one determine what constitutes "what works," or "which way of reading makes the best sense of a text"? Two criteria decide: (1) What kind of document is being interpreted? and (2) For whom is the document being read? (1) The New Testament is a religious book. It is expressive of a particular religious community's world, of its assessment

---

[3]J. Neusner ("Judaism within the Disciplines of Religious Studies," *C S R Bulletin*, 14 [1983] 143) wrote: "Even though, through philology, we understand every word of a text, and through history, we know just what happened in the event or time to which the text testifies, we still do not understand that text. A religious text serves not merely the purposes of philology or history. It demands its proper place as a statement of religion. Read as anything but a statement of religion, it is misunderstood."

[4]Geertz (*The Interpretation of Cultures.* [New York: Basic Books], 18) wrote: "A good interpretation of anything—a poem, a person, a history, a ritual, an institution, a society—takes us to the heart of that of which it is an interpretation. When it does not do that, but leads us instead somewhere else...it may have its intrinsic charms; but it is something else than what the task at hand...calls for."

238   *Charles H. Talbert*

of serious life issues and ultimate questions. If it is read properly, it is read to enter that world and to hear its assessments. So the interpretative method that "works" is the one that better enables the final form of the biblical text to confront us with its own perspective, a distinctively Christian one. (2) For a Christian in the community of faith, the question is whether or not a method of reading enables her to enter the Christian world, to appropriate its norms, and to be who she is as a Christian. For a humanist in the liberal arts environment of a college or university, the question is whether or not a method of reading enables her to gather up this part of our cultural heritage in a coherent form so that she and her students may be confronted with it and may be enabled to understand better who they are as men and women with this history. That is, interpretation has practical ends in both cases.

Is this a comprehensive literary model? From my perspective, it is comprehensive enough to enable me to do my work (pragmatism again!). It also influences *how* I do it. (a) It determines the style of my current writing. *Reading Luke* (1982d) and *Reading Corinthians* (1987a) are both written for as wide an audience as possible although they are cutting edge research. Early twentieth-century liberals like Shirley Jackson Case and Shailer Matthews, for example, wrote this way; we fail to emulate them at our peril. Biblical research has practical ends which can only be realized if scholars communicate with as wide an audience as possible. (b) It determines the orientation of my current writing. I do not feel the discontinuity between homiletical concerns in biblical study and faithfulness to a biblical author's world of thought that Parsons does. In fact, *Acts* (1984a) in the Knox Preaching Guides uses, usually, the summary of Lukan theology in a large thought unit as the homiletical suggestion. This is, in my judgment, as it should be when one's interpretative community is the church. It is hardly a violation of the Lukan world of thought.[5] (c) It determines how I evaluate other types of biblical criticism. " Testing the spirits" in various methodologies is a part of a theologian's critical task (so Käsemann). Does a method yield the religious results for which I am seeking? That tool is to be appropriated. Does a method fail to yield the fruit desired? That tool may be of value for someone else but not for me. The desired end, not what is the traditional way to read or what is the latest literary theory, provides the criterion for appropriation of methodological tools. This

---

[5]For the early church, "real interpretation of Scripture is church preaching." (Ellen Van Leer, *Tradition and Scripture in the Early Church* [Assen: Van Gorcum], 92-96).

criterion caused me to eschew structuralism a decade ago and makes me hesitant about Parsons' type of literary criticism now. It is long on theory and short on results. Norman Petersen's *Literary Criticism for New Testament Critics* (1978) is a prime example, as are the dissertations done in this way that I have read in the past six years as editor of the SBL Dissertation Series. Their interpretation does not lead naturally to Christian proclamation and parenesis, or for that matter to a human encounter with the religious world of the early Christians.[6] Why then cite its protagonists?[7]

The Difference a Method Makes

(4) Did the changes in my methodology at various stages affect my reading of the text? Parsons says that "by observing the way he applied different methods to the same passage, we may gauge the degree to which Talbert's method does or does not inform his interpretation (Parsons, 168). He then chooses two examples. (a) The treatment of martyrdom in the different "stages of my method's evolution (redaction criticism, architecture analysis, the method of *Reading Luke*) demonstrate that "for Talbert, a change in method does entail a change in emphasis or interpretation" (Parsons, 169) (b) The interpretation of Luke 7:1-10 in Talbert's redaction critical stage and in *Reading Luke* (1982d), however, shows that, except for the cosmetic elimination of any references to Q the interpretation is the same. Parsons concludes: "Talbert drew conclusions regarding the meaning of Luke 7:1-10 based on Luke's redaction of traditional material, rather than on his conformity to or deviance from literary conventions of contemporary Greco-Roman parallels" (Parsons, 169) This is described as a "lapse" of the type that "occur often enough to question how much previous conclusions based on intensive redaction-critical analysis have shaped Talbert's interpretation of certain passages, and how much 'new' his new interpretative method really discovers" (Parsons, 169).

---

[6]Continuity between classical and modern literary theory and practice was broken by the theories and practices of romantic writers, English and German, in the nineteenth century (M. H. Abrams, *The Mirror and the Lamp: Romantic Theory and the Critical Tradition* [New York: Norton, 1958]). A poetics developed in a post-romantic era to read post-romantic fiction cannot, without justification, be assumed appropriate for interpreting literature from the pre-romantic period.

[7]If I were to cite literary critics with whom I have sympathy, the names would include R. Alter and M. Sternberg.

In this instance, Parsons is raising the question whether or not suspending source theories offers any gain to interpretation. Remember his statement of this part of my method in *Reading Luke*.

> The earlier approach, using a synopsis, involved a careful scrutiny of every variant between the Lucan text and an alleged source. The later tendency has been to *start* with the continuous text of the Gospel and to do a close reading of it as a finished product by either rhetorical criticism or modern narrative criticism. *Then* a synopsis is used to compare Luke with the other Gospels, which are viewed not as alleged sources but as independent developments of the same basic tradition (Parsons, 151-52).

Keep in mind that this is not the method as a whole about which he speaks but one fourth of it, the part involving suspension of any source theory for a study of a gospel. Note further that this component has two parts: (a) where one starts, that is, with a continuous reading of the text; and (b) where one ends, that is with a comparison of one gospel with the others using a synopsis. The only difference between assuming a source theory and not assuming one at this level is how one regards the other gospels, either as a real source of the text under consideration or as an independent development of the same tradition. If there is anything "new" to be had, it ought to be derived from the continuous reading. The comparison of Luke with the other gospels to discern differences between them is to guarantee that nothing will be lost that was gained from assuming a source theory. The second part of this component of the method is not supposed to discern anything new but to preserve the insights gained from a study of a synopsis, yet without assuming a source theory. *To compare Luke with Mark and Matthew yields the same results whether one assumes the two source theory or no source theory.* If there is a lapse here, it is in Parsons' logic.

Conclusion

Such a conversation with one's colleagues in the profession ought to go on until clarity is achieved. Perhaps these sometimes critical responses on my part will suffice to insure enough dialogue in the future to move us further along the road toward understanding. In no case should my responses detract from the very real appreciation I feel for their time spent on a serious engagement of my perspectives on the New Testament, especially on Luke-Acts. Dare I say, "May their tribe be legion"?

BIBLIOGRAPHY OF CHARLES H. TALBERT

Mikeal C. Parsons

1965a Review of Hans Conzelmann, *The Theology of St. Luke.*
       RevExp 62:97-98.
1965b Review of A. Q. Morton and G. H. C. MacGregor, *The
       Structure of Luke and Acts* and D. M. Smith, Jr., *The
       Composition and Order of the Fourth Gospel. RL* 35:158-
       59.
1966a Review of M. D. Goulder, *Type and History in Acts. RevExp*
       63:101-3.
1966b *Luke and the Gnostics: An Examination of the Lucan Purpose.*
       Nashville: Abingdon.
       Reviewed:
       RevExp 4 (1967) 537. (F. Stagg)
       JR 47 (1967) 78. (P. Kjesth)
       CurTM 39 (1968) 54. (E. Krentz)
       JBL 85 (1966) 264-66. (E. Ellis)
1966c "A Non-Pauline Fragment at Romans 3:24-26?" *JBL* 85:287-96.
1966d "II Peter and the Delay of the Parousia." *VC* 20:137-45.
1966e "The Gospels." Pp. 3-64 in *Studies in Christian Living.* N.p.:
       Board of Education of the Methodist Church.
1967a "Again: Paul's Visits to Jerusalem." *NovT* 9:26-40.
1967b "The Problem of Pre-existence in Philippians 2:6-11." *JBL*
       86:141-53.
1967c with Cheryl Exum. "The Structure of Paul's Speech to the
       Ephesian Elders (Acts 20:18-35)." *CBQ* 29:233-36 .
1967d "The Lukan Presentation of Jesus' Ministry in Galilee."
       RevExp 64:485-97.
1968a "An Anti-Gnostic Tendency in Lucan Christology." *NTS*
       14:259-71.

1968b   Review of James Kallas, *Jesus and the Power of Satan*, and Fred Craddock, *The Pre-Existence of Christ*. RL 37:477-78.

1968c   Review of R. P. Martin, *Carmen Christi: Philippians 2:5-11 in Recent Interpretation and in the Setting of Early Christian Worship*. JBL 87:480-81.

1968d   "The Anatomy of Stand-Taking." *The Baptist Student* 47:13-15.

1969a   "Tradition and Redaction in Romans 12:9-21." NTS 16:83-94.

1969b   Review of Issac Asimov, *Asimov's Guide to the Bible, Volume II: The New Testament*. *Winston-Salem Journal and Sentinel*, Sunday, November 9, Section D4.

1970a   "The Redaction Critical Quest for Luke the Theologian." Pp. 171-222 in *Jesus and Man's Hope: Proceedings of the Pittsburgh Festival on the Gospels*, vol 1. Ed. D. G. Miller and D. Y. Hadidian. Pittsburgh: Pittsburgh Theological Seminary.

1970b   "Artistry and Theology: An Analysis of the Architecture of John 1:19-5:47." CBQ 32:341-66.

1970c   Editor. *Reimarus: Fragments*. Trans. Ralph S. Fraser. Lives of Jesus Series 1. Philadelphia: Fortress. Reprinted, Macon, GA: Mercer University, 1985.
         Reviewed:
         Encounter 32 (1971) 248.
         Int 25 (1971) 530-31.
         CBQ 34 (1972) 119-21.
         Dialog 11 (1972) 308-9.
         JBL 91 (1972) 120-21.
         Theology 75 (1972) 211-13.
         RevExp 71 (1974) 399-400.

1970d   Review of Lesslie Newbigin, *The Finality of Christ*. *Encounter* 31:195-96.

1971   Review of Robert H. Smith, *Concordia Commentary: Acts*. *Encounter* 32:168-69.

1972   With E. V. McKnight. "Can the Griesbach Hypothesis Be Falsified?" JBL 91:338-68.

1973   Review of Eckhard Plümacher, *Lukas als hellenistischer Schriftsteller: Studien zur Apostelgeschichte*. JBL 92:302-3.

1974a Review of Mgr. de Solages, *La composition des Evangiles: de Luc et de Matthieu et leurs sources. JBL* 93:464-65.
1974b "A Historical Introduction to Acts." *RevExp* 71:437-49.
1974c Review of Morton Smith, *The Secret Gospel. ANQ* 14:283-85.
1974d *Literary Patterns, Theological Themes, and the Genre of Luke-Acts.* SBLMS 20. Missoula: Scholars Press. (Japanese trans. by Koji Kayama. Tokyo: Kyodan, 1980.)
       Reviewed:
       CurTM 3 (1976) 361. (D. Miesner)
       JAAR 45 (1977) 85-86. (P. Minear)
       CBQ 38 (1976) 131. (G. Graystone)
       Int 31 (1977) 94. (D. Reeves)
1974e Review of Frank Stagg, *Polarities of Man's Existence in Biblical Perspective*, and R. E. Brown, ed., *Peter in the New Testament. RL* 43:388-89.
1975a Review of Hans-Joachim Michel, *Die Abschiedsrede des Paulus an die Kirche Apg 20:17-38. JBL* 94:145.
1975b "The Concept of the Immortals in Mediterranean Antiquity." *JBL* 94:419-36.
1975c "Nicodemus and the Challenge of Christ." Pp. 24-34 in *To Be a Person of Integrity*. Ed. R. James Ogden. Valley Forge: Judson.
1976a Review of Michi Miyoshi, *Der Anfang des Reiseberichts, Lk 9:51-10:24. JBL* 95:138-39.
1976b "The Myth of a Descending-Ascending Redeemer in Mediterranean Antiquity." *NTS* 22:418-40.
1976c "Shifting Sands: The Recent Study of the Gospel of Luke." *Int* 30:381-95.
1976d Review of Ward Gasque, *A History of the Criticism of the Acts of the Apostles. JBL* 95:494-96.
1976e Review of Eric Franklin, *Christ the Lord: A Study in Luke-Acts. RL* 45:517-18.
1976f Review of Roger Hazelton, *Ascending Flame, Descending Dove. ANQ* 16:232-33.
1977a *What is a Gospel? The Genre of the Canonical Gospels.* Philadelphia: Fortress. (Reprinted, London: SPCK, 1978; and as Reprints of Scholarly Excellence 9, Macon, GA: Mercer University, 1985.)
       Reviewed:
       JBL 98 (1979) 439; 440. (P. Shuler)

Int 33 (1979) 215. (R. Hiers)
Dialog 19 (1980) 72. (W. Pilgrim)
PSTJ 31 (1978) 45. (V. Furnish)
Theology 82 (1979) 301. (J. K. Riches)
AUSS 17 (1979) 130. (S. Kubo)
JAAR 47 (1979) 314. (N. Petersen)
See also:
    David E. Aune, "The Problem of the Genre of the Gospels: A Critique of C. H. Talbert's *What Is a Gospel?*" in *Gospel Perspectives: Studies of History and Tradition in the Four Gospels* (ed. R. T. France and D. Wenham; Sheffield: JSOT, 1981) 2:9-60.

1977b   "Response to Alan Dundes." Pp. 64-65 in *The Hero Pattern and the Life of Jesus Protocol of the 25th Colloquy, 12 December 1976.* Ed. Alan Dundes. Protocol Series of the Colloquies of the Center for Hermeneutical Studies in Hellenistic and Modern Culture 25. Berkeley: The Center for Hermeneutical Studies in Hellenistic and Modern Culture.

1978a   "Biographies of Philosophers and Rulers as Instruments of Religious Propaganda in Mediterranean Antiquity." *Aufstieg und Niedergang der Römischen Welt: Geschichte und Kultur Roms im Spiegel der neueren Forschung* II.16.2: 1619-51. Ed. Hildegard Temporini and Wolfgang Haase. Berlin and New York: Walter de Gruyter.

1978b   "Oral and Independent or Literary and Interdependent? A Response to A. B. Lord's 'The Gospels as Oral Traditional Literature.'" Pp. 93-102 in *The Relationships Among The Gospels.* Ed. William O. Walker, Jr. San Antonio: Trinity University Press.

1978c   Review of Millar Burrows, *Jesus in the First Three Gospels.* *CBQ* 40:432-33.

1978d   *"The Birth of the Messiah*: A Review Article." *PersRelSt* 5:212-16.

1978e   Editor. *Perspectives on Luke-Acts.* Perspectives in Religious Studies: Special Studies Series 5. Danville and Edinburgh: Association of Baptist Professors of Religion/T. & T. Clark.
Reviewed:

     ATR 61 (1979) 410-12. (P. Parker)
     ExpT 90 (1979) 280. (I. Marshall)
     PersRelSt 6 (1979) 254-58. (E. Hamrick)
     TS 40 (1979) 351-54. (R. O'Toole)
     RTR 38 (1979) 88-89. (R. Maddox)

1979a Review of John Drury, *Tradition and Design in Luke's Gospel.* *JBL* 98:151-53.

1979b Review of Fridolin Keck, *Die öffentliche Abschiedsrede Jesu in Lk 20:45-21:36: Eine redaktions und motivgesschichtliche Untersuchung.* *CBQ* 41:341-42.

1979c Review of Richard J. Cassidy, *Jesus, Politics, and Society: A Study of Luke's Gospel.* *RL* 48:123-24.

1979d "The Gospel and the Gospels." *Int* 33:351-62.

1980a "Prophecies of Future Greatness: The Contribution of Greco-Roman Biographies to the Understanding of Luke 1:5-4:15." Pp. 129-41 in *The Divine Helmsman: Studies on God's Control of Human Events Presented to Lou H. Silberman.* Eds. J. L. Crenshaw and Samuel Sandmel. New York: KTAV.

1980b Review of Robert F. O'Toole, *Acts 26: The Christological Climax of Paul's Defense (Acts 22:1-26:32).* *CBQ* 42:130-31.

1980c Review of Hans-Theo Wrege, *Die Gestalt des Evangeliums: Aufbau und Struktur der Synoptiker sowie der Apostelgeschichte.* *CBQ* 42:395-96.

1980d Review of Augustin George, *Etudes sur l'oeuvre de Luc.* *JBL* 99:622-23.

1980e Review of David R. Cartlidge and David L. Dungan, *Documents for the Study of the Gospels.* *PersRelSt* 7:243-46.

1981a Review of Frank Zimmerman, *The Aramaic Origin of the Four Gospels.* *JAOS* 101:450.

1981b Review of Howard C. Kee, *Christian Origins in Sociological Perspective.* *Int* 35:322-23.

1981c "The Gospel and the Gospels." Pp. 14-26 in *Interpreting the Gospels.* Ed. James L. Mays. Philadelphia: Fortress. (Reprint of 1979c.)

1981d "The Recent Study of the Gospel of Luke." Pp. 197-213 in *Interpreting the Gospels.* Ed. James L. Mays. Philadelphia: Fortress. (Reprint of 1976c.)

1981e   Review of Albert Fuchs, *Die Entwicklung der Beelzebulkontroverse bei den Synoptikern.* CBQ 43:464-65.

1981f   Review of David Tiede, *Prophecy and History in Luke-Acts.* JAAR 49:681.

1981g   "Athens and Jerusalem: Allies or Antagonists?" *Mission Journal* 15:3-7.

1982a   Review of Gerhard Schneider, *Die Apostelgeschichte 1: Einleitung, Kommentar zu Kap.1,1—8,40.* CBQ 44:162-63.

1982b   Review of Joseph Fitzmyer, *To Advance the Gospel: New Testament Studies.* BTB 12:96.

1982c   *The Certainty of the Gospel: The Perspective of Luke-Acts.* Annual Lectures on Christian Theology 5. DeLand: Stetson University Press.

1982d   *Reading Luke: A Literary and Theological Commentary on the Third Gospel.* New York: Crossroad.
        Reviewed:
        JBL 104 (1985) 341. (J. Tyson)
        TS 44 (1983) 533. (R. Karris)
        PersRelSt 11 (1984) 284. (M. Parsons)
        Faith and Mission 1 (1983) 96. (A. Nations)
        CumSem 21 (1983) 26. (R. Brawley)
        BTB 14 (1984) 158. (J. Kodell)
        CBQ 46 (1984) 377. (F. Danker)

1982e   "The Way of the Lukan Jesus: Dimensions of Lukan Spirituality." *PersRelSt* 9:237-49.

1983a   "The Contribution of the View of Martyrdom in Luke-Acts to an Understanding of the Lukan Social Ethic." Pp. 99-110 in *Political Issues in Luke-Acts.* Eds. R. J. Cassidy and P. J. Scharper. Maryknoll: Orbis.

1983b   "The Gospel Genre: The Seminar and Its Context." Pp. 197-202 in *Colloquy on New Testament Studies: A Time for Reappraisal and Fresh Approaches.* Ed. Bruce Corley. Macon: Mercer University Press.

1983c   Review of Frederick W. Danker, *Benefactor. Mission Journal* 17:23.

1983d   Review of Jürgen Roloff, *Die Apostelgeschichte: Übersetzt und erklärt. CBQ* 45:506-7.

1983e Review of Franz Georg Untergassmair, *Kreuzweg und Kreuzigung Jesu: Ein Beitrag zur lukanischen Redaktionsgeschichte und zur Frage nach der lukanischen "Kreuzestheologie."* JBL 102:342-43.

1983f Editor. *Luke-Acts: New Perspectives from the Society of Biblical Literature Seminar.* New York: Crossroad.
Reviewed:
CurTM 13 (1986) 55-56. (R. Smith)
CTQ 49 (1985) 217-218. (A. Just, Jr.)
BTB 18 (1988) 37-39. (J. Via)

1983g "Promise and Fulfillment in Lucan Theology." Pp. 91-103 in 1983f.

1984a *Acts.* Knox Preaching Guides. Atlanta: John Knox.
Reviewed:
RevExp 82 (1985) 443. (R. Omanson)
Lexington Theological Quarterly (1986) 29-30. (R. White)

1984b Review of Gerhard Schneider, *Die Apostelgeschichte: II. Teil, Kommentar zu Kap. 9:1-28:31. CBQ* 46:368-69.

1984c "Once Again: A New Series of Commentaries." *PersRelSt* 11:167-71.

1984d Review of *Colloquy on New Testament Studies: A Time for Reappraisal and Fresh Approaches,* ed. Bruce Corley. *CBQ* 46:805-6.

1984e "Paul's Understanding of the Holy Spirit: The Evidence of 1 Corinthians 12-14." *PersRelSt* 11:95-108.

1985a "New Testament." Pp. 698-701 in *HBD.* Ed. P. J. Achtemeier. San Franscisco: Harper & Row.

1985b Review of Sandra Wackman Perpich, *A Hermeneutic Critique of Structuralist Exegesis, with Specific Reference to Lk 10:29-37. CBQ* 47:559-60.

1985c Editor. *Perspectives on the New Testament: Essays in Honor of Frank Stagg.* Macon: Mercer University Press.
Reviewed:
CBQ 49 (1987) 176-77. (C. Rhyne)

1985d Review of Allan J. McNicol, *Apostolicity and Holiness: The Basis for Christian Fellowship. Mission Journal* 18:17.

1985e "Expository Article: Luke 1:26-31." *Int* 39:288-91.

1985f "Discipleship in Luke-Acts." Pp. 62-75 in *Discipleship in the New Testament.* Ed. Fernando Segovia. Philadelphia: Fortress.

1986a   Review of Joseph A. Fitzmyer, *The Gospel According to Luke (X-XXIV)*. *CBQ* 48:336-38.

1986b   "The Bible as Spiritual Friend." *PersRelSt* 13:55-64.

1986c   Editor. *Perspectives on 1 Peter*. NABPR Special Studies Series 9. Macon, GA: Mercer University Press.
Reviewed:
SWJTh 29 (1987) 57-58. (T. D. Lea)
CBQ 49 (1987) 690-91. (J. H. Neyrey)
PerRelSt (1988) 286-88. (M. R. Michaels)

1986d   "Once Again: The Plan of 1 Peter." Pp. 141-51 in 1986c.

1986e   Review of Graydon Snyder, *Ante Pacem: Archaeological Evidence of Church Life Before Constantine*. *PersRelSt* 13:175-76.

1986f   Review of Alan Culpepper, *Anatomy of the Fourth Gospel*; Peter Ellis, *The Genius of John*; Ernst Haenchen, *A Commentary on John*; and Robert Kysar, *John's Story of Jesus*. *PersRelSt* 13:278-80.

1986g   "Inerrancy: The Central Question." *SBC Today*. February:14.

1986h   "Biblical Criticism's Role." *SBC Today*. November:8-9.

1987a   *Reading Corinthians: A Literary and Theological Commentary on 1 and 2 Corinthians*. New York: Crossroad.
Reviewed:
Cumberland Sem 26 (1988) 29-30. (R. L. Brawley)
SwJTh 30 (1988) 48. (E. E. Ellis)
CBQ 50 (1988) 733-34. (M. A. Getty)
TS 49 (1988) 157-58. (A. C. Mitchell)
CTR Register 77 (1987) 46-47. (G. Snyder)

1987b   "Paul on the Covenant." *RevExp* 84:299-313.

1987c   "Reimarus." Pp. 263-64 in *The Encyclopedia of Religion*, vol. 12. Ed. Mircea Eliade. New York: Macmillan.

1987d   Review of Gerald F. Hawthrone, *Philippians*; Ralph P. Martin, *2 Corinthians*; and Stephen S. Smalley, *1, 2, 3 John*. *PersRelSt* 14:183-85.

1987e   Review of David Aune, *The New Testament in Its Literary Environment*. *TS* 48:736-37.

1987f   "The Bible's Truth is Relational." Pp. 39-46 in *The Unfettered Word*. Ed. Robison B. James. Waco: Word.

1987g   "Biblical Criticism's Role: The Pauline View of Women as a Case in Point." Pp. 62-71 in *The Unfettered Word*. Ed. Robison B. James. Waco: Word.

1987h Review of Klaus Wengst, *Pax Roman: Anspruch und Wirklichkeit. Erfahrungen und Wahrnehmungen des Friedens bei Jesus und in Urchristentum. CBQ* 49:522-23.

1988a "Once Again: Gospel Genre." *Semeia* 43:53-73.

1988b Review of Robert A. Oden, Jr., *The Bible Without Theology. TS* 49:339-40.

1988c Review of Robert Tannehill, *The Narrative Unity of Luke-Acts: A Literary Interpretation. Volume One: The Gospel According to Luke. Bib* 69:135-38.

1988d Review of Abraham Malherbe, *Moral Exhortation: A Greco-Roman Sourcebook. Int* 42:206-8.

1988e Review of George R. Beasley-Murray, *John. PersRelSt* 15:177-78.

1988f Review of Bruce C. Johanson, *To All the Brethren: A Text-Linguistic and Rhetorical Approach to 1 Thessalonians. CBQ* 50:531-33.

1988g Review of Demetrius Dumm, *Flowers in the Desert: A Spirituality of the Bible. En Christo* 1:12-13.

1988h Review of H. Stephen Shoemaker, *The Jekyll and Hyde Syndrome: A New Encounter with the Seven Deadly Sins and Seven Lively Virtues. En Christo* 1:16-17.

1988i Review of William Powell Tuck, *The Way for All Seasons: Searching Reflections on the Beatitudes. En Christo* 1:9.

1988j Review of Norman Kraus, *Jesus Christ Our Lord: Christology from a Disciple's Perspective. En Christo* 1:4.

1988k "Where is Biblical Research Headed?" *Foundation* 11:2.

1988l Review of Mark A. Noll, *Between Faith and Criticism: Evangelicals, Scholarship, and the Bible in America. PersRelSt* 15:300-301.

1988m Review of Donald McKim, ed., *A Guide to Contemporary Hermeneutics: Major Trends in Biblical Interpretation. PersRelSt* 15:300-301.

1989a "Luke-Acts." Pp. 297-320 in *The New Testament and Its Modern Interpreters*. Ed. E. J. Epp and G. W. MacRae. Philadelphia and Atlanta: Fortress Press and Scholars Press.

1989b "Money Management in Early Mediterranean Christianity: 2 Corinthians 8-9." *RevExp* 86:359-70.

1989c Review of David Gooding, *According to Luke: A New Exposition of the Third Gospel. CBQ* 51:151-52.

1989d   Review of Julia Gatta, *Three Spiritual Directors for Our Time: Julian of Norwich, The Cloud of Unknowing, Walter Hilton. En Christo* 2:10-11.

1989e   Review of Nicolas Caballero, *Silence and the Liberation of Consciousness. En Christo* 2:7.

1989f   Review of Sidney Callahan, *With All Our Heart & Mind: The Spiritual Works of Mercy in a Pyschological Age. En Christo* 2:13-14.

1989g   *Reading Corinthians.* Second edition. Revised. New York: Crossroad.

1989h   Review of Francis Bovon, *Luke the Theologian: Thirty Three Years of Research (1950-1983). JBL* 108:345-346.

1990a   *Review of Matthias Klinghard, Gesetz und Volk Gottes: Das lukanische Verständnis des Gesetzes nach Herkunft, Funktion und seinem Ort in der Geschichte des Urchristentums. CBQ* 52:158-59.

1990b   "Apocryphal Gospels." Pp. 40-41 in *Mercer Dictionary of the Bible,* ed. Watson E. Mills. Macon, Ga.: Mercer University Press.

1990c   "Critical Study of the Gospels." Pp. 343-346 in *Mercer Dictionary of the Bible,* ed. Watson E. Mills. Macon, Ga.: Mercer University Press.

1990d   "Gospel Genre." P. 324 in *Mercer Dictionary of the Bible,* ed. Watson E. Mills. Macon, Ga.: Mercer University Press.

1990e   "Gospel of Luke." Pp. 529-531 in *Mercer Dictionary of the Bible,* ed. Watson E. Mills. Macon, Ga.: Mercer University Press.

1990f   "Theophilus." P. 908 in *Mercer Dictionary of the Bible,* ed. Watson E. Mills. Macon, Ga.: Mercer University Press.

1990g   Review of Ched Myers, *Binding the Strong Man: A Political Reading of Mark's Story of Jesus;* Eduardo Hoornaert, *The Memory of the Christian People;* Leonardo Boff, *Trinity and Society, PersRelSt* 17:189-92.

1990h   Review of Hubert Frankemölle, *Evangelium—Begriff und Gattung: Ein Forschungsbericht. JBL* 109:345-46.

1990i   Review of Joseph A. Fitzmyer, *Luke the Theologican, TS* 51:367-68.

1990j   Review of Eugene H. Peterson, *Reversed Thunder: The Revelation of John and Praying Imagination, En Christo* 3:4.

1990k   Review of Oliver Davies, *God Within: the Mystical Tradition in Northern Europe, En Christo* 3:21.

1991a   *Learning Through Suffering: The Educational Value of Suffering in the New Testament and in Its Milieu.* Collegeville, Minn.: The Liturgical Press.

1991b   Review of James D. G. Dunn, *Word Biblical Commentary, 38A: Romans 1-8 and 38B: Romans 9-16;* and Ralph P. Martin, *Word Biblical Commentary, 48: James, PersRelSt* 18:189-91.

Forthcoming   "Worship in the Fourth Gospel and in Its Milieu." *Perspectives on John.* Eds. Mikeal Parsons and Robert Sloan. Macon, Ga.: Mercer University Press.

Forthcoming   "Once Again: The Gentile Mission in Acts." *Der Treue Gottes trauen. Beiträge zum Werk Lukas.* Eds. Walter Radl and Claus Bussman.

Forthcoming   "Luke, History of the Interpretation of," in *Dictionary of Biblical Interpretation.* Ed. John H. Hayes. Nashville: Abingdon.

Forthcoming   Review of Susan R. Garrett, *The Demise of the Devil: Magic and the Demonic in Luke's Writings, CBQ.*

Forthcoming   Review of E. E. Ellis, *Pauline Theology: Ministry and Society, Int.*

Forthcoming   Review of Jan Wojcik, *The Road to Emmaus: Reading Luke's Gospel, Critical Review of Books in Religion.* Ed. Beverly R. Gaventa. Atlanta: Scholars.

CONCLUSION:
THE FUTURE
OF
LUKAN STUDIES

THE FUTURE OF THE STUDY OF THE LUKAN WRITINGS IN NORTH AMERICAN SCHOLARSHIP

David L. Tiede

I. "How do you read?" (Luke 10:26): A Plausible and Productive Future

Prognostication is more the inspired art of the prophet than the analytic craft of the scholar, but scholars must also plan their work on the basis of assessments of which methods, topics, and issues hold the greatest promise for productive study. This volume surveys the study of Luke-Acts in the twentieth century while a decade still lies ahead. The "three American contributions" and the evaluations in this volume already indicate challenges and promising avenues of inquiry. This essay extends the survey lines into the future, seeking to identify plausible and productive ways to read the Lukan writings.

No augury is required to observe the continuing high level of interest in the interpretation of Luke and Acts. The number of dissertations, monographs, articles, and essays is still growing. A student of the sociology of knowledge could have a productive project analyzing why so many scholars are interested in this religious literature of the first century. The persistence of Christian communities in North America is a crucial, but somewhat indirect factor.

The social context of New Testament interpretation is not simple. Contemporary scholarship does not immediately serve communities of faith or their interests in the theological significance of Luke's narrative. Current North American "readings" of Luke and Acts are attentive to more phenomenological assessments of the text as narrative, as commentary, and as window on the social history of early Christianity. The primary community for these studies is the guild of scholars itself.

Promising avenues of interpretation, therefore, have been staked out by methods and discoveries in non-theological fields of academic inquiry. These methods are consistent with the wealth of North American literary, historical, and empirical study of Luke-Acts earlier in the century. Their mode also contrasts with the prominence of theological agenda in the scholarship on Luke and Acts in post-war Germany, especially in the work of Conzelmann and Haenchen.

The sociology of North American scholarship also reflects a different economic and political base than in Europe. Biblical scholars of the European universities have traditional responsibilities for exegetical and theological interpretations in established churches, while their counterparts in the departments of religion in North American colleges and universities distance their work from the theological encyclopedia. The theological faculties in the United States and Canada seek to sustain sound expository interpretation, but their academic commitments are a step removed from popular interest in the religious and ethical significance of the text. The subject to be interpreted is more immediately the narrative itself, Luke's distinctive reading of Israel's scriptures, or the social realities underlying the text.

To be adequate to the subject matter of the text of Luke-Acts, however, any "reading" must finally be concerned with the convictions about God, Jesus, the Holy Spirit, Israel's history, and the nations implied and expressed in the narrative. This is literature of an ancient community of faith, and its relevance to modern communities of faith may be essential to sustaining a lively future of research and scholarship.

North America offers a distinct context for a reading of the Lukan writings. This context of interpretation will require literary, historical, and sociological disciplines, resisting direct theologizing or exposition to sustain the convictions of particular Christian communities. These disciplines promise to yield fresh assessments of the literary integrity of the narrative, Luke's distinctive hermeneutic of the Jewish scriptures, and the context of social and religious conflict within which this text was produced. A decade of such study will also provide a broader foundation for the exposition of Luke-Acts within the faith communities of North America.

II. The Literary Integrity of Luke-Acts

North American scholarship on Luke-Acts has been interested both in British assessments of the historical verifiability of the narrative and in Germanic efforts to isolate Luke's theological tendency as revealed by the redaction of sources, but neither of these concerns has dominated the discussion. The literary lessons of Henry Cadbury and Charles Talbert have had a more enduring effect, teaching North American interpreters to read Luke-Acts in comparison with other literature. At least two kinds of assessments of the literary integrity of Luke-Acts have proved significant: comparison with historically contemporary Jewish and Hellenistic literature and assessment of Luke's narrative by the canons of modern literary criticism. Both of these approaches will continue to be productive.

William S. Kurz,[1] Vernon K. Robbins,[2] and Richard I. Pervo[3] exemplify the efforts of a new generation of scholars to assess Luke's appropriation of Greco-Roman literary conventions and genera. This work is very specific and technical in its comparisons, perhaps straining its credibility by explaining so much on the basis of formal parallels. Nevertheless, such detailed analysis has illumined the traditions and techniques of Hellenistic rhetoric and revealed Luke's thorough familiarity with them. These studies move beyond Cadbury's rich collections of literary comparisons, demonstrating how an author's adaptation of conventional forms will exhibit both the traditional consistency of rhetorical education and the distinctive emphases and cultural biases in a given narrative.

Choosing the literatures with which to compare Luke-Acts is itself a fundamental issue. The traditional bias toward Luke's "Hellenistic" provenance has been reinforced and culturally typed in the selection of comparable texts. The persistence of Hellenistic rhetorical education is, of course, more readily demonstrated in Greek and Roman sources. But how does Luke's familiarity or debt in this aspect compare to certain

---

[1]William S. Kurz, "Hellenistic Rhetoric in the Christological Proof of Luke-Acts," *CBQ* 42 (1980) 171-95, and "Luke 22:14-38 and Greco-Roman and Biblical Farewell Addresses," *JBL* 104 (1985) 251-268.

[2]Vernon K. Robbins, "Prefaces in Greco-Roman Biography and Luke-Acts," *SBL 1978 Seminar Papers* (ed. Paul Achtemeier; Missoula, MT: Scholars Press, 1978) 193-207.

[3]Richard I. Pervo, *Profit With Delight: The Literary Genre of the Acts of the Apostles* (Philadelphia: Fortress, 1987).

Hellenistic Jewish authors, such as Josephus, Philo, or the Alexandrians cited in Eusebius' *Preparation for the Gospel* IX?

Studies of Josephus may prove to be especially instructive for future comparative work, reviving a field of research which held great interest at the turn of the last century but investigating new topics. Both Josephus and Luke demonstrate their knowledge of several conventions of Hellenistic historiography, such as a handbook knowledge of how to write proper prefaces. Both wove their sources and their stock speeches so thoroughly into the narrative that it is almost impossible to distinguish source from text. The issue is not whether Luke or Josephus knew the other's text or a common source or even who is more historically accurate. But what do the comparisons reveal about the way each understood the historian's task and the meaning of history?

Both Luke and Josephus are also thoroughly acquainted with Jewish biblical lore and hold the law, prophets and writings in sacred regard. How does this heritage affect their literary mode and concepts of divine involvement in human affairs? Both wrote with a heightened conviction that the destruction of Jerusalem was due to divine judgment. Perhaps neither would have been fully accepted in the synagogues of Judea in the era of the Flavians.

Many other literatures from Luke's era also invite comparison, and current North American studies on Josephus are not as strong or extensive as the work of recent decades on Qumran, the apocrypha and pseudepigrapha, and early rabbinic texts. Nevertheless, Josephus offers a particularly attractive instance of a Hellenistic construal of the events of the first century as a fulfillment of biblical history.[4]

Productive avenues of research have also been opened by several studies of the literary integrity of Luke-Acts. Drawing upon more modern methods of literary analysis, such scholars as Luke Johnson,[5] Jerome Neyrey,[6] Robert Karris,[7] Donald Juel,[8] and Susan Garrett[9] have

---

[4]Harold W. Attridge's study (*The Interpretation of Biblical History in the Antiquitates Judaicae of Flavius Josephus* [HDR 7; Missoula: Scholars Press, 1976)] is an excellent example of the kind of analysis of Josephus which will be most productive for comparison with Luke.

[5]Luke Johnson, *The Literary Function of Possessions in Luke-Acts* (SBLDS 39; Missoula: Scholars Press, 1977).

[6]Jerome Neyrey, *The Passion According to Luke: A Redaction Study of Luke's Soteriology* (New York: Paulist Press, 1985).

[7]Robert Karris, *Luke: Artist and Theologian: Luke's Passion Account as Literature* (New York: Paulist Press, 1985).

[8]Donald Juel, *Luke-Acts: The Promise of History* (Atlanta: John Knox Press, 1983).

heightened critical appreciation of the coherence and claim of Luke's narrative. These studies rely upon the assessments of Hellenistic conventions mentioned above, but now the larger picture emerges of Luke's sense of plot, characterization, narrative structure, and the reliability of the narrator. And if it is possible more exactly to describe the beginning, middle, and end of the story, then will not also the "point" of the whole be more precisely articulated?

Robert C. Tannehill's masterful study of *The Narrative Unity of Luke-Acts: A Literary Interpretation*[10] is the most comprehensive North American attempt to answer this question of the literary whole. His project has already established a new point of departure for the coming decade of research. Like the studies which precede it, Tannehill's analysis does not begin with a specific theological question, as was so often the case in European scholarship. For example, is Jesus or Paul a "divine man" or "philosopher" in Luke's Hellenistic portrait or biography? Does Luke's understanding of spiritual power and ecclesiastical authority reflect an "early catholic" form of the Christian movement? Has Luke compromised Paul's "theology of the cross" by the way the story of Jesus' death is told?[11]

None of the studies mentioned is focused upon isolating Luke's sources, either to verify their historical reliability or to make finely honed judgments about Luke's theological redaction. The questions are more comprehensive. How does Luke use sources, appropriate conventions, and develop themes and characters? Finally, how does this narrative persuade the reader of the truth of Luke's construal of history?

III. Luke as Interpreter of the Jewish Scriptures

Luke's ethnic identity is probably irretrievable, and if it were known how this author understood his bond to Israel, it might well offend both modern Christians and Jews. The intervening centuries have not been kind to relationships among those with competing convictions about the fulfillment of God's promises to Israel. But Luke has been rediscovered

---

[9]Susan Garrett, *The Demise of the Devil: Magic and the Demonic in Luke's Writings* (Minneapolis: Fortress Press, 1989).

[10]Robert Tannehill, *The Gospel According to Luke, Volume 1* (Philadelphia: Fortress Press, 1986); *The Acts of the Apostles, Volume 2* (Philadelphia: Fortress Press, 1990).

[11]For an interesting literary critique of the Bultmannian assessment of Luke as a theological "triumphalist," see Beverly Roberts Gaventa, "Toward a Theology of Acts: Reading and Rereading," *Int* 42 (1988) 146-157.

as an interpreter of the law, prophets, and Psalms. His thesis is that all
the Scriptures find their fulfillment in the death, resurrection, and
exaltation of the Messiah Jesus (Luke 24), and the audience for his case
was composed of those who were willing to examine the Scriptures to
see if these things are so (Acts 17:11). By Luke's own standards, he was a
member of the community of true Israel, while some others who claimed
the name "Judean" or "Jew" have been "utterly rooted out of the
people" by rejecting Jesus as Messiah (Acts 3:23).[12]

This difficult topic is of public interest in North America and will
surely stimulate further studies in the 1990's.[13] Even scholars are not
adverse to relevance, but the disciplines of research require careful
attention to several prior questions. What were the contents and form(s)
of the Scriptures of Israel known to Luke? By what canons, principles,
and convictions did Luke construe these Scriptures to be fulfilled in the
history of Jesus and the apostles? What was the sociology of knowledge
or community of understanding within which Luke's interpretation
could have been received as plausible and persuasive?

Some of these matters are very technical, inviting the kind of
meticulous research on ancient versions which has characterized the
efforts of F. M. Cross and his students at Harvard University. Previous
debates about "semitisms" in Luke-Acts and the complexities of studies
of the Semitic and Greek versions indicate the difficulty of knowing
precisely the form of the text which was accessible to Luke and Luke's
readers. How did Luke's Scriptures compare with Philo's or Josephus' or
even Paul's? No simple contrast between "Hebrew" and "Greek"
versions can be sustained, and direct comparisons to the way the rabbis
used the Hebrew text may be misleading in both similarities and
contrasts.

These concerns have already proved to be interesting and significant
in the work of several scholars. In *Luke-Acts: New Perspectives from the
Society of Biblical Literature Seminar*,[14] T.L. Brodie argued for viewing

---

[12]Jacob Jervell is clearly not a North American, but his analysis of Luke's
understanding of "The Divided People of God" has been profoundly influential
in this context. See note 18 below.

[13]See Joseph B. Tyson, ed., *Luke-Acts and the Jewish People* (Minneapolis:
Augsburg, 1988).

[14]Charles H. Talbert, ed., *Luke-Acts: New Perspectives from the Society of
Biblical Literature Seminar* (New York: Crossroads, 1984) 17-46. See also Brodie's
studies, "Luke 7:36-50 as an Internalization of 2 Kings 4:1-37: A Study in Luke's
Use of Rhetorical Imitation," *Bib* 64 (1983) 457-85; and "Towards Unraveling

"Greco-Roman Imitation of Texts as a Partial Guide to Luke's Use of Sources." Donald Juel has explored the "Social Dimensions of Exegesis: the Use of Psalm 16 in Acts 2", as a preface to his larger study of *Messianic Exegesis: Christological Interpretation of the Old Testament in Early Christianity*.[15] And David P. Moessner has undertaken a series of studies of Luke's appropriation of the Scriptures of Israel, leading to his monograph, *Lord of the Banquet: The Literary and Theological Significance of the Lukan Travel Narrative*.[16] The cutting edge of Moessner's work is his argument for Luke's interpretation of Jesus as the "prophet like Moses" promised in Deuteronomy.

Many other studies could be mentioned, but these suffice to indicate the range and depth of this new stage of investigation of Luke's use of the Scriptures. Brodie's work is intriguing because of his clear demonstration that "imitation" or "archaizing" was a common Hellenistic technique. But which text or authoritative tradition did the author imitate? Only those which were commonly received as authoritative could be used in this indirect and direct fashion. Then what does that suggest about the author and audience of Luke-Acts and their relationship to the Scriptures of Israel?

IV. The Context of Conflict

In 1976, Charles H. Talbert described the previous twenty years of Lukan studies as "like shifting sands" leading to a present where "widespread agreement is difficult to find, except on the point that Conzelmann's synthesis is inadequate." He also observed that only clearer agreement in method could produce a higher level of consensus in Lukan interpretation.[17] Now another decade and a half have passed, and still no single interpretation has taken Conzelmann's place. But on the basis of a growing coherence of literary, inter-textual, and social-historical methods, a new understanding of the plausibility and appeal of Luke's narrative is emerging.

Luke's Use of the Old Testament: Luke 7:11-17 as an Imitatio of 1 Kings 17:17-24," *NTS* 32 (1986) 246-267.

[15]Donald Juel, "Social Dimensions of Exegesis: The Use of Psalm 16 in Acts 2," *CBQ* 43 (1981) 543-556; *Messianic Exegesis: Christological Interpretation of the Old Testament in Early Christianity* (Philadelphia: Fortress Press, 1988).

[16]David P. Moessner, *Lord of the Banquet: The Literary and Theological Significance of the Lukan Travel Narrative* (Fortress Press, 1989).

[17]Charles H. Talbert, "Shifting Sands: The Recent Study of the Gospel of Luke," *Int* 30 (1976) 395.

Even those who differ on the specific social setting for which Luke's extended account was written agree that fundamental issues of truth and meaning were at stake, and the level of dispute was high both outside and within the primary community of the text. Luke's "orderly account of the events that have been fulfilled among us" was a concerted effort to make a persuasive witness to "the truth concerning the things about which you have been instructed" (Luke 1:1-4). But that testimony was offered in a context of intense conflict about the truth concerning Israel, Jesus, God, and the Roman order.

Jacob Jervell's 1965 essay on "The Divided People of God"[18] has continued to be a point of departure for North American interpretation, largely because of Jervell's insight that Luke had entered into an intra-Christian dispute about the identity of true Israel. Studies of the competing claims among Jewish groups concerning who is faithful and apostate in the era of formative Judaism have broadened the context for understanding Luke's project.[19] No clear agreement has emerged about the specific ethnic identity of the author of Luke-Acts.[20]

North American interpreters have disagreed sharply over Luke's relationship to the Pharisees.[21] Even those who underscore Luke's irenic style, however, recognize that Luke saw the challenge which the

---

[18]Jacob Jervell, "The Divided People of God," *Studia Theologica* 19 (1965), reprinted in *Luke and the People of God* (Minneapolis: Augsburg, 1972) 41-74.

[19]A host of significant North American studies could be mentioned. A few which typify the approach and insights would be: Jacob Neusner, *Judaism in the Beginning of Christianity* (Philadelphia: Fortress Press, 1984); Jacob Neusner, Peder Borgen, et al, eds., *The Social World of Formative Christianity and Judaism: Essays in Tribute to Howard Clark Kee* (Philadelphia: Fortress Press, 1988); Alan F. Segal, *Rebecca's Children: Judaism and Christianity in the Roman World* (Cambridge: Harvard University Press, 1986).

[20]See the extensive discussion of this issue in Joseph A. Fitzmyer's masterful commentary, *The Gospel According to Luke* (AB 28, 28a; Garden City: Doubleday, 1981 and 1985). The complexity of Luke's "Jewish identity" was also explored in a fresh way in E. Earle Ellis, *The Gospel of Luke* (NCB; Greenwood, S.C.: Attic Press, 1966). See also David L. Tiede, *Luke: Augsburg Commentary on the New Testament* (Minneapolis: Augsburg Press, 1988).

[21]See Robert L. Brawley, *The Pharisees in Luke-Acts: Luke's Address to Jews and His Irenic Purpose* (Ph.D. Diss. Princeton Theological Seminary, 1978); Jack T. Sanders, "The Pharisees in Luke-Acts," *The Living Text: Essays in Honor of Ernest W. Saunders*, ed. Dennis Groh and Robert Jewett (Lanham, Md: University Press of America, 1985) 141-188; Marilyn Salmon, "Insider or Outsider? Luke's Relationship with Judaism," *Luke-Acts and the Jewish People*, ed. Joseph B. Tyson (Minneapolis: Augsburg, 1988) 76-82.

Christian movement posed to various Jewish groups.[22] Luke's strong affirmations of Jesus as the exalted Messiah and Lord had profound social consequences, as the narrative itself emphasized. Luke could not testify to Christian claims to legitimacy in the divine plan without conflict with others who understood themselves to be heirs to God's promises to Israel.

Old debates about whether Luke was ingratiating toward Rome also have taken new forms in the light of a more complex model of Luke's relationship to various Jewish groups in the late first century. Comparisons with Josephus might again be instructive for fresh assessments of Luke's political philosophy as related to his literary heritage and sense of relationship to conquered Israel "until the times of the Gentiles are fulfilled" (Luke 21:24). Luke not only minimized the possibility that the Christian movement might be a danger to the Roman order, but also recognized that the conflicts over the law and the Messiah were Jewish problems of little interest to Roman governors (see Acts 18:15; 23:29; 24:12-14; 25:5, 8, 18-19, 25-27; 26:3).

Conclusion

A very productive future is, therefore, emerging in studies of Luke-Acts. No longer preoccupied with theological modifications of Mark or "Q" or even contrasts with Paul or the Paulinists, this scholarship will focus upon Luke-Acts as a literary narrative, an artful rendition of Hellenistic rhetoric through which the author builds a case, enters into Israel's argument about how to "read" the Scriptures and how to discern the work of God's Spirit in "the present time" (see Luke 12:56). And the theological consequences of this narrative testimony will be evident in their relevance to the context of conflict in first-century Israel to which this testimony was addressed.

Whether Luke's narrative will support the theological concerns of particular modern communities will remain to be seen. The irrelevance of Luke-Acts to some of these agenda may even challenge the purposes for which some would lay claim to Luke's narrative. But the recovery of Luke's narrative as a lively testimony to concrete human realities will not only stimulate further literary, scriptural, and historical scholarship. This grasp of the rhetorical force of Luke's witness also promises to

---

[22]See Robert L. Brawley, *Luke-Acts and the Jews: Conflict, Apology, and Conciliation* (SBLMS 33; Atlanta: Scholars Press, 1987). See also David L. Tiede, *Prophecy and History in Luke-Acts* (Philadelphia: Fortress Press, 1980).

instruct modern readers in historical appreciation of Luke's uncompromising claims to knowledge of the truth about God, Jesus, the faith of Israel, and the role of the Roman order in the divine plan.

DATE DUE

HIGHSMITH 45-220